The **Bedside Guardian 38**

The Bedside Guardian 38

A selection from *The Guardian* 1988–89

Edited by
Nicholas de Jongh

With an introduction by
Ian McKellen

Cartoons by
Steve Bell
Doonesbury

COLLINS
8 Grafton Street, London W1
1989

William Collins Sons & Co. Ltd
London · Glasgow · Sydney · Auckland
Toronto · Johannesburg

BRITISH LIBRARY CATALOGUING IN PUBLICATION DATA

The Bedside Guardian – 38
1. English essays – Periodicals
I. The Guardian
082'.05   PR1361

ISBN 0-00-223572-2

First published 1989
© Guardian Newspapers 1989

Photoset in Linotron Century Schoolbook
by Rowland Phototypesetting Ltd,
Bury St Edmunds, Suffolk
Printed and bound in Great Britain
by William Collins Sons & Co. Ltd, Glasgow

Editor's note

Editors of the *Bedside Guardian* are traditionally mute selectors and compilers, leaving the business of introducing the year's selection to some famous outsider. But this year a small break with tradition is required. I have given the *Bedside Guardian*, edited for so long with such distinctiveness and distinction by Bill Webb, and by Hugh Hebert in 1988, a face-lift or at least a change of face. Explanations are required.

An annual publication facing up to almost forty years of life is a suitable candidate for retouching. And just as the *Guardian* itself, with its recent redesign, put on a new and vivid face, so too, in a smaller sense, has the *Bedside Guardian*. This year, the book is arranged chronologically rather than in a stream of editorial consciousness. Each item is preceded by the writer's name and the date when the piece was originally published; in years gone by you had to reach the end of an article before you discovered who had written it and when. There is also, for the first time, a selection of photographs from the *Guardian* – an acknowledgment of the increasingly important role that they play in our newspaper.

The old magic dip approach had its obvious advantages. But the new format allows those who so wish, to read their way through in sequence, following the year's events chronologically. As a result of this format, there may be a slightly greater emphasis on the epochal events of the last twelve months, but there has been no attempt to make the *Bedside* a commemorative museum of 'big news'. The small sweep of the strange, the individual and the unusual continues to jostle with the great happenings.

In the last analysis, the *Bedside Guardian* remains, inevitably, one person's idiosyncratic and partial reminiscence of a year in the life of the *Guardian* newspaper.

Nicholas de Jongh

Introduction

Like most of us, I'm a consumer of habit and loyal to the brand names of my childhood. No denigrating campaign could ever dissuade me from Kelloggs (my nickname at primary school) nor from Heinz, who used to can beans in my home town of Wigan. My shelves, these days, would seem bare without Marmite and Bird's Custard, stalwarts from the old days, as comforting as the memory of my mother's cookery, to which they contributed so reliably. Under the stairs is a Hoover still. When I smoked it was always Benson's, and I finally stopped earlier this year only by pretending to myself that B&H had gone out of business. Rather than cope with unfamiliar lungfuls of Rothmans, I gave up overnight. In my moped decade, through the biennial progression from 49 to 95cc, it was Honda all the way. My current car, of course, is a Prelude.

Thrift annually draws me to 'the sales' and more frequently to 'the special offer'. On my monthly supermarket binge, common sense has converted me from Lever Brothers to Azda's own soap-powder. I once even subscribed to *Which* magazine. But mostly, against all reason, I prefer to consume what I'm used to.

I hope the *Guardian* won't mind sharing the shopping bag with Ryvita and Basildon Bond. But it has been my only regular newspaper since we were first introduced across the breakfast table forty or so years ago. It was then published only ten miles from our house. We familiarly dropped the 'Manchester' long before the *Guardian* itself did. We scorned the London-based *Times*, whose early editions up north contained so many silly spelling mistakes.

No self-respecting middle-class Lancashire family would

have been without it. We lit our coal fires with the *Guardian*. We also wrapped chips in it, lined drawers with it; even walked on it, a home-made felting under the carpet. My mother dried the woollens between its absorbent pages. Under the Anderson Shelter, which filled half the back living room, throughout the war I slept on the *Guardian*, insulation between mattress and lino. There was no Sunday rival in our non-conformist, strict church-going household. Once a week, however, the *Wigan Observer* was delivered, packed with the really boring, really local news.

As a boy, I only skipped through the *Guardian*. Despite an obsession with acting and theatre-going, I mostly missed Philip Hope-Wallace's reviews. But then his patch was the West End, as far distant as the rainbow's end, six hours by steam train along the London and Midland Railway, which passed along the cricket field at the bottom of our garden. I was deputy scorer for the Wigan Second Eleven at weekends, when Sunday School didn't intervene. Yet I didn't discover Neville Cardus on cricket until I read his gradely autobiography, so much of its early years on my home ground.

In the forties the *Guardian*'s first page was a bore. It was all Gothic script and adverts. (On 25 May 1939 it had announced my birth.) There weren't enough photos inside. My own boyhood journal was the enticing *Eagle*, emblazoned with full-colour strips of Dan Dare and St Paul. (Its creator, Revd Marcus Morris, died this year.) I loved the sheen and smell of the *Eagle* even more than its pictures.

At this time, when they asked, I said I'd be an actor when I grew up; an evasive stock answer, just plausible enough to cause a wise incline of the head and a sympathetic wink at my worried parents. A bit later, being a dab-hand at apple crumble, I fancied myself as a chef and filled in application forms for a catering school in Blackpool. Another dream was to imagine I might be a professional journalist.

My father fixed up an interview with the editor of the local evening paper. He said that there were more applications per day than he had jobs to dispose of in a year. So I settled for the nice safe life of acting. But I was allowed to submit 100-word pieces for Anon.'s 'Chit Chat' column. I once achieved a by-line with 'School-leaver's Notebook'.

The apprenticeship, which led nowhere, at least got me reading the professionals with an admiring eye. By the time I left university and had a letterbox of my own, I subscribed to the *Guardian* regularly and I haven't stopped. I was also left with an abiding respect for all those whose job is writing to a deadline. It's really too much to expect that their words, delivered on time, should also be entertaining or wise even. The pieces in this year's *Bedside Guardian* are often both. I hope, before you go to sleep, that you, too, marvel a little.

Ian McKellen

P.S. It's time the *Guardian* had a regular Gay Page. And if you don't know why, then it's *high* time. Like all the media, my daily paper sees the world from the heterosexual point of view. Yet, considering its liberal attitudes, I bet that 20 per cent of its readers are lesbian or gay. Too often we see ourselves distorted in the press or reviled and, even by the *Guardian*, ignored. The only major piece touching on homosexuality in this book is about a sensation. Maybe it was expected that I might rectify the balance. But like the *Guardian*'s other gay contributors, perhaps, I have censored myself to fit in with what it's expected the readership wants.

What did I miss out? Just a few words about how the local paper editor, having printed my juvenilia, invited me out to the ballet, took me to his home, his wife being away, and chased me round the sofa. Being 17, I knew I was gay and that if I made love to another youth, we'd be breaking the law. (Still true in 1989 where one or both of you is under 21.) There were then no sympathetic switchboards for advice or friendship. I wish the bisexual editor, witty and kind, had talked to me about sexuality instead of about sex. His clumsy (and unsuccessful) advances quite put me off journalism. That's probably why I became an actor. I'd heard everyone in the theatre was queer. As it turns out most of us are, in one sense or another.

The rise of the Eurothug

ED VULLIAMY
15 June 1988

Over the last five days, the prosperous city of Düsseldorf has been host to three groups of foreign visitors for the European soccer championships. First the Italians, who descended on the city in their voluble thousands and left peacefully. Then the English, up from the weekend's drinking and brawling in Stuttgart, and now settling in for tonight's match with Holland and already fighting. And lastly the Dutch who began truckling in last night and will arrive en masse today.

Between them, these visitors afford a survey of football madness at its ugliest (usually among the English), at its most enviably effervescent (usually among the Italians), and then in a curiously hybrid form of those who envy and seek to emulate the ugliest – and who sometimes pull it off (usually among the Dutch or indeed the Germans).

The arrival of some 4000 Italians last Friday constituted a carnival – sometimes no doubt annoying and sometimes very funny – which derived from a football ethos utterly outside the experience of England's beleaguered game.

It was more like a sacrament of the second national religion than the beefy assertion of a perverted patriotism as practised by the English mobs. It was a more celebratory national fervour that felt and observably was very different from the now hardened and abusive xenophobia of the lads who humped about in their Union Jack shorts, Nazi saluting and bellowing, smashing bottles and occasionally attacking people, never without the obligatory can or bottle of beer.

The Italians follow a game which commands huge legal and illegal wealth in their own country. The managers are national figures. There are three national daily soccer newspapers in Italy. During the last World Cup, the usually hectic streets of Rome and Florence were deserted when there was a big match on television.

In Italy, football is by and large the 'family game' beloved of English wishful nostalgia. Nor is it the preserve of a single class. Football captivates people who are male, female, poor, rich, unemployed and in between. The Italians came to Düsseldorf in a bubbly mood, making a tremendous amount of noise but sticking, apparently and remarkably, to coffee and Coca-Cola rather than to Germany's more noted beverages of which the English are so fond.

Some drove in motorcades and spent the day circling the city tooting and hooting and flying their gigantic tricolour flags – a few had even painted their cars red, white and green. The Italians are more likely to take their girlfriends to matches than are the English – a seat for a big game in Italy is a prestige date. On Friday, couples – and even groups of girls – meandered admiringly around Düsseldorf's pricey boutiques and through the little streets of the *Altstadt* – the old town.

Although the majority came from Italy itself, many were from the European diaspora of waiters and restaurateurs. They pored over glossy magazines in which the players are adored more like pop stars than footballers. They hung around the team's hotel anxious for autographs or photos arm-in-arm with the stars and former stars. Paolo Rossi, the now retired darling of Italy who scored the World Cup-winning goal in 1982, duly obliged to the loud delight of the girls. A team official warned the boys: *'Non fate casino.'* Don't make trouble.

They didn't. In a pretty market square, fans pointed to the cages of exotic parrots for sale and asked the girl selling them *'Parlano Italiano?'* A group of men spent a long time trying to teach a bird to say *'Forza Italia'*, but without success.

Several older men, wearing very smart suits and ties –

but with silly football hats on, nevertheless – had a quick browse around the jewellery and chocolate shops before settling down to expensive lunches at the Carl Haaffen restaurant on Bernerstrasse or, indeed, at the Ristorante Ponte Vecchio, predictably festooned with flags. After the match, the *Altstadt* restaurants were again packed with Italians dining fairly handsomely.

There were rougher-looking types, of course. Soccer hooliganism is a problem in Italy, and it stretches back a long way – in 1965, *The Times* carried an ironic warning that English football might one day become as bad as that of Italy. In Italy, the hard-core fans are called *ultras*, small and vicious bands often armed with knives – and nobody dares to suggest that they are not in Germany now, even if they are more sober, less visible and better dressed than their more numerous English counterparts. But the *ultras* are far more isolated within the body of Italian supporters than are the British hooligans among their tribe. If there is a fight at an Italian match, it is common for the seated crowds to shout *basta, basta* (enough, enough).

In Düsseldorf on Friday, some young Italians mocked their hosts, waltzing down the street singing *Jawohl, Jawohl* to the tune of 'The Blue Danube'. But even the hard boys seemed unwilling to ruffle the effect of their pressed Aertex shirts and fashion jeans – and next to even the meanest-looking German lads, they looked pretty tame prey. Two posses of opposing fans joined together for a joint photo. If the *ultras* were in town, they didn't do anything. There were eight arrests: six German and two Italians.

The other figures for arrests in the tournament until yesterday afternoon point the contrast. Two at Spain v Denmark, five at Holland v USSR, 107 at England v Ireland and 46 in Cologne, Düsseldorf and Frankfurt since the English arrived.

Within hours of *their* arrival in the *Altstadt*, a gang of English fans had wrecked an open-air theatre performance, slung a bottle through a restaurant window and thrown bottles at a Dutch couple at dinner on a pavement.

Politicians like to refer to the thugs as a 'minority' or a 'hooligan element'. Certainly there were the two lads from Exeter, bronzed and on a month of Interrail, hoping to take in a Bruce Springsteen concert too. But it is they who are now the minority.

A boorish and thuggish patriotism has in recent years become the central pillar rather than a nasty sideshow among the English national following. The foul abuse of foreigners and conducting the whole affair in a wash of beer are integral to the operation. One of the more commonly sung chants is now the National Anthem, here, at least, invariably accompanied by a Nazi salute. Shaking his head warily, the affable police spokesman in Stuttgart, Fritz Bacholz said: 'They are doing what we were doing one thousand years ago.'

He meant 50 years ago, surely, but there is something about the primitivism of the territorial urge in these fans that made the millennial distance appropriate. It recalls the Crusades, hordes of bigots on their way to get rid of some ill-defined infidel, stampeding through whatever alien culture they happened to encounter, and probably to envy, on the way.

The Englishmen's talk was about 'taking' the station or the *Altstadt*. 'England here, England there, England every fucking where,' they sang in the station square, cans aloft. The English left the Irish largely alone in Stuttgart. Their victims tended to be Germans, black Americans or immigrant Arabs, and now an Italian. The whole thing has become more ideological – tattoos read 'England, my country' – and also more racial.

Up to a point, at any rate. For the people whom these English fans really *hate* are the Dutch. Ironically, this is because the Dutch have dared to imitate the behaviour, the imagery and the racial purity of the English thug. Hooliganism has become a serious problem in Holland, too. There have been stabbings and there was fighting at the recent Dutch cup final. The PSV Eindhoven fans recently flew a swastika at a match in Belgium. The Dutch supporters who trickled into Düsseldorf last night were a mixed bunch. Some were older and raucous, showing little regard for the English spread out in the sun. Others, who began to gather in the *Altstadt*, came from a youth culture that looks to England anyway – for its rock music, its language and its soccer style.

They were much younger than their English counter-parts, but they swaggered none the less. They had imported the style: shaven heads or layered 'casual' cuts, tattoos, and even the vocabulary. Some had sewn on patches saying 'Hooligan'. One of them sported a Liverpool scarf. In the bars of the *Altstadt*, they raised their glasses self-consciously, sometimes shouting 'Holland'. Occasionally they were joined by Germans – ugly skinheads, tattooed, who because the swastika is illegal, are sometimes draped in the flag of the Reich navy with its Maltese Cross. For these lads, and for the Dutch, the English are the 'real thing'. To beat them on the streets would be a triumphant validation of their imitation.

This latest British export has, however, reached further. Some months after the Heysel deaths of 1985, fans of Sampdoria of Genoa smashed up the promenade at La Spezia, carrying the British naval ensign and chanting 'Liverpool'.

Herr Volker Grünnewig, vice-chairman of the Düssel-dorfer Altstadt hotel and bar managers' association, said yesterday: 'To have the Italians here was delightful – if the final is Germany v Italy we will have a super party. But I wonder if we will be having one tomorrow night.' He isn't the only one.

Dark, satanic mills

ERLAND CLOUSTON
17 June 1988

It was the chairs that did it. I mean, really, could you imagine Mr Coats or Mr Viyella, to whom ultimately the chairs belong, expecting their wives, sisters or daughters to flop gratefully into these after struggling through the 6 a.m. – 2 p.m. shift?

No. You would not ask a dog to sit on these chairs, for the simple reason that there is no surface for a dog to adhere to. Backless, baseless, sideless, useless, these are not so much chair skeletons as chair corpses.

But Mr Coats and Mr Viyella are not inhuman. The rest area at their Spring Mill, in Heywood, Lancashire, is equipped with the finest low-tech sofa the Coats and Viyella millions could buy. At least three members of the weaving shed's 25-strong shift can flop on to the six-inch plank suspended between two oil drums. In their playful way, Mr Coats and Mr Viyella encourage their staff to put their feet up after seven-and-a-half hours of guarding Mr Coats's and Mr Viyella's looms. 'Do Not Use A Table Cloth In This Room' barks a notice pinned to the rest-room's walls.

'Diabolical, isn't it?' shouted Mrs P. She had to shout because the walls in the rest area do not extend to the ceiling. On the other side of the partition several dozen looms thrash and crash away cheerfully, mincing yarn into beer towels.

'Ninety decibels,' screamed Mrs P. 'Have to put your plugs in. If you don't, the company can fine you fifty pounds – they've had that many claims.'

Every Tuesday for the past four weeks the workers at Spring Mill have staged a 24-hour strike. This is part of a general action for an 11.5 per cent pay claim. They, and thousands of other Lancashire textile workers, have just been balloted by their union on a 6.5 per cent offer by the employers' negotiating body, the British Textile Employers Association. This is a 1 per cent advance on the employers' original offer; as the average textile worker's pre-tax weekly wage is £125 and the average manufacturing wage is £197.92, the textile workers are now in a fearful quandary. Each 24-hour action costs them between £15 and £27. I walked in with a 6 a.m. shift to see a little of what life is like for people who swathe us in their products from birth to death.

In brief, it is not pleasant. Half-an-hour was sufficient to put me off mill working for life. The weaving shed measured 60 by 60 paces. It was hard to tell precisely how many looms it contained because the machinery was packed together extremely tightly. The girls were quite plucky about it. 'All them bloody cogs and wheels going round,' roared Miss B. 'I've seen factory inspectors in here, but they never spoke to any of us.'

The lady workers work a seven-and-a-half hour shift. Their job is to load the loom and watch out for 'ends' – breakages in the weft that a pick pulls backwards and forwards across the warp. When an 'end' materializes, the loom should stop to enable the weaver to tie the threads together. If the loom doesn't stop, the weaver has to call for help from a tackler.

Also involved are platers, tape sizers, twisters, pickers, slitters, beamers, and rollers. It was hard for the ladies to explain what these did, partly because I do not lip read very well, and partly because they have to keep such a close eye on the shrieking shuttlecocks.

'If the manager catches you reading he becomes hopping mad,' bawled Miss L. 'He grabs the book and throws it under the looms. He also comes into the toilet and drags us out, saying: "Right, weavers you've been here long enough".' In the winding room they have a two-minute limit on going to the toilet.

'They've all got BA," screeched Mrs R. 'Bad Attitude.

They don't know how to talk to people. You'd think you were away back 100 years! One foreman's got a nice manner but he's only been here two months.'

It was 6.20. The weaving shed was getting extremely hot. My nostrils were beginning to silt up with fibres which had escaped being pummelled into beer towels. As the official rest area was obviously no good, I was invited, for the first and probably last time in my life, to take shelter in a ladies' toilet. Others were there before me, grabbing a quick fag before the manager leapt in. 'This place is a dump,' affirmed Miss T. 'When it rains, it's like a colander. You have to cover the beams with polythene!' This met with general agreement.

'They say they can't pay us the money because they've been investing it. But where, I'd like to know. These Picanol looms, they're scraps, really. Make do and make mend, that's the policy here.'

'If your face fits, you're in.'

'Too many chiefs, not enough bloody Indians.'

'Look at these filthy towels. You wouldn't think we worked in a towel mill, would you?'

Fags extinguished, we marched out and straight into the arms of a male supervisor. 'Excuse me, sir . . .' Feeling rather faint, the *Guardian* allowed itself to be escorted off the premises. Later that morning I managed to have a word with Mr Robert Peel, Spring Mill's general manager. Mr Peel is not one of life's information givers.

'If I'd seen you there you wouldn't have got past t'bloody gate,' he roared down the telephone.

It was surprising he hadn't seen me. News travels fast in textile management circles. 'You were the bloke that took pickets to pub yesterday. This was all reported to me, on paper. I've got a file on you now.'

Mr Peel did not want to hear from me, let alone discuss any employees' complaints. He puts his faith in pro-ceed-ures.

'We've all got pro-ceed-ures. It's wrote down in books between the union and BTA. As long as I cross my t's and dot my i's, Mr Longworth is happy with me. Mr Longworth is the guy who looks after our affairs. If the people have something to say, there are pro-ceed-ures.'

Yes, but, would Mr Peel, who sounded a nice old gent under that scallywaggish manner, really like a wife of his to breathe in all that fibre, dry her hands on those filthy towels, fall off those pathetic chairs?

'My wife,' boomed Mr Peel, with the relish of a man who has just run over his neighbour's troublesome cat, 'my wife works in t'mill.'

Sparrows can sing

NANCY BANKS-SMITH

11 July 1988

In *Monte Carlo* (ITV) Joan Collins is Katrina Petrovina, a world-famous singer: 'I have sung before the crowned heads of Europe. I have sung before the Emperor of Japan.' One considers the crowned heads of Europe and the Emperor of Japan with a new and sympathetic eye.

I have never heard a tinier voice. It was like a sparrow singing in a bubble bath. Of course, as she demurred: 'I have the most terrible laryngitis' – and this may well be true as she dresses almost exclulsively in snoods and off-the-shoulder ostrich feathers, both notoriously draughty. Secretly, of course, she is a beautiful spy. The British War Office is pretty keen to know what is going on in Monte Carlo and she taps it all out on the transmitter concealed in her commodious jewel case.

The resemblance to *'Allo 'Allo* is positively eerie. There is Peter Vaughan as Herr Pabst of the Gestapo, grinding a tooth or two: 'We can crush you like so many ants.' I once travelled on the tube with Peter Vaughan. Those who had no tickets got out hastily at the next station. Some who had tickets got out and bought another to be on the safe side. He induces uneasiness. Philip Madoc gets to play Humberto, the comic Italian colonel, and clank around Miss Collins's boudoir in uniform: 'Oh, your medals are squashing me.'

There is something about Miss Collins's delivery of a line, however innocent, which gives it a slight air of impropriety. I am increasingly impressed by her resemblance to Mae West, whom I once saw wearing what appeared to be a diamond-studded sausage skin with aplomb. Aplomb is a necessary accessory.

Anyway, there is the whole *'Allo 'Allo* scenario. The transmitter in the bedroom, Miss Collins's version of 'The Last Time I Saw Paris' so reminiscent of Edith's musical evenings at the café and, of course, the British twits.

The War Office seems to be run by Leslie Phillips, a consideration which would have unnerved us if we had known it at the time. He has a brainwave: 'I think we ought to send planes into Monte Carlo to strafe the beach club.' This punctures every rubber duck for miles around, thus, I suppose, delaying the invasion of England.

Coming to with a start somewhere along the line – *Monte Carlo* runs for four hours over two nights – I realized who Miss Collins really was. Neither singer nor spy but the Grand Duchess Anastasia of Russia. She was snuggling up to George Hamilton, a novelist with a writer's block and a large selection of cravats. It was George's mother who once said to Alan Whicker: 'How can I lie about my age when my son's had a facelift?' Mothers come out with remarks like that and there's not a thing sons can do about it. Miss Collins confides that she is really a Russian princess: 'When I was seventeen my parents were executed by the Bolsheviks.' Now, which Russian princess was 17 when her parents were executed by the Bolsheviks? Anastasia. I rest my case. Picking it up again, briefly, to add that at one point Miss Collins leaps off a bridge into a river, a feat which Amy Irving duplicates at the start of *Anastasia* (BBC1).

Unlike *Monte Carlo* where the action seems to take place

in an unpretentious guest house, *Anastasia* runs to palatial sets with chandeliers and the usual touring company of Stars For Soaps – Olivia de Havilland, Omar Sharif – who add a dash of class to this kind of thing. As the Grand Duke Cyril, who has a promising future as a TV critic when the bottom falls out of the monarchy market, Rex Harrison delivers the most crunching criticism: 'Drivel. Never heard such patent drivel in my life. I suppose it might appeal to the hausfraus of the world. It's a fairy tale.' It is, of course, a fairy tale. Anna Anderson (Amy Irving) was not a pretty thing with curls. There was no Prince Erich. No love story. There may well have been no Anastasia. But it is very pretty to look at.

What it is really like to adopt an entirely different identity can be gauged from *Final Run* (BBC2), a four-part thriller, in which an IRA informer is given an entirely new existence – new P60, new UB40, new parents, new past. And a new house in the Midlands, poor beast, possibly because this is a Birmingham production. *Final Run* has been postponed twice, once last year because of Enniskillen, once this year because it clashed with the not dissimilar *Crossfire*. Which is why, most unusually, we have an original drama in July. Everyone on that side of the screen will consider it thrown away on the summer schedules. Everyone on this side will barely believe their luck.

A return to Auschwitz

MICHAEL SIMMONS
16 July 1988

In 1492, after wandering for many months, it is written, some Jews who had been expelled from Spain finally reached a land of many forests. Suddenly, a heavenly voice called out to them in Hebrew, *Poh-lin* (Here shall ye rest); and from that day on, the country was known as Poyln, or

Poland. Today, almost 500 years later, though only 40-odd years after millions of their number were exterminated by Nazis on Polish soil, they are heading towards Poland again – on study tours.

The other week a group of them were on a tour which took them to the silent, graveless sites of the Nazi camps. Under the trees in the vicinity of these places the wandering, prayerful Jews of 1988 have stubbed their toes against human bones. Each stubbing has led to an impromptu burial ceremony.

There have been many Jews in Poland this year. Partly it is the doing of 'the authorities'. Diplomatic relations between Poland and Israel were broken off after the 1967 war, but they're now in the laborious process of being mended again – in spite of an unhelpful remark from Menachem Begin, when he was Israel's Prime Minister, that he would never set foot in Poland again.

But other people have been to Poland, sometimes with next to no Polish and often with a Brooklyn or some other American accent, to remember relatives who were murdered for the simple reason that they were Jewish; to remember one of Judaism's 'golden ages' (Poland before the war); or to revisit houses of learning which are now something else. Adolf Hitler, in other words, has set new parameters for tourism in Europe. There are queues now to get into Auschwitz (Dachau, Mauthausen, Buchenwald, and the rest) and there is great demand for memorabilia and souvenirs of the holocaust. On Hitler's count, Poland before the war had just 3,547,896 Jewish inhabitants. They constituted 10 per cent or more of the population. Every third person in Warsaw was Jewish, and in some towns the figure was as high as three out of four.

Today, nobody quite knows. Perhaps there are 12,000 Jews in Jaruzelski's Poland, perhaps 10,000, or possibly 14,000. Many have 'lost' their faith, and authorized Jewish associations boost their memberships by admitting non-Jews. The textile city of Lodz (population nearly 900,000) used to be 'a Jewish city'; today it is home for about 250 Jews.

Many Polish Jews during the 'golden age' before the war were easily assimilated into everyday life. Many, as in Germany before 1933, rose to high positions in the arts and professions, their Jewishness accepted and not seen in any sense as a reason for discrimination. Some, however, kept themselves to themselves, and Isaac Bashevis Singer has depicted in impeccable detail the way they lived in the latter period of this 'golden age'.

Even before the arrival of the Nazis, ominous clouds had begun to gather. A Gentile hairdresser in Singer's novel *Shosha* speaks shortly before the outbreak of war: 'They've taken over all Poland . . . The cities are lousy with them. Once they only stank up Nalewki, Grzybowska, and Kroch-malna Streets, but lately they swarm like vermin every-where. They've even crawled as far as Wilanow. There's one consolation: Hitler will smoke them out like bed-bugs.'

The novel's narrator says that he could barely keep from trembling. 'The man held the edge of the razor at my throat . . .' Today's tourists go for usually private and some-times inexplicable reasons. Certainly not for morbid curiosity; Jews have been through too much for even that to be bearable. They return nonplussed by the experience. 'Apart from anything else,' says one of the visitors, back in the security of her south-east London home, 'it is totally confusing as to why the Poles have always been so anti-semitic . . .'

But the Polish economy needs hard currency and, since it is intermittently a beautiful and always an interesting country, tourism is a way of meeting that need. Six days in Poland for about £440 (although that includes the cost of imported kosher meals) can be counted a nice little earner.

This year, furthermore, an anniversary has been found and a new memorial erected with due ceremony, marking 45 years since the beginning of the Warsaw Uprising in the spring of 1943. The 25th anniversary, which would perhaps have been more appropriate and would obviously have drawn more survivors, couldn't be marked because the Polish authorities at the time were busy blaming Jews for their troubles and, despite protests from every corner of the conscience-ridden world, driving them from Polish soil.

The other day, not long after the public ceremony was over, an old man, in clean but threadbare clothes, came pattering along Warsaw's Stawki Street, carrying a plastic bag containing some rather tired flowers. At a bend in the road next to a petrol station, he reached the giant slabs of white marble, three or four times higher than himself, which constitute the new memorial.

The man looked at the endless list of names carved into the wall in front of him, reflected for a second or two, and with minimal ceremony placed his flowers on the ground. It did not matter that on such a relentlessly hot day the flowers would quickly wither. What mattered was that this man had remembered the holocaust. This was Umschlagplatz, the point from which hundreds of thousands of Jews – and Poles – were herded by the Nazis into cattle-trucks to make the trip to the death camps. The memorial may be modest in comparison to the scale of the events it recalls, but the Polish government is poor.

Henry Israel, an organizer of one of this year's study tours, lost several close relatives in the holocaust, but he will never be sure how they died. 'I had a feeling that I wanted to go to Poland,' he says. 'I can't articulate the reasons. I think we all had that feeling . . .'

The group has a crowded itinerary and goes everywhere by coach. They pray as they go – three times a day – and listen to lectures or sing Jewish songs. In places where there were once dozens (in Warsaw, hundreds) of houses of learning and several places of worship and prayer, they seek out the remains, cemeteries from which the grave stones have been removed or smashed, a revered house of learning which is now a medical school, synagogues which are now furniture stores or museums.

The itinerary takes in, as it has to, the once predominantly Jewish cities of Lublin and of course Krakow, and all sorts of places in between that are known to Jews and frequently celebrated in Singer's novels. Appropriately, at the approach to what used to be the centres of the Hassidic dynasties, Hassidic songs are played and sung on the coach. A Jerusalem University researcher fills gaps in the group's knowledge.

Some of the most important buldings are not easily discovered. Plaques denoting their previous, illustrious use are out of sight from the street, to be found only on side walls. Doors are locked and a key-holder has to be found. But there are still marks on door posts where the mezuzah, containing a prayer, was kept. There are still Hebrew signs on some Krakow houses, and some streets are still named after biblical characters.

Communication with local Poles, even of an older age group, is difficult. Questions like, 'Did you know so-and-so?' or 'Were you here when . . . ?' are greeted with a suspicious reserve, or silence. Group members feel these Poles fear these visiting Jews may suddenly reclaim the houses in which they, the Poles, now live. Poles who speak little Yiddish feel they are being accused by visitors who speak little Polish.

In the medical school at Lublin, once a distinguished Jewish centre, one of the group finds '*Juden raus*' carved into the wooden desk top. In a street in Warsaw, a small posse of teenagers walks along behind other group members, quietly but audibly chanting, '*Zhid, Zhid, Zhid.*'

The shatteringly gloomy climax to the tour occurs when the group comes to Majdanek, Treblinka, and Auschwitz. At these places, the group quietly disintegrates, each one of them preferring his or her own thoughts and recollections. Every group member seemed to feel they had lost a relative at one of these places. Auschwitz today, with the less visited Birkenau next door, is the most disturbing of all; for the most bizarre reasons. 'Auschwitz,' says one of the group now, 'is like Disneyland: queues of coaches and people, ice-cream vans, post-cards, a hotel . . .'

There are flowers now in the ovens of the crematoria ('But we don't use flowers that way,' says one of the group) and the grass plots between the old accommodation blocks are neat and trim. The Polish guide is quickly faulted on facts and dispensed with. Those who recall the horrors of the place now see the whole complex as an affront. 'Sanitized is the word for it,' says Henry Israel.

In the main watch-tower above the entrance gate into Birkenau, the one Auschwitz survivor in the group cannot stop herself remembering. The very calmness of the way she speaks induces deep emotions, followed by prayers, followed by tears. 'This tour has marked me ... for life,' says Israel.

A last view of the country

ENID WILSON
25 July 1988

KESWICK: I came home recently from a month's enforced absence which had begun just as the hot fine weather was giving promise to all growing things. I stayed on my way home in a high open country of moors, spinneys and older fields, with ripe blueberries on some hedge banks and each with its own range of birds. There were linnets, spotted flycatchers and goldfinches with south-headed warblers. My garden, by contrast, has many ordinary little birds like wrens. Some young bullfinches have taken over a tall heath tree and there are small blue tits everywhere. They are still far from elegant fliers but are real experts in pancake landings. All the birds, big or little, have been having the time of their lives in the soft fruit – black and red currants and raspberries – and now they are netted there is little left for me. However, I can boast of the fittest, most sleek, birds anywhere near. When it comes to mice or voles I am not competing. I can see a field of allotments from here where they lie below Castle Head, and fine they look too, but all that burgeons, sadly, is not green. They have a strain of sophisticated gourmet mice. The usual thieving of a few peas or strawberries is not for them; they chew the rhubarb in spring when it is being forced under cover, they eat the lowest brassica leaves, but they also take new potatoes from under the soil and parsnips, too. Last winter a hard-working plot-holder went to get leeks and met a mouse coming from the hedge bottom on exactly the same quest. There must be an answer to mice with such mixed tastes.

● *This was Enid Wilson's last contribution to* Country Diary. *She died soon afterwards at the age of 83.*

White mischief

JEAN SARGEANT
16 August 1988

When a school friend asked me, 'Have you got a poor child yet?' I said, 'Yes, I'm getting one from the plantation.' Each year, pupils at my school were instructed to bring a child from the poorer classes to be a guest at our school's Christmas party. Victorian ideas of charity lingered at the two schools in the West Indies where, in the late 1940s, I was educated to be an English young lady 4000 miles from England.

The first school was in Antigua and run by a formidable trio of maiden ladies, the Misses Branch. Miss Millie and Miss May wore floor-length dresses and could quell insubordination with a look; Miss Mamie was pious, shepherding us regularly to the nearby Anglican cathedral. 'It's because she lost her fiancé in the First World War,' girls would say knowingly.

Our education was wholly geared to the British system and passing examinations like the Cambridge Local School

Certificate, later GCE. We learnt a lot about English kings; nothing about West Indies history. But sometimes there was a tropical tinge to our curriculum. We acted Shakespeare out-of-doors, for instance, and I discovered the magic of doing *A Midsummer Night's Dream* in a place where it was always midsummer. I was Puck, running beneath shady tropical trees, carrying a hibiscus and proclaiming, 'This flower's force in stirring love.'

I was one of a minority of school boarders. I missed my home on the plantation, with its waving green sheaves of sugar cane. One day I telephoned my father, who was a doctor in the colonial service, and persuaded him to come and take me home.

'Jean is not a brave soldier,' said Miss Millie. Next day my father persuaded me to return.

'Jean *is* a brave soldier,' Miss Millie conceded.

I decided to found a secret society dedicated to the French Revolution (I had enjoyed *A Tale of Two Cities*). To aid the overthrow of the established order, my friends and I would chant slogans like '*A bas les aristos*' from a mahogany tree and greet each other frequently in the prescribed mode: '*Bon jour citoyenne!*'

Not everyone was impressed.

'Three white monkeys up a tree,' Freddie, a black girl, called scornfully. The school was multi-racial and black girls outnumbered the white. There was little racial tension and I was sorry to go, aged 12, to Codrington High School in Barbados which offered wider educational opportunities for sixth form work, but was virtually whites-only and even more closely modelled on traditional English boarding school lines. Here the headmistress, newly arrived from England, even tried to introduce hockey – an unsuitable game for the tropics.

The school was set on a hill from which you could see the sea gleaming silver on moonlight nights – an archetypal scene of West Indian tranquillity; at the bottom of the hill, Codrington theological college, a Palladian building in a park with 80-foot palm trees and a lake filled with water lilies, had its origins in the vast 18th-century plantation wealth of Christopher Codrington in whose honour the school too was named. (We learnt nothing about the history of the slave trade.)

Near by was a boys' boarding school whose headmaster taught Latin to our fifth formers. After the lesson, he would make a ceremony of getting one of us to pour tea, usually Helen, a nubile 16-year-old who was good at Latin. So was I but, at 13, I was too young to take his fancy. One day, offering me cakes, he whipped the plate away laughing, just as I put out my hand to take one; but I had the last laugh when I won the Latin prize.

There was a certain ambivalence about girls' academic success which was expressed in school reports in the phrase 'good, but . . .' For example, 'Good, but Jean tends to be excitable.' Deportment and poise were as important as good marks for young ladies. As one West Indian teacher commented in *Women of the Caribbean*, 'Middle and upper class girls were being educated to be good mothers, wives and companions worthy of educated husbands.'

The education I received was deficient because it distanced me from the West Indies, making England, the 'mother country,' the cultural and educational focus; a form of psychological absenteeism which reflected the physical absenteeism of the English plantation owners in earlier times. In social terms, absenteeism meant that white West Indians never created a culture of their own, while West Indians of African descent had been robbed of theirs by slavery and the Middle Passage; the result was a cultural void. In personal terms, the logic of my education was that I would leave the West Indies and live in England, which I did.

But what has been excluded can return with a force which shatters comfortable illusions. Enoch Powell's 'rivers of blood' speech and reactions to it forced me to confront the reality of racism in England; I was struck by the contradiction between racist talk of the black immigrants' 'alien culture' and the Englishness of the education I knew many black West Indians had been given during the colonial period.

I began to educate myself by reading books by black West Indians such as Eric Williams, Frantz Fanon, and C. L. R. James whose *Black Jacobins* showed me the links between the French Revolution and the Haiti slave rebellion. From novelists like Lamming and Selvon I learnt about the West Indian 'poor child'.

Today, as a result, I feel a link to the West Indies and the Third World which has influenced the way I see things – radicalizing my politics for one thing. My memories, too, have taken on a different colour. Now I believe the significant part of my schooldays was the early period when I mixed on equal terms with black girls who formed the majority in that school. That, at least, didn't do me any harm.

Moore revalued

TIM HILTON
21 September 1988

There is too much of the atmosphere of a solemn feast at the Royal Academy, where Henry Moore's career is now installed in galleries that murmur with the patter of received opinion. Nobody blurs the line between a major and a minor artist as well as Moore, and this is why his admirers find it easy to take a reverential tone. But why, if Moore is an artist for all time, do we never read new thinking about his sculpture?

Moore himself, growing of age in the 1920s, thought about sculpture incessantly, with the application and quick understanding of an exceptional student. He decided to understand the whole of the world's art at the period when the modern impulse mingled with appreciation of the 'primitive' (to use the word then current). This led to a remarkable endeavour in self-education. When Moore left Leeds for London in 1921, on a scholarship, he had decided to become a great modern artist with the help of the British Museum rather than the Royal College of Art.

Moore later recorded 'hundreds' of visits there. He drew every time he went there and filled his study shelves not only with Paris magazines but with German anthropological art books. This latter interest was exceptional. Who in England in the 1920s knew about, say, Carl Einstein's *Negerplastik* of 1915? Moore had a copy. Or Ernst Fuhrmann's *Afrika* and *Reich der Inka*, both of 1922? Moore had the books in his library by the next year. Up to Leo Frobenius's *Kulturgeschichte Afrikas* of 1933 illustrations of non-European sculpture are transferred via sketchbooks to Moore's own sculpture. And the list of his sources is staggering. He looked at African and Oceanic, Palaeolithic and Neolithic sculpture, Sumerian, Babylonian and Egyptian too, then early Greek, Chinese, Etruscan, Mayan, Indian, Mexican and Peruvian work, while always looking at more familiar Romanesque, Byzantine and early Gothic sculpture at the same time as studying South Sea Island, North American Indian, Pre-Columbian and Eskimo art. Moore's capacity for ingestion of art from other cultures has no parallel I can think of, or imagine. At the Royal Academy are the results of his survey of 30,000 years (his figure) of sculpture.

Two points are relevant. Without feeling for historical continuity he assumed his own art was timeless. and his derivation from a large number of sources dulled the edge of his talent. His art has been of synthesis rather than innovation. Moore, who is said to have been so opposed to the Royal Academy that he walked on the other side of the street when passing, was himself the academician of primitivism.

His instincts led to summary, generalization, repetition. These highly academic characteristics are not only in the shapes and outlines of Moore's sculpture, but also reside in his smooth modulations of form, in the silken surfaces that swell and delve yet live by polish.

For instance, the once notorious holes, popularly supposed to be an innovation, depend for their best effect on evenness and continuity; otherwise they would seem merely dug or gouged. But like the whole of which the hole is a part, they seem to reflect a suddenly frozen Parian marble. The holes would not be surprising, still less intriguing, if they did not share the inviolably perfect execution of Renaissance tradition.

Moore continued marmoreal art by other means. The direct carving and 'truth to materials' was never important as the preservation of tasteful dignity in sculpture. It is not original to say that Moore made art whose modernism was acceptable to the cultivated bourgeoisie in their old rectories and converted oast houses. But it is worth repeating that his rapid translation from a miner's cottage to the luncheon tables of the rich was owed to art school. At Leeds he first found himself. Then, social and commercial good fortune took him to the most fashionable of colleges. The Royal College of Art gave him a seven-year lectureship; then he walked down the road to Chelsea, where he had status as department head and an income all through the Thirties.

Moore's inherent lack of aesthetic daring became ossified by his teaching routines. Here is a contrast with the modern practice of Anthony Caro, whose own career haunts the compilers of the Royal Academy's catalogue. By the late Fifties, when his teaching at St Martin's was at its height, Caro could use its sculpture department as a vehicle of his own advance, driving towards half-visible desires. Moore could not have done this at Chelsea in the Thirties; not only because art schools were then quieter places, but also because he never dreamt of fervour.

Unlike Caro, Moore lacked artistic comrades. Membership of Unit One, association with the Surrealists, was more like joining a club than a movement. Again unlike Caro, he had not the benefit of creative criticism. He was accompanied by the inert mind of Herbert Read: Caro used the visual intelligence of the best of modern art critics, Clement Greenberg. But the crucial dissimilarity between Moore and Caro is in drawing. Caro has never drawn in order to make a sculpture.

Moore, it appears, was mentally and physically unable even to begin work on a piece without having previously drawn something to which the future sculpture would conform. In a precise sense of the word, therefore, Moore's sculptures are picturesque; his longing to have them placed outdoors, and on hills rather than lawns, comes from a desire to liberate them from his sketchbooks and his library.

The long sequence of drawings, saddening to eye and mind, begins with ordinary exercises: then, in 1927, there is an emotional portrait of Moore's mother. The emotion is fear. After that date (just before his first one-man exhibition) he never again attempted to draw a living and distinct human being. His thousands of mother figures are not only generalized but petrified.

Why did he refuse to read beyond the first chapter of Erich Neumann's *The Archetypal World of Henry Moore*, whose Jungian argument claimed that he was bound to the archetype of the 'primordial feminine'? Moore admitted there were things in Neumann's book that he did not want dredged up. The overpowering theme of maternity in Moore's art may well have psychological roots. We cannot know about such things but we can see that there was something crippled in his drawings.

Moore's work on paper suffers – even more than that of most modern sculptors – from his three-dimensional imagination. His figures never properly occupy the sheet, and he has neither touch nor finesse. Once Moore had established his subject's volume, which he did by exaggeration or by his unlovely 'sectional lines', the drawing's impetus was over. The better ones often make use of crosshatching right to the edge of the paper. But because he could not draw with a single, supple line he cooked and finished off his drawings with methods remarkably opposed to 'truth to material'. Pen, for instance, has to be smothered with top layers of wax crayon, colour wash, chalks and so on, which characteristically render flesh into stone. The vastly overrated 'shelter drawings', done from life at Belsize Park tube station in the war, are of this sort. They are not really about life, despite their strange sentiment, but tell us quite a lot about the impasse of Moore's art.

He had been at his best about five years after he first discovered his rough gift for carving. The 1929 *Reclining Figure*, carved from a single block of brown Hornton stone, is still a powerful work. It is not as receptive as the sculptures that followed in the Thirties in which the influence of modern European artists was added to the imitation of the primitive. Moore got some of his roundedness from Arp, his strings from Gabo, and many lessons in anatomical freedom from Picasso. None the less the *Composition* of 1931 and the elmwood *Reclining Figure* of 1935–6 are notable. The latter sculpture, lent by the Albright-Knox Gallery in Buffalo, is one of the few pieces that give one a new feeling for Moore. Much else in the exhibition is either familiar or disappointing. The Academy has done well, I suppose, to have borrowed the 1943–4 *Mother and Child* from its church in Northampton.

This was the first sculpture Moore made after his enforced two-year break when he served as a war artist. Dependent on Renaissance models, it still is more than pastiche. Yet can we truly say that this is sculpture that belongs to our time and condition?

Moore, of course, had no real desire to be a contemporary artist. For him the eternal was of more interest than the present. Perhaps this has some bearing on the absence of a genuine maturity in his work. In the Forties and Fifties he produced his most misconceived, grandiose and sometimes ludicrous sculpture. Yet in old age, when his art was generally made by assistants, he was often able to approach a convincing majesty. The huge *Knife Edge Two-Piece* of 1962–5 is of this sort. So are *Goslar Warrior* of 1973–4; and *Reclining Figure, Hand* of 1979, as well as a number of outdoor sculptures that cannot, for physical reasons, find a place in the Academy. Could the fact that he gave up drawing for almost all of the Sixties have helped him towards his best late work?

Dangerous refugees

23 September 1988

ANGELA CARTER reviews *The Satanic Verses* by Salman Rushdie

Somebody switches on a tape recorder; a meretricious disco version of a psalm of David, 'How shall I sing the Lord's song in a strange land,' booms and twitters into a semi-apocalyptic version of London. Ellowen Deeowen, as the children's rhyme has it. And even in its vicious decay, Salman Rushdie still accords the glamour of a child's dream to this 'great, rotting, beautiful, snow-white illuminated city, Mahagonny, Babylon, Alphaville'.

But the vexed question of the Lord's song and how to sing it in Mahagonny, Babylon, Alphaville, concerns most of the characters in Salman Rushdie's new novel, for they are mostly displaced persons of one kind or another. Expatriates, immigrants, refugees. Perhaps, finally, the answer lies in the 'satanic verses' of the title; might not the Lord's song be utterly transformed by time and distance, just as the two heroes of this long, complicated, exhilarating novel are transformed in the course of a journey.

Formally, *The Satanic Verses* is an epic into which holes have been punched to let in visions; an epic hung about with ragbag scraps of many different cultures. In Bombay, another city this novel celebrates, the beautiful Zeenat Vikal, doctor, activist and art critic, seeks 'an ethic of historically validated eclecticism, for was not the entire national culture based on the principle of borrowing whatever clothes seemed to fit, Aryan, Mughal, British, take-the-best-and-leave-the-rest?' Rushdie gleefully follows this prescription. *The Satanic Verses*, as if in tribute to Zeeny's Indian ethic, is eclectic as hell.

It kicks off *in medias res*, astonishingly: two brown men, clasped in a reluctant embrace, hurtle out of the clouds towards the English coast, singing at the tops of their voices in raucous discord. They have burst out of the exploded pod of a hijacked aircraft, miraculously to survive impact and be extraordinarily reborn.

Mind you, one of them, Gibreel Farishta, the movie star, has already scraped through a brush with death and is now prey not only to an obsessive, clearly doomed passion for the iceblonde mountaineer, Allelia Cone, but also to hauntings from a former mistress who killed herself for love of him. In addition, he suffers from halitosis; and strange, terrible dreams in which he features as his own namesake, the archangel.

These dreams form a phantasmagoric narrative within the novel itself, with themes and characters that echo and reflect the rest of the action and inventions such as the city of Jahilia, 'built entirely of sand', that gives a nod to Calvino and a wink to Frank Herbert; and a girl who subsists on a diet of butterflies such as might have sprung from the pen of Gabriel Garcia Marquez, himself another archangel.

These dreams have a cineramic quality that befits the unconscious of a Bombay superstar, even if their intellectual content seems pitched high for someone as gloriously, irrepressibly vulgar as Gibreel. Indeed, his vulgarity is so irredeemable, so comic, so full of vitality as to seem a kind of grace, and yet his author punishes him for it with madness and a brief incarnation as Azreel, the worst of all possible angels.

Seduced at an early age by the imperial promise of those magic syllables, Ellowen Deeowen, the other hero went to great lengths to tailor himself to fit his adopted city, paring down his hilariously unwieldy name to Saladin Chamcha, only to find the slimline version makes him a laughing stock – champcha means 'toady' – when he returned to his native Bombay.

Like Gibreel, he is an actor but an actor in England; his face 'is the wrong colour for their colour TV' so he has pursued with success a uniquely late-twentieth-century career, that of delivering the voice-overs for television commercials. This week, he personates a ketchup bottle; next week, a packet of crisps. It is a bizarre way to sing the Lord's song and that return visit to Bombay has revealed his inner emptiness to him, whilst Gibreel, full of himself, is hastening to meet his love when he sits down beside Saladin on that fateful flight.

After they tumble through the air entwined, they find, when once again on terra firma, that one has grown horns and the other a halo. At first the devil fares worse. Picked up as an illegal immigrant, Saladin joins in a mass escape from a detention centre – a scene of great power and strangeness. He finds his wife in bed with his best friend. And moment by moment he grows hairier, smellier, goatier. He takes refuge in the Shandaar Café, an establishment you might find in a Hanif Kurishi film script, or on the next corner – home cooking, skinhead whites who spit in the meals of Sikhs, roomsfull of rackrent tenants upstairs, outside the mean streets of a marvellously evoked eighties London.

These mean streets team with deracinated flowers who are tough as old boots. Mischal, for instance, the nubile daughter of the café, with her enthusiasm for the martial arts. And the clients of the Club Hot Wax, with its effigies of Mary Seacole, and Ignatius Sancho, and other, sometimes anonymous black men and women who once lived by the waters of Babylon. In this wilderness of a city, haloed Gibreel pursues a career as a full-fledged archangel that ends in blood and fire and disaster and a veritable massacre of supporting players before the two actors return, separately, to Bombay, there to finally engage with the complicated dialectic of good and evil that occasioned their transformations in the first place.

The novel, after its roller-coaster ride over a vast landscape of the imagination, ends calmly – for one of the protagonists, at least – in reconciliation and home-coming and a necessary grief.

As to the fate of the other, and which one of the twinned pair of opposites it is who achieves such wholeness in the teeth of the mess and horror of the world, you must read this populous, loquacious, sometimes hilarious, extraordinary contemporary novel to find out.

Mr Eliot's secret rooms

23 September 1988

DAVID LODGE reviews *The Letters of T. S. Eliot: Volume I 1898–1922*, edited by Valerie Eliot.

One of the most striking impressions made by this first eagerly awaited instalment of Eliot's letters, beautifully produced and meticulously edited by his second wife, Valerie, is Eliot's clear-eyed dispassionate sense of his own literary identity, and shrewd management of his own literary career, long before he became famous. Although he often doubted his fertility (in 1916 he feared *Prufrock* might be his 'swan-song') he never doubted the quality of the work he published, and he was prepared to wait for the general public to catch up with the taste of the small audience for whom he wrote. 'There is a small and select public which regards me as the best living literary critic, as well as the best living poet, in England,' he wrote to his mother in that same year, 1919, with a calm matter-of-fact confidence in the justice of an assessment which would have seemed bizarre to the literary world at large at that time.

From the moment in 1914 when, with Ezra Pound's encouragement, he decided to abandon an academic career in philosophy for the more precarious life of a man of letters in London, he seems to have set his sights on becoming a modern classic – and of course he succeeded. Though Yeats was arguably the greatest modern English language poet, Eliot was undoubtedly the most important and influential, and this was due in part to his understanding of how literature works as an institution, and how it can be persuaded to accept the new.

Major writers are not necessarily jolly or lovable human beings, and there has always been something rather chilling and clenched about Eliot's public persona which this collection of mostly private correspondence does little to modify. To be sure, there is some humour and high spirits in the youthful letters – it is a pleasant surprise to find Eliot joining in a pillow fight on board ship in 1914 and entertaining his cousin Eleanor Hinkley with comic sketches and a serial parody of cinematic melodrama.

We also learn a lot about the day-to-day circumstances of Eliot's early years in England – the struggle to make ends meet, the grind of teaching and reviewing, the surprising satisfactions of his work at Lloyds bank, the state of his health, even the state of his underwear. There are some vivid glimpses of the incongruities and discontinuities of life in war-time London which anticipate the kaleidoscopic technique of *The Waste Land*. 'Life moves so rapidly over here that one never hears twice of the same person as being in the same place or doing quite the same thing. It is either killed or wounded, or fever, or going to gaol, or being let out of gaol, or being tried, or summoned before a tribunal or some kind . . . If I have not seen the battlefield, I have seen other strange things, and I have signed a cheque for £200,000 while bombs fell about me. I have dined with a princess and with a man who expected two years hard labour; and it all seems like a dream. The most real thing was a little dance we went to a few days ago . . .'

But even when writing to his closest friends and relatives, Eliot never seems to reveal the naked core of his being, as did his great contemporaries, Lawrence and Joyce, in their letters. Each of his letters is a rhetorical exercise, the verbal projection of a persona appropriate to the occasion. To his mother he is soothing and solicitous; to the gossipy denizens of Bloomsbury he is sprightly but wary; to his literary cousin Eleanor he presents epigrams like nosegays ('Meredith knew what he was doing, but unfortunately it wasn't worth doing'); to his poetic mentor Ezra Pound he is unbuttoned and ribald ('good fucking, brother' he concludes one letter). Like the poetry, the correspondence is a polyphonic tissue of borrowed voices and styles in which we search in vain for the authentic Eliot.

Scholars will be excited by the exchanges between Eliot and Pound about *The Waste Land*, so drastically revised under the latter's advice, and by fragments of early unpublished verse. But this volume will be scrutinized with particular interest for the light it throws on Eliot's sexual life, and on his first marriage to Vivien (sometimes 'Vivienne') Haigh-Wood. A troubled sexuality has often been seen as the dark heart of Eliot's poetry.

Vivien was vivacious, but not an intellectual. More ominously she was physically delicate – a prey to neuritis, colitis, migraine, toothache and every other pain under the sun – and psychologically unstable. She was certainly not the woman to help Eliot achieve sexual fulfilment, and there is evidence that the marriage was a sexual disaster from the honeymoon onwards. In 1932 Eliot separated from Vivien, and she ended her life in a mental home.

In her brief introduction, Valerie Eliot quotes from a fascinating 'private paper' written by Eliot in the 1960s: 'To explain my sudden marriage to Vivien Haigh-Wood would require a good many words, and yet the explanation would probably remain unintelligible. I was still, as I came to believe a year later, in love with Miss Hale (the American girl whom he had met in Cambridge, Mass., and with whom he had an intimate, platonic relationship in later life). I cannot however even make that assertion with any confidence: it may have been merely my reaction against my misery with Vivien and desire to revert to an earlier situation. I was very immature for my age, very timid, very inexperienced ... I think that all I wanted of Vivien was a flirtation or a mild affair: I was too shy and unpractised to achieve either with anybody . . . To her the marriage brought no happiness . . . to me, it brought the state of mind out of which came *The Waste Land.*'

This statement is more revealing than all the letters put together. Never, in all his recitals of his wife's endless indispositions does Eliot betray any exasperation or give the slightest hint that he regretted his marriage. He remains to the end of this volume the image of a patient, stoical and caring spouse. Seldom has a private misery been so carefully and consistently guarded.

If there is a revelation in this book, it is of the character of Vivien rather than of Tom. She has always been a rather shadowy and sinister figure on the margins of the Eliot legend – jealous, neurotic and threatening. In the letters by her which Valerie Eliot has included, however, she emerges as a much more human and sympathetic figure: spontaneous, honest and, in spite of her hypochondria, vital. Although fiercely loyal to Eliot, and appreciative of his care, she does occasionally give vent to exasperation in a way he never allowed himself to do. 'I wanted to go to the ballet tonight,' she writes to Mary Hutchinson in 1919, 'but Tom is *IM*possible – full of nerves, really not well, very morbid and grumpy. I wish you had him!'

In 1921, Eliot's mother met her daughter-in-law for the first time. In a fascinating letter to Henry written shortly after their return to America, Vivien apologises for behaving hysterically at the leavetaking. Evidently the reserve and emotional repressiveness of the Eliot family had proved too much for her. It is as if Vivien is addressing her husband through his brother, especially in the touching conclusion to this letter: 'Good-bye Henry. And be *personal*, you must be personal, or else it's no good. Nothing's any good.'

It is ironic – and poignant – to reflect that at this time Eliot was formulating his famous theory of the necessary 'impersonality' of the poet. 'The progress of an artist is a continual self-sacrifice, a continual extinction of personality,' he wrote in *Tradition and the Individual Talent.* And there are several passages in these letters which echo that sentiment. 'The best promise of continuing is for one to be able to forget, in a way, what one has written already,' he wrote to the poet Robert Nichols, in 1917, 'to be able to detach it completely from one's present self and begin quite afresh, with only the technical experience preserved. This struggle to preserve the advantages of practice and at the same time to defecate the emotions one has expressed already is one of the hardest I know.' The metaphor is startling but symptomatic.

It may be that subsequent volumes of Eliot's correspondence, and the huge collection of letters to Emily Hale sealed until the year 2020, will reveal more of the tormented inner life of T. S. Eliot, but for the time being the poetry, with its baffling, tantalizing, infinitely suggestive profusion of personae and voices, resists any attempt to unlock its secrets with a simple biographical key. Which is exactly what Eliot intended.

The gender blender

BRENDA POLAN
29 September 1988

When, in 1982, Michael Kimmel first offered a course in the Sociology of the Male Experience at Rutgers University, his students were not taken too seriously by some of their peers. One student reported that his fraternity brothers had expressed the nervous hope that he was not about to become a 'libber lover' or a 'faggot'. Another fraternity brother suggested in irrational anger that the course was probably 'for fags taught by fags'.

The homophobic reaction and the anger were both predictable. By giving a course which studied masculinity, which treated it as a social construct rather than the immutable biological norm and which addressed it as a problem,

Michael Kimmel was breaking ranks, indulging in a kind of gender-treachery and casting himself as a weak-sister fellow-traveller to feminism. *And* subverting other red-blooded guys to his pernicious philosophy.

Thirty students signed on for the first course. Their numbers have doubled every year and men's studies courses are now on offer in many American universities. Michael Kimmel is now, at 37, Assistant Professor of Sociology at State University of New York, Stony Brook, and he was in Britain last week for the first International Conference on Men and Masculinity at Bradford University, under the auspices of the British Sociological Association.

'The work of academic feminists put masculinity on the agenda twenty to thirty years ago,' he says. 'Men's studies doesn't seek to supplant women's studies. It seeks to buttress, to augment women's studies, to complete the radically redrawn portrait of gender that women's studies has begun.'

Ten years ago, when he was doing his PhD at Berkeley, Michael Kimmel sat in on graduate seminars in feminist theory, the only man in the room. 'At one seminar I witnessed an exchange between a white woman and a black woman. The white woman said that all women share the same oppression; whatever their colour or class, all are equally oppressed. The black woman did not agree. She asked the white woman: "What do you see in the morning when you look in the bathroom mirror? You see a woman. I see a black woman. For you race is invisible because that is where you are privileged."

'When I look in the mirror,' says Michael Kimmel, 'I see a human being – a white, middle-class male. Gender is invisible to me because that is where *I* am privileged. I am the norm. I believe most men do not know they have a gender.'

Other academics have responded suspiciously to Kimmel's field of study. 'Aren't all courses that don't have the word "women" in them about men?' asked one. That's the point. Men have dominated society and shaped it to their own convenience. Men's experience has been read as 'human' experience not as exclusively masculine experience. Men as men have never been studied.

Men's studies explores what it means to be a man in our society and investigates how masculinity figures in the lives of influential men. 'You cannot, for instance, explain Baden-Powell and the Boy Scout movement unless you examine the crisis in masculinity in late Victorian England. You still have to take into account imperialism and class relationships but it can't be explained without reference to gender.

The founder of the American Boy Scouts, Ernest Thompson Seton (they argued endlessly about who stole the idea from whom) established the organization in 1910 explicitly to revitalize American masculinity gone soft through "enervating brain work and emasculation by women" – mothers and teachers.'

The period between 1880 and 1920 has been identified as the first 'crisis in masculinity' and there are significant parallels with the 1980s. The 1880s saw a closing down of frontiers – America's wild West and the limits to Europe's imperialist adventures – and the taming or feminization of Western culture. In the 1980s the rise of the multinationals, the shift to a service economy and the 'deindustrialization' of advanced countries combined with the acceptance of feminist ideas and a visible gay culture which challenges traditional definitions of masculinity; this resulted in the panicky perception that the West is decadent, soft, its masculinity seriously undermined and in need of reinforcing. Step forward, Rambo. On with the backlash.

'No one should be surprised at the backlash,' says Michael. 'But it is only a product of the moment. The old ideas of masculinity do not work for most men. Most men are confused and confusion makes people angry. In our public, working lives, we are finding an increasing number of women; they are our colleagues, our bosses, our bank managers. We have no skills to deal with them if we only know women in the private sphere. We have to learn to deal with them.

And then our expectations in the private sphere are not being met either. Wives and lovers are working from choice or necessity and are not there to take care of us in a way we have been led to expect. So there's disappointment and more anger. If women are no longer able to give men the comfort they once did, then we must find comfort in each other. We must develop our skills for friendship. And, for heterosexual men, that's scary.

'Parenthood is another greatly confusing area. One of the achievements of the women's movement is that by demanding men take an equal share of parenting, it has given men permission to want it for themselves. But they have no role models. Their own relationships with their fathers were based on the "absent breadwinner" principle. And when men contemplate this, they feel cheated and angry.'

Women who have studied women as women have inevitably related what they have learned to their own lives and then sought change; so too the men who have embarked on men's studies. In the new book which he has edited, *Changing Men: New Directions in Research on Men and Masculinity* (Sage), Michael Kimmel describes how, although eager to give personal anecdotal evidence, students were strangely reluctant to make sociological generalizations based on them.

'Of course one's conclusions have to affect one's private life. The work has had a remarkable impact on *my* personal relationships. One student jokingly complained that the course made it impossible to read a book, see a movie or look at a magazine without thinking about how it portrays men and gives subtle messages about appropriate masculine behaviour. It was, also, the only course in which they discussed what happened in class with their friends and families.'

Men *are* changing, he insists, slowly. Women's expectations after two decades of the women's movement mean that there can be no going back. Men *have* to adjust. 'I have been accused of jumping on a bandwagon. Well, it's the right bandwagon. I have no intention of leading this parade. Most of my feminist women friends are very supportive while expressing a hint of suspicion. They are right. We, in men's studies, know we must beware of "premature self-congratulation".

'It would be premature to say that new man has arrived. It would be outrageous to imply that now we have discovered masculinity and are beginning to deal with it, the women can go home and leave it to us. That would be just like what happened when the male medical profession discovered obstetrics, stepped in and took the practice away from the midwives. That's the history we have to understand and account for.'

And, he obviously believes, live down and give up. His optimism is contagious.

Seven steps that curse apartheid

DAVID BERESFORD
7 October 1988

At the back of a church hall on the slopes of Table Mountain lie several granite slabs. Abandoned – but not forgotten – they are the Seven Steps.

They were most recently remembered in a musical which earlier this year played to packed houses in the Cape:

> So kneel down and listen
> When you are all alone
> And maybe you will hear the sound
> Of the seven steps of stone.
> The rattle of a cheap guitar
> The squeal of a saxophone . . .

went the lyrics of one song.

The children will avenge us
For better or for worse
'Cause they can clearly hear the steps
And understand its curse.
For they too have been broken
And scattered like the bricks
The stones, cement and concrete
That once was District 6.

It is now nearly a quarter of a century since District 6 – a cauldron of gangs, bands, whores, beggars, itinerant preachers and the myriad others who make up an urban slum-land – was declared 'white' and wiped off the map by apartheid. All that is left today of that vibrant community of 35,000 to 70,000 is a scar on a hillside.

It is a scar made up of nothing more than disconcertingly empty land in a highly desirable location – overlooking one of the world's more beautiful cities. There are acres of green grass, a couple of pockets of gentrified homes, a big 'for sale' sign erected by a daring property developer and a street called Kaiser Boulevard. But the community which used to live there has been very much on South Africa's mind over the past ten days, thanks to an extraordinary battle being waged in the 'Great Chamber' of the Houses of Parliament.

It has been one of the most traumatic parliamentary debates in this country, as newly enfranchised Coloured and Indian politicians lambasted the government over its attempts to both 'liberalize' and entrench one of the pillars of apartheid – the notorious Group Areas Act, providing for residential segregation. Coloured MPs, in particular, took the floor one after the other to confront their white counterparts with personal accounts of their suffering under apartheid.

'God made me a man, you made me a Coloured man,' accused their parliamentary leader, the Rev Allan Hendrickse. 'You can shake your head, but you stole my land, my people's land. That is the legislation of theft.'

Although National Party MPs have been clearly shaken

by the debate, the State President, Mr P. W. Botha, is expected to steam-roller the legislation through. Under the complex constitution of the Tricameral Parliament he can, after a statutory waiting period, rubber-stamp the legislation into law despite its flat rejection by two of the three Houses of Parliament. But even if he does, the fight against residential segregation will continue.

One of the battle-grounds is likely to be that scar on the slopes of Table Mountain. And the chief protagonist will be the oil giant, British Petroleum. While the public controversy has been raging over residential segregation, BP has had a team of town-planners, architects and others beavering away at a scheme for the rehabilitation of District 6, with the declared intention of using it to destroy the Group Areas Act.

BP has been working on the scheme to raise District 6 from the dead since 1982. The project was born of a 'corporate responsibility' programme of the type which has become familiar to the operations of multi-nationals around the world – as a counter to public perceptions of the 'unacceptable face of capitalism' – but which have been fuelled in South Africa by the pressures of the international disinvestment campaign.

At the beginning of this decade, the South African subsidiary of BP, under the chairmanship of a New Zealand expatriate, Ian Sims, decided to use its 'social responsibility' funds to attack the system, choosing Group Areas as a priority target and District 6 as a model of how a harmonious multi-racial society could be created. It was a highly ambitious project, because they had to take on not only the State, but anti-apartheid sentiment which – as the song suggests – saw District 6 as cursed, 'salted earth' to be left empty as a monument to the iniquities of the authorities.

The authorities, of course, had no intention of allowing such a monument and had been busily working to ensure that the land was occupied and entrenched in white hands, as BP discovered when it made an exhaustive study of property ownership in the area. The land had become so stigmatized by the removal of the Coloured community that the government had been initially unable to sell the expropriated properties. It managed to do so by perverting the land registration system – encouraging speculators to purchase by suspensive deeds of sale, so they did not have to register ownership.

More seriously for the BP project, the State had sold a giant slab of the land to the local polytechnic, the 'Cape Technikon', which has already started work on a new campus intended to cut a huge concrete swathe through District 6. The multi-national began intense lobbying to persuade the polytech that they were building in the wrong direction, producing their own detailed proposal for a more attractive campus running down into the city. Simultaneously they produced their plans for District 6.

Enthusiastic young town planners and architects have produced a blueprint for over 4000 homes in styles reminiscent of the old Victorian terraces which used to characterize the area. BP has used its business clout to persuade the banks into backing low-cost loan schemes. They estimate that families with joint incomes of little more than £300 a month will be able to buy their own homes. They have now launched a hunt for the residents of District 6, preparing to persuade them to return to their old community.

The scheme is developing momentum. The City Council has voted almost unanimously in favour. The Cape Technikon is believed to be wavering. And the country's Group Areas supremo, the Minister of Constitutional Development and Planning, Mr Chris Heunis, has referred vaguely to the possibility of the area being declared 'open' (multiracial). A major obstacle remains – the attitude of the Coloured community.

One former denizen of District 6 is Dr Richard Rive, a PhD from Oxford, teacher and writer who remembers as a child playing on the Seven Steps – a thoroughfare between two main streets, where the gangs used to gather and pretty girls preened themselves and which became a social hub to the community.

Dr Rive describes the BP project as 'so artificial as to be almost schmalz'. He says: 'One mustn't see District 6 in isolation. It has to be seen in the context of the Group Areas Act. What we have to have is an end to the Act, not the rehabilitation of District 6. The rehabilitation of D6 within the framework of the present legislation means absolutely nothing.'

He points out that District 6 was a slum – 'it can never be what it was before; one doesn't want it to be what it was before' – and argues that its importance is rather that of 'a powerful myth for a people who have been emasculated of a history'.

And it is perhaps as a myth that those abandoned slabs of stone at the back of the Holy Cross Community hall raise not only a question for BP, but one of significance to the future of South Africa.

As the song from District Six the Musical has it:

> It was here you must remember
> Our children played their games
> And the skollie gangs smoked dagga
> Young lovers scratched their names.
> These seven stones bear witness
> Can these stone steps forgive
> The people who destroyed our homes
> And told us where to live?

Rock in the sky

JOHN VIDAL
10 October 1988

Huddled in space blankets in the shelter of a crumbling wall more than a mile from Jean-Michel Jarre's much-vaunted, long-delayed £5 million Docklands extravaganza, two kids who can't afford the spectacular entry-price sit, with a tranny and a couple of cans between them, listening to the simultaneous Radio 1 broadcast, trying to imagine the sky explode around them like doomed supernova. 'Spacy,' says one. 'Like the hitch-hiker's guide to the galaxy,' says the other.

And in the windswept, muddy nave of M. Jarre's cathedral of light, safe from the stench of the nearby brewery, the uninterested police sit playing cards in their vans, the donut sellers clean up and the staff of Wembley Arena, block-booked for the night, watch the poor sodding paying crowds begin to stream away before half-time. 'I've seen better shows in my fridge,' says a programme-seller, unkindly. 'I'll watch it on telly later.'

Well, it probably looked fine on telly where fireworks can fill the screen like they can never quite fill the sky and M. Jarre on his floating stage is made imaginary flesh as he strums his laser harp in front of a choir of schoolgirls wearing lifejackets. Or from a mile away where there is still room to try and grasp all those statistics – like these being the strongest lights, the biggest crowds, the most powerful sound system on earth, the concert of the decade etc. But right there in the eye of the wild, wet Saturday night, M. Jarre is revealed as little more than a post-modern glow worm – afar off shining bright but, as John Webster observed, seen closely having neither real heat nor light.

Take away the hype and the humbug, and what have you? Little but bland, derivative, sub-New Age synthesized music-to-surf-by, accompanied by thousands upon thousands of clichéd images of quasi-revolution. Only the scale is interesting. Only the statistics and the technical superlatives. All the rest is pastiche; as depressing and meaningless as waking up in a postcard shop.

Destination Docklands was conceived as a one-off audio-visual celebration of three British 'revolutions'; the industrial, the cultural Sixties, and the 'coming' communications one. So, incongruously, sub-Russian revolutionary images of spanners and designer workers flashed on buildings like giant postage stamps in a kid's album, followed by

Rousseauesque scenes of jungles, detached compass points, Bond, Caine, the Avengers and Hitchcock, all moving inexorably into satellites and silicon chips; random motifs becoming mere televisual jottings for the muddle-aged.

The night, of course, didn't help. Under a warm starlit sky those fab-sounding lasers and starguns might have reached further than the miserable, low grey clouds which reduced them to the level of the Royal Artillery searchlight display at the Shrewsbury Flower Show and the splendid, breath-catching fireworks might have been more celebratory and less swept off in the wind.

It was a joyless situation too; in the wastelands of East London, far beyond the shiny new developments and the London Docklands Development Corporation's brash showpiece city, the true regeneration of devastated Docklands seemed like pie in the sky, a glossy brochure for an imaginary planet.

Three scenes stand out: a young woman clutching her eight-week-old child and wondering aloud whether baby will be permanently affected by it all; the tiny Jean-Michel, almost unnoticed but looking as if he were about to be mobbed as he made his way through the champagne-swilling crowds in the VIP club; and Jean-Michel's charming, loyal mother-in-law, tottering down the rain-lashed steps of the pier to catch the boat back to the safety of the hotel: 'He's such a sweet boy, isn't he, but it's all become a bit gimmicky. He should concentrate on his music.'

A very British misery

GERMAINE GREER
14 October 1988

According to Anthony Thwaite, editor of *Philip Larkin: Collected Poems*, Larkin 'sometimes feared ... that the appearance of what he considered to be his inferior poems, would encourage critics to tear his reputation to pieces'. If Larkin was afraid of being better known, we should not be surprised, for Larkin was capable of producing a negative emotion in virtually any circumstances.

We discover, for example, from a hitherto unpublished poem of 1949, *On Being Twenty Six*, that he feared being in his middle twenties, 'when deftness disappears'. Rejection discouraged and depressed him; then recognition terrified him. Yet in the negativity of his feelings lies the secret of Larkin's success; inability to love, to persevere, to commit oneself, to risk all, is nowadays understood to be real, and poetry that expresses such non-sentiments to be honest, genuine, true.

Philip Larkin: Collected Poems gives us 83 poems which have not appeared in print before; these include 22 poems from 1938–1945, described as a 'substantial selection' from a total number which is not given. Anthony Thwaite judged that it would have been a mistake to have included all the juvenilia; his selection is included at the end rather than the beginning of the volume, evidently so that Larkin fans will not be put off by the unfamiliar bursts of rhapsody amid the well-worn imagery of winter nights that leave 'the world alone' etc. which can be found in the earliest poem included, printed in Larkin's school magazine of 1938.

Larkin's best-loved poems cannot lose their lustre simply because they are now to be seen beside others that he himself considered to be inferior. Given the extreme diffidence with which the unfamiliar poems are at last produced, the reader is obliged to find them not so bad, many not bad at all, some of them certainly better than a lot of the stuff that Larkin included in his *Oxford Book of Twentieth Century Verse*.

What is surprising is that Larkin so readily internalized the rejections that he suffered at the end of 1947, when *In the Grip of Light*, his own collection of 25 poems, was rejected by Faber and Faber, John Lane, J. M. Dent, Macmillan, Methuen and John Lehmann, all of whom had published worse poetry in their time.

This disappointment choked off the prolific vein of juvenile pastiche, from the 'pseudo-Keats babble' of his schooldays, to the Eliot and Auden of his time at Oxford, and the Yeats of his early twenties, and with it exuberance and arrogance. Larkin drew in his horns, deliberately limited his compass, concentrated on the spare, severe diction that we now call Larkin's authentic voice, and what he called 'the authority of sorrow'.

Ever since Matthew Arnold defined a classic in terms of 'high seriousness', and produced various gloomy runes as touchstones for determining whether other examples ring true, it has been taken for granted that poetry ought to be short, lyric, melancholy and sincere. Comic poetry, the poetry of compliment, narrative poetry (especially the epic) and the poetry of statement, can be chucked out without a pang.

This kind of philistinism announces with certainty that Dryden and Pope are classics of our prose. Larkin himself dumped Milton and Spenser along with the rest.

The tradition he succeeded in belonging to was the thoroughly English one of the dramatic lyric. The logical extension of this view, which holds 'O Rose, thou art sick' to be a *ne plus ultra*, is complete silence, at which Larkin arrived somewhere around 1974. There are signs in the poems written between December 1975 and May 1977 which Thwaite has managed to assemble – 'When first we faced and touching showed', 'Morning at last: there in the snow', 'The little lives of earth and form' – that the silence had something to do with a visitation of happiness that momentarily banished the cultivated misery which usually drove Larkin's pen.

It is an obvious mistake to take the 'I' of Larkin's poetry to be co-extensive with the reality of Larkin, the man, or even Larkin, the poet. His prose writing, and in particular his writings on jazz, reveal a human, prejudiced, enthusiastic, playful character who is seldom encountered in the poems. Though Larkin himself was not a miserable cuss, the persona he favoured for his poetry from about 1950 was just such a one. In another poem now published for the first time, *The Literary World* (1950), this persona presumes to teach even Kafka about depression.

Larkin's poetry pretends to be sired out of sleeplessness, by fear of failure, impotence, disillusion. Such negative emotions engender silence, not the painstaking formulation, reformulation, streamlining and polishing that went on for months before Larkin considered he had a poem worthy of being seen by others. He claimed to need large amounts of solitude in order to get through the day, but he used some of that time to scratch a message on the wall of his cell, and in that very act denied his own stated set of priorities.

In Larkin we come to the end of the tradition that began with those who found a 'pleasure in the pathless woods and a rapture by the lonely shore, a society where none intrudes' etc. Larkin is seldom to be found striking attitudes with his sea-gown scarfed about him; his solitary landscape is a city-scape viewed by an insomniac, the same bald street on which the blank day broke in Tennyson's *In Memoriam*. Larkin shares the acute apprehension of entropy that tormented Tennyson, who is the first post-Darwinian poet, bereft of God. Echoes of Tennyson crackle throughout Larkin's work, but like all such echoes in Larkin they are muted, almost subliminal.

Larkin's persona has never obviously read anything. The direct reference to Tennyson in Part II of *The Literary World* is a particularly nasty sneer at Tennyson's productivity. This poem was written a day after the better-known poem *Spring* in which the Larkin persona is defined forever as 'an indigestible sterility', threading his way across the park. Larkin was then 28.

Those who favour the view that Larkin is not promoting the insularity and curmudgeonliness of his persona hold that his lyrics are in fact dramatic monologues. This is a difficult argument to sustain, for, despite Larkin's virtuoso manipulation of tone and colloquial ellipsis, the reader is seldom allowed any role other than complicity in what is being confided. Browning, the architect of modern dramatic monologue, always provides indications of perspective and distance. In any case, Larkin expresses similar views in poems of bald generalization where no I is adduced to be rejected. The snottiness of *Nothing to be Said* (one of Larkin's favourites among his own poems) is Larkin's own snottiness. Just as the reader is about to jettison Larkin as the poet of inadequacy, a poem like *A Writer* turns up and jigs all the perspectives yet again:

> He lived for years and never was surprised:
> A member of his foolish, lying race
> Explained away their vices: realized
> It was a gift that he possessed alone:
> To look the world directly in the face;
> The face he did not see to be his own.

This poem was written in early 1941; Larkin was 19. Chaotic though the syntax may be, the evocation of the poet's solipsistic world of mirrors does partake of the higher cynicism that has been claimed for Larkin as a major poet. It is perhaps because of Larkin's awareness of the inescapability of self-deception that his poetry is so often in the avowal mode, and seems so self-centred, only to be in turn distanced by the semi-ironic treatment that Seamus Heaney once called 'sleight of tone'.

The effect of such diffuse irony is to absolve the poet of direct responsibility for what is being said. It is the perfect cop-out. One is neither surprised nor disappointed to find that the verses Larkin penned in Oxford during the war never mention any of the cataclysmic events that were destroying his faith in humanity. He appears to have resented the Welfare State far more vividly than the Holocaust or Hiroshima.

Ours is not a likely time for the emergence of a major poet. It is doubtful whether Larkin himself would have sought the appellation. He was attracted to Hardy because

Hardy encouraged him to feel that he did not have, as he put it, to 'jack himself up' to write poetry.

His verse is deceptively simple, demotic, colloquial; the attitudes it expresses are also anti-intellectual, racist, sexist, and rotten with class-consciousness. Larkin early became the poet we wanted, but some of us will mourn the passing of the boldness of imagination that produced *Mythological Introduction* (1943). *Philip Larkin: Collected Poems* adds another set of poignant signposts to the many roads that Larkin did not take.

Hurd silences the IRA

LEADER
20 October 1988

Whenever a terrorist outrage occurs in Northern Ireland there is wide cross-party agreement that every measure which might conceivably impede the IRA and mitigate the province's monstrous death toll must be properly and pragmatically explored. The measures announced in the Commons yesterday, echoing legislation already in force in the Republic, to prevent radio and TV interviews with people connected with terrorist groups or their political extensions, deserve to be judged first of all on that test. The Home Secretary gave two main grounds for his action. First, the broadcasting of such interviews after episodes of violence offend many who see and hear them. That is true, but it would surely alienate such people rather than building support for terrorism. Second, the terrorists draw support and sustenance from getting direct access to an audience rather than operating through intermediaries as they do when they talk to the press. What Mr Hurd no doubt has in mind is the image of gentle reason which Sinn Fein spokesmen attempt to exude, in contrast to the bloody death-dealing methods they elsewhere support; the epitome of this approach is Mr Gerry

Adams, who with his cosy sweater and pipe might almost be mistaken by the unwary for an advertisement for St Bruno. But where the Home Secretary errs is in his apparent assumption that viewers are fooled. It seems odd that a government which in so many other spheres trusts people to judge for themselves, and condemns the nanny state, should think them incapable of scenting such duplicities. Even so, it is possible that such interviews do help Sinn Fein build support among young people, and the Government would be right to take that very seriously.

But on the basis of yesterday's statement there is much to be weighed on the other side. So much that is crucial has been left imprecise that it is bound to create extensive problems in the coverage of Northern Ireland for the broadcasters who are already bound by its contents. What happens if on a demonstration a crowd (some of them IRA or Sinn Fein members, many others merely sympathizers) is chanting IRA slogans: must the sound be blanked out? How do you cope with Sinn Fein's presence, unparalleled in the Republic, in local government? Whatever its over-riding purpose, it is deeply embroiled in arguments over finance, the environment, roads and the rest. Can its views be reported? If they can't, won't that greatly boost its chances of representing these measures, however dishonestly, as discrimination against the wider republican community? And how will the exemption for election coverage work? Couldn't it, as Mr Hattersley suggested in the Commons yesterday, set off a whole new propaganda campaign with Sinn Fein candidates running at Govan, Richmond and Epping?

These and other problems and anomalies threaten the whole design. But Mr Hurd's initiative needs also to be considered in the light of the baleful attitude of this Government to the broadcast media (in sharp and eloquent contrast to its complacence in the face of newspaper excesses.) The introduction of this new prohibition through the medium of existing legislation covering the BBC and IBA would be worrying at any time; with *Spycatcher* and GCHQ so fresh in the mind it becomes positively alarming.

YOU SEE RAYMOND, THE THING IS, THERE'S NO MONEY IN REPAIRING THESE CRUMBLING VICTORIAN SEWERS...

WHO GIVES A TOSS?

EXACTLY, AND THE COLLAPSE OF THE SEWERS WILL HERALD A RETURN TO THE 1830's, WHICH, AS WE ALL KNOW, WAS THE GOLDEN AGE OF RATKIND, WHEN WE WALKED THE STREETS WITH PRIDE

...ONLY NOW THERE'LL BE A BONUS: MORE PEOPLE, MORE DISEASES AND A GREATER CHOICE OF SHIT THAN EVER BEFORE

...SO LET'S SUIT UP AND GO FOR IT!! 1992 HERE WE COME!

© Steve Bell 1989

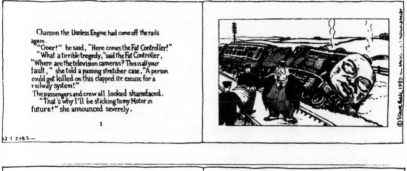

Channon the Useless Engine had come off the rails again.

"Ooer!" he said, "Here comes the Fat Controller!"

"What a terrible tragedy," said the Fat Controller, "Where are the television cameras? This is all your fault," she told a passing stretcher case, "A person could get killed on this clapped ite excuse for a railway system!"

The passengers and crew all looked shamefaced.

"That's why I'll be sticking to my Motor in future!" she announced severely.

1

Nigel the Fat Engine had fallen into Shit Creek again.

"Doesn't worry me a bit," he said, "I like it here!"

Just then the Fat Controller came along in her motor boat.

"Hello Nigel, everything going swimmingly?" she asked.

"We're getting there, ma'am," said Nigel.

"How are the passengers taking it?" she asked.

"Screw the passengers!" they both laughed.

2

Hurd steals priceless liberties

ANDREW RAWNSLEY
21 October 1988

Douglas Hurd, a 58-year-old Home Secretary, was last night wanted for questioning over a series of disturbing robberies throughout the country.

A tall, white-haired man, answering to Hurd's description, has for the last two days run amuck over large areas of democracy, causing incalculable damage to some of the country's most precious civil liberties. The right to silence, a particularly well-loved monument, dating back to before the Magna Carta, was said by distraught custodians to be beyond repair.

A tall, blonde woman, already wanted for a series of similar offences over the last nine years, is also sought. She is said to answer to the name Thatcher, though prefers Your Majesty. It was from her home in Downing Street that the two are believed to have planned their raids on a series of priceless liberties previously thought to be completely secure.

Also wanted is a short, mousy-haired man called King, responsible for the Northern Ireland end of the operation. Hurd is thought to be the Mr Big in the affair; King is said to be its Mr Little. Both are thought to have been acting while the balance of their minds was disturbed.

Hurd is widely described as deceptively mild-mannered with a sophisticated command of beguiling patter. Over the years he has adopted a variety of disguises: bookish thinker, suave diplomat, trusty policeman, even successfully posing as a liberal Tory.

His favourite ruse for gaining entry to public confidence is posing as a guardian of liberty. He then proceeds to rob and loot it of some of its most valuable assets.

He has no previous convictions, and his behaviour suggests that he is unlikely to develop them. Angry callers gathered at Hurd's home address in the House of Commons last night to demand their rights back, but could raise no answer from the Home Secretary when they banged on the despatch box. His legal advisers are thought to have told him: 'Whatever you say, say nothing.'

Hurd declined to answer questions using the novel technique of simply not turning up to hear them. Some aspects of the right to silence, it was confirmed in subsequent questioning to the Leader of the House during Points of Order, will be preserved. The right to silence remains absolute for Government ministers in a tight corner.

It was alternatively suggested that the Home Secretary may have decided to extend his earlier ban on radio and television interviews with political organizations to himself, lest he say anything else which will encourage the IRA.

Roy Hattersley, the Opposition spokesman on Home Affairs, said Hurd had clearly gone on the run, leaving only a written Commons statement admitting responsibility for his latest attack. It was an act of mindless vandalism on 'an essential aspect of our free society'.

He pleaded with the Government to get Hurd to turn himself in before he did any further damage. One of the wanted man's neighbours, John Wakeham, confirmed that they were not expecting him on the Government front bench all day. Members of the public seeing Hurd are asked immediately to report his whereabouts to their nearest Opposition MP.

On no account should members of the public approach Hurd. He is highly dangerous and may steal their rights without warning.

From Vienna to Victoria Station

HELLA PICK
22 October 1988

Victoria Station in March 1939. Clusters of young children, bewildered, shivering, in a large bare reception hall, staying close to their possessions. Grown-ups uneasily surveying the scene as a functionary from the Jewish Community in London reads out a roll-call of the new arrivals from Nazi-occupied Vienna. Hella Pick is called. I move forward, and one of the adults comes towards me.

We shake hands. She is to be my surrogate mother. I pronounce the only phrase of English that I know: 'Goodbye'. But, of course, I remained.

The scene is etched on my mind, together with a handful of other significant snapshots; although far too much about the events that uprooted me, and irrevocably changed my life, are blotted from memory.

This year has been marked by a series of anniversaries, recalling Hitler's progression, 50 years ago, into Austria and Czechoslovakia, and his drive to erase the Jewish presence in the Greater Germany, horrifyingly accelerated by the anti-Jewish pogroms of the Kristallnacht on 9 November 1938.

It is impossible to look back with clinical detachment. But I no longer react with personal anger. I am surprised how dispassionately I have been able to watch some of the old newsreels of Hitler, delivering his harangues on racial purity, or of cheering crowds as they welcomed the Nazis, strutting into Vienna. Or to read the spate of recent articles aimed at rehabilitating Neville Chamberlain and asserting that appeasement in Munich won Britain time to re-arm against certain defeat.

For good or ill, I seem more able to distance myself from

it all these days. The Nazis still remain the personification of evil. But from deeply private, personal grief, Hitler and his works have shifted into a broader context of general history. I no longer rush from the room crying, as I once did in my late teens from a cinema which showed scenes at Belsen concentration camp.

Perhaps I could even return to Auschwitz without again freezing into incoherence, unable to utter a word for two or three days afterwards – as happened to me after covering the German Foreign Minister's visit to the former concentration camp in the late 1970s.

These days when I am in Vienna I feel like a tourist – neither victim nor native. Kurt Waldheim's election as Austria's President was, to put it mildly, an inept choice. But it did not arouse the same bitterness it provoked among many of my friends. Sometimes I wish it were otherwise. But the fact is that my native country is not really part of the fabric of my life. The centre of my universe is Britain.

But what if there had been no Hitler; if I had been formed in Vienna's cultural environment; if Austria had remained my home; if I had not become 'a victim of Nazi aggression'?

Such questions, of course, can never be satisfactorily answered by my generation. Our parents could compare their pre-refugee existence with the life they made for themselves in Britain. But those of us who came here as children can only speculate what might have been. We know we were brutally uprooted. We have become British citizens and most of us are probably indistinguishable from our British contemporaries. We like to believe that we have put down firm roots here. Yet there is a certain rootlessness that never quite disappears; a basic insecurity that cannot be erased.

I had been brought to London in 1939 on a 'Children's Transport' – Jewish children, bought out for cash in cloak-and-dagger deals negotiated between representatives of the Jewish community in Palestine and Hitler's men in Vienna. I have a hazy memory of waving to my mother, forlornly left behind as the train left Vienna's Westbahnhof. Neither of us knew whether we would ever meet again.

We were among the lucky ones. A couple of months before the outbreak of the war, she managed to secure a visa to Britain, arriving in London with two or three suitcases, a few pounds in her pocket and the promise of a job as a cook. Hardly the kind of comfortable middle-class existence of her earlier incarnation. But it was a salvation not vouchsafed to my mother's mother – last heard of in a concentration camp. My father had emigrated to the US, and he died there before a reunion could be arranged.

When war broke out, the refugees in Britain were treated with considerable suspicion. Initially, most of the men were interned, while the women were restricted to domestic work. Even the children's documents carried the label 'enemy alien'.

Living on the Westmorland side of Windermere, I was supposed to have police permission before being allowed to visit school friends on the Lancashire side of the lake – because that was a restricted area, not freely open even to juvenile enemy aliens: it housed the VIP prisoner-of-war camp where Rudolf Hess came to be lodged.

In retrospect this seems quite absurd. At the time, it must have reinforced my determination to blend into my surroundings, to anglicize, to integrate. Rapidly learning English, I flatly refused to speak German to anyone. If my mother pronounced so much as a sentence of German within hearing distance of another human being, I shushed her angrily. For a long time I read no German literature and only gave up my boycott when I developed a teenage crush on one of my language teachers, who convinced me that I must relearn my mother tongue.

The drive to assimilate also meant trying to blot out the fact that I was Jewish. Grasmere Church became a haven, and I even succeeded in dragging my mother, an agnostic, to regular church services. It was only years later, on my first visit to New York with its large Jewish population, that I finally managed to absorb the fact that there is no shame attached to being a Jew, and that I abandoned the attempt to hide my Judaism.

My flirtation with Christianity also stopped, although it was never replaced by any great feeling for the Jewish faith. Nor did I ever develop the urge to live in Israel.

There was heavy pressure on me, at one point, to emigrate to Israel. I was already working as a journalist, and during a trip to Ghana I had gone to interview Israel's ambassador in Accra. It turned out that the ambassador, Ehud Avriel, had been the man in charge of negotiating the evacuation of Vienna's Jewish children. Quite possibly I owed my life to him.

We became the best of friends and he influenced me deeply. But he never convinced me – although not for want of trying – that Israel would provide a better answer to my search for a secure identity. During visits there, I have never been quite comfortable; I lacked the emotional involvement and excitement which surely ought to have been there if I had felt any sense of homecoming in Israel.

After the war, in Britain, most of the Austrian and German refugees settled comfortably and were advancing in business and the professions. We all became naturalized British citizens. My mother, who had turned from cook to milliner, had a small group of friends, all refugees, who met regularly and spent much time delving into the past. Some of them held that every Austrian and every German had been, if not a Nazi, at least an anti-Semite, and they swore they would never go back, even on the shortest of visits, to their former countries. My mother belonged to the minority who resisted such wholesale condemnation, and seized every opportunity for holidays in Austria. While she was quite happy in Britain, it really never became her country. From 1939 until her death in 1971 she lived in limboland.

I never felt any scruples about visiting Austria. But I did find it hard to come to terms with Germany. There was no rhyme or reason to that – after all, Hitler had been an Austrian and anti-Semitism was rife in Austria before the

Anschluss. But that did not stop me from believing that the Germans had to be blamed as instigators of the holocaust far more than the Austrians.

It was Willy Brandt who finally convinced me that there was moral integrity in post-war Germany. History has yet to give its verdict on Brandt's political achievements. But I have no doubt that he comes out a champion in the leadership he gave to millions of Germans to confront their past and rebuild their nation on honourable foundations.

My talks with Willy Brandt erased the remnants of rancour and make it possible now to condemn the events of 50 years ago without feeling endlessly and very personally betrayed.

My wives and I

DEREK BROWN
31 October 1988

Today, at an auspicious hour, His Majesty Jigme Singye Wangchuk, King of Bhutan, will wed Their Majesties Ashi Dorgi Wangmo, Ashi Tshering Pem, Ashi Tshering Yandon and Ashi Sangye Choden.

It will be a solemn ceremony, and something of a family get-together. The four brides are not only sisters, but already queens. They first married the king nine years ago, and have between them borne him four sons and four daughters.

The eldest son, Prince Jigme Gesar Namgyal Wangchuk, will play a central role. He will formally become Crown Prince, destined to be the fifth Wangchuk to rule.

The glad, multiple matrimonial tidings were borne to the Indian capital by the Foreign Minister, Mr Dawa Tsering. He told reporters yesterday: 'I will hold a reception for all the diplomats here, and tell them that they can't come to the wedding.'

For, even in their second, ceremonial form, the nuptials are to be conducted in relative privacy. They will be witnessed only by those members of the royal family not actually getting married, and by a formidable gathering of lamas, monks and lalops (senior monks).

The king will receive nine royal scarves of noble colours from the sacred presence of the Shabdung Machey whose role is central, but passive, as he has been embalmed for 337 years.

Although dead, he remains a towering figure. In the 17th century he unified and ruled Bhutan. And he went on ruling it for two and a half centuries, through a series of 55 reincarnations. As Foreign Minister Tsering nobly explained yesterday: 'This was not a very workable system.'

The first of the Wangchuks took over in 1907. The present king is the fourth of the line. Happiest when working for the advancement of his desperately poor nation, he relaxes by playing basketball. He used to play soccer, as goalkeeper, but his subjects thought it undignified.

The king's simple tastes were reflected in his first multiple marriage nine years ago, a homely affair with a few monks in attendance. Today's marriages will be much more elaborate, though no more public.

'People felt that a private ceremony was not good enough for the king, and that the line of succession should be formally laid down,' the Foreign Minister said.

The ceremony will be in Punakha, the ancient capital, and will be followed by three days of public celebrations in Thimphu. Keen royal watchers may expect a certain discreet elevation in the status of Ashi Tshering Yandon, who, as the mother of the new Crown Prince, has moved from third sister to first queen, second time round.

A rent-boy's story

MARIANNE MACDONALD
5 November 1988

Marianne Macdonald, a 20-year-old student reading English at Oxford, won the *Guardian* Student Journalist of the Year award with this article.

To me David was always the wild one, completely irresponsible, dangerous. Champagne, expensive meals, alcohol, alcohol. He brought out the sense of danger in other people; he had the power to transmute situations, to draw people as cruelly as gnats to a flame.

This was years ago. I'd heard rumours that lately he was subdued, had settled down. I might have known that predictable is one thing David will never be.

Knee-length riding boots, jeans and leather jacket, driving back from the station, his talk was all rent-boy. If that was what we were expecting, that was what he would be.

David wasn't supposed to be drinking; he'd just been released from a clinical dependency clinic. We had cocktails and champagne. Later, in the college bar, he kept on nudging me to point out the gay men in the vicinity. I had to tell him I didn't think there were any, at least any attractive ones. Still his huge brown eyes kept swivelling all night.

Sunday was interview day. Coffee, chains of cigarettes, red wine: David started to talk . . .

'I slipped into it as though I was made for it. My prostitution was a punishment: of myself, of other people – of men. Of my father for leaving and to hurt my mother because I knew she'd find out. And for the first time there was a number to what I was worth . . . the only ones who disturbed me were the ones who wanted more for their money – who wanted to kiss you – that's something I've never been able to do.'

David got into prostitution after his expulsion from public school. Deciding to go to Paris ('as far away as my 16-year-old mind could comprehend') his only contact was a man who ran a string of porn cinemas in Saint-Germain, a rent-boy area. It was hardly surprising that David was approached one night for sex. What is perhaps more surprising is that he said yes. 'I felt horrendous about it afterwards, not because of the prostitution but because he was married. The thing that made me cry as I walked out, was that he sounded like what I would have wanted my father to have sounded like. He was very sad, very lonely.'

His words are down-to-earth, even flippant. But it hurts me every time he describes himself as a whore ('if you've got to, put yourself down first'). And it hurts me when he tells me about how he burned the hand of his lover in a nightclub with his cigarette ('I watched it turn red, then purple') and I don't know what to think.

'When you're whoring you make the whoring unreal. And because you're only so clever and you can only be selective up to a certain point, your whole life becomes unreal. You're giving yourself total freedom because the consequences will not happen, or if they do happen, it doesn't matter.'

After returning from Paris, David moved to a squat in Brixton. All day would be spent in pubs and bars, with the punters. Everyone would get very drunk. 'Even on the punters' side as much as yours there was as much effort to put the actual doing as far away as possible, timewise. You've got to get as much lubricant in as you can.'

It was during this period that he first met Harvey Proctor. Another rent-boy, whom he knew by sight, asked if he wanted to go back to a punter's house. It was 'a very ordinary one-bedroom flat in Fulham with this guy who was wildly into school-boy scenes. He asked me out the next night, then he asked me to move in.' The guy was Harvey Proctor, MP.

Having moved in with Harvey Proctor, life became –

mostly – more comfortable. 'Every day he'd give me £20 and I'd go out and do another punter – just an hour-job – and get very, very slaughtered ... He liked having a real situation to punish me for, so the next morning it would be: "David, you've been a very bad boy, haven't you? What did you do last night?" "Came in drunk, sir." He liked me, I'd been at public school, I knew what I had to do.

'There was no sex involved at all. He'd start off with his hand, then move on to his slipper, then the cane. And it was horrendous. It brought being at school to me in a big way. Which I hated then and how much more did I hate it now. I was feeling that same fear of being hit and of knowing you are putting yourself in that situation, and that he wants to do it. It's very odd and scary. Once I actually enjoyed it and that scared me as well. But generally I didn't.'

Even out of the 'filthy disgusting squat' David kept up his links with the rent-boy scene, which thrived at that time around the Victoria and Piccadilly Circus Tube stations. It was becoming a need, and at the same time a fear: 'You become old very quickly. Physically and in every way. If only because of the hours you're keeping and the drink you're consuming. Not eating. It's soul-destroying as well. But the older you get, the less attractive you are, because on the whole gay men are paying for youth. The older you get the less you're worth. So you'll do it for a quarter-pounder and chips.

'There's no caring. There's no one to care. It makes you feel lonely, yes, but at the same time you feel you belong, because you don't care either. The rent-boy scene is very much its own society with its own laws, its own rules. You're very aware of the danger because you read about it in the papers. People you know, faces you recognize, have either got Aids or just disappear.

'I was very lucky on the whole. I knew that. I was very aware of going to be dying young. And I still feel that way ... I think we make a bit too much of death perhaps. There was a certainty in this – through all the destruction I felt creative . . . But it has to happen. My life has always been manipulative. I think it's the crowning joke in bad taste that you can't choose the time of your death.'

This double life – half rent-boy, half diner at the House of Commons – continued for three months. It was then that he went to the *Sunday People* with his story. They couldn't believe their luck – having followed Proctor on a round-the-world tour in an unsuccessful attempt to nail him. One practical point for David about going to the press was that he would no longer be able to get punters – the trust was no longer there. This didn't actually happen. The career of Harvey Proctor, however, had been effectively destroyed. And David's mother rang him up the morning it came out: 'I want to die today.'

How did he feel about it?

'There was this feeling of climax, and going as far as you could go. Down. The night before it came out I spent £20 in a bar on my own and literally drank myself sick . . . The ridiculous thing is three days after that I went and sat an English A-level.'

'Did the contrast strike you?'

'Oh, not really. I went in and wrote a story about prostitution. It was one called "Smiles".

'I tried to kill myself. I was absolutely off my head, I was too drunk to do it properly. I tried to cut my wrists and passed out and came to an hour later with the mattress covered in blood, and me bleeding. I just wandered round, it was rather Lady Macbeth-like . . . I was tripping because I'd lost some blood and I was – empty. My mind was empty.

'There *are* certain times when you can't carry on pretending, when it does come to you – a recognition of what you've done. And it was bound up with the fact that I was turned down that night. Someone didn't want to have sex with me, which disturbed me immensely. The worst thing is recognizing that you don't think you're going to be happy, and you don't think you've ever been . . . Apparently I was once. My mother said that up until the age of six when I was sent to boarding school I was the happiest child she'd ever known. So maybe I was happy once.

'My fantasy has taken over totally! I've been manipulated by myself. I had everything going for me: I was intelligent, young, well-educated and healthy. And with those tools that I had, I set out and said, I'm going to be a writer. This is what I need to write novels. And this is what I need to do, full stop. I've gone back to it and back to it just as people go back to heroin or to alcohol. It's an addiction in itself I think. And now I'm so far into fantasy I ask myself whether it's really true. It may all be a lie, you know.'

It may well be a lie. But one thing I'm most sure of right now is just how sad I feel. David feels it too. What can follow and make sense? What is there left apart from to write? But if he can write with the truth with which he speaks, then perhaps people will begin to understand that David's life does not rise from the gutter, because the pain he has expressed is part of the lives of the vast majority. He's just a little more honest about being sad.

Goodbye, Ronald Reagan

ALEX BRUMMER
9 November 1988

As Ronald Reagan journeyed triumphally from Texas to California in the closing hours of campaign '88, tipping his stetson to the crowds lining the streets for a glimpse of the Gipper on his last hurrah, it was plain that, whatever his failings, the American people are both forgiving and adoring.

More than any other modern President since John Kennedy, Mr Reagan has restored the ceremonial functions of the presidency. Although his popularity slipped during the Iran–Contra debacle, it is now back at its peak, and the

Reagan era is being hailed as one in which America found heart and confidence again.

Although we have come to know over the years that everything sensible Mr Reagan says is scripted, down to small talk with child visitors to the Oval Office, his engaging style of saying it, his natural sense of humour, and his goodwill always come through.

Intellectually, he has never left Hollywood. Even his own favourite nickname, the Gipper, based on his role as the ill-fated quarterback in the film *Knute Rockne – All American*, was culled from silver screen archives. As Mr Reagan formally handed the baton to Vice-President George Bush in New Orleans this August he used his famous catchphrase once again: 'Win one for the Gipper.'

Mr Reagan's record is likely to be debated by historians for years. There have been achievements: the INF treaty with Moscow; the moves towards settling conflicts in Afghanistan, Angola, and the Gulf; successful military operations in Grenada and Libya; the reduction of inflation and interest rates; and the longest period of sustained economic growth in the post-war era. In short, he has provided the agenda of peace and prosperity on which Mr Bush seeks the White House.

However, the roots of these accomplishments, particularly on the foreign policy side, are more tangled than the conservative fans of Mr Reagan would admit. Moreover, economic prosperity has been built on a fragile base which means that young Americans may be required to pay the cost for generations to come with depressed living standards.

While American conservatives would argue that the US's new relationship with the Soviet Union was built on the firm defence policy of the Reagan team and on the modernization of the strategic triad of the intercontinental MX missile, the Trident 2 submarine and the B-1 bomber, together with research on Star Wars, critics might argue that he was simply lucky.

He was the American President who happened to be in

office when the most important changes in the Soviet Union since the revolution were set in motion. There could have been no INF deal without Mr Gorbachev, as there could have been no movement on Afghanistan or Angola without the newly elevated Soviet President's contribution. However, Mr Reagan's conservative credentials enabled him to achieve the extraordinary rapprochement with the Soviet Union more easily than might have been possible for a Democratic President.

But whereas Mr Reagan has been reasonably successful in managing big-power relations, he has often failed in his dealings with the little countries.

He began his presidency with the return of the 50 US diplomats held in Iran. But he has nothing to compare in the Middle East to the Camp David accord won by President Jimmy Carter. In Lebanon he was forced to retreat after the loss of 241 marines.

His amateur attempts at freeing hostages in Iran brought the greatest crisis of his presidency – the Iran–Contra affair. Mr Reagan has had good fortune with the economy. After the oil price shocks of the 1970s he came to office when an age of cheap energy was just beginning. This, together with the firm grip on monetary policy imposed by Mr Paul Volcker of the Federal Reserve – the other towering American figure of the 1980s – meant that the spiral of ever-higher inflation and interest rates was broken.

Under the guise of supply-side economics, the movement born in California where resentment of high taxes was at its peak, Mr Reagan built prosperity on an old-style Keynesian boom. But instead of using the fat years of prosperity to pare back the deficits and federal debt he allowed them to burgeon, creating a domestic debt legacy of $2100 billion – or 43 cents for every dollar of US income – which will take generations to eliminate.

Moreover, the value of the dollar became caught up in the nationalist burst which Mr Reagan brought to the presidency, sending it soaring to new heights on the international markets and pricing US goods out of competition.

The result was a decline in basic heavy industry and agriculture and a foreign investment and takeover binge in the US which has created a bizarre value system. The Ivan Boesky affair and the Michael Deaver lobbying scandals provided grim evidence of a society which had abandoned self-discipline and had a value system out of kilter. It has also given rise to a fierce strand of economic populism, and potentially isolationism, should the next Administration begin the long task of correcting fiscal and trade imbalances.

The darker side of the Reagan legacy is already being explored in popular books such as *Landslide* by the reporters Jane Mayer and Doyle McManus; *Day of Reckoning* by the Harvard economist Benjamin Friedman; and *Rendezvous with Reality* by Muray Weidenbaum, the former Reagan chief economic adviser.

Such works, written even before the old campaigner has ridden off to the sunset years at his ranch, lack the perspective history will bring. President Truman left office widely despised: in the 1988 campaign he was the President whose name was most invoked by both parties as the epitome of fighting American values.

Escaping the fire – and after

RICHARD BATES
II November 1988

Richard Bates, a subeditor on the *Guardian*, was caught in the King's Cross fire on his way home from work.

I suppose it was the poster that saved my life. I'd just walked along the platform for a closer look when the policemen shouted at us to get out. I found myself towards the back of the queue for the escalator thinking, 'Don't panic

or no one's going to make it. Stand on the right as usual.'
Two strides into the ticket hall it happened.

First there was the noise like a blast furnace. Then the
flames ripped across the ceiling as if they'd been shot from
a flamethrower. Then choking smoke, so black and thick it
seemed you could grab it by the handful. People who had
walked past me further into the hall staggered around
unable to see and unable to escape. Their bodies bumped
into me.

I got out, the only one to stagger down the escalator out
of that cauldron where 31 people had just died in a heat so
intense it melted metal. I found out later that a fireman
was on the escalator alongside, swearing at me to keep me
conscious and keep me going. My hair and jacket were on
fire. I reached the bottom and the fireman, Peter Osborne,
shouted at me to lie down. He handed someone a fire
extinguisher which was emptied over me. The two policemen tried to get me out of the station but the gates were
locked. After five minutes keys were found. Another set
of gates. Shut. Twenty minutes of shouting, rattling and
kicking the gates by the policemen as frightened and confused as me. I walked around in circles screaming with the
pain from my hands. I imagined the fire snaking its way
down the tunnels and there I was with my back to the wall.
I thought I was going to die.

And then, thank God, someone with keys heard the
desperate shouts for help. Suddenly we were out on the
street and I was walking round to the front of King's Cross
vaguely aware of people staring at me, of crowds gathering,
of lights and sirens. Into an ambulance after making the
policeman promise to ring my wife. There was a man
already in it. He wore an oxygen mask. We gave our names
to the ambulanceman. In hospital a few weeks later I
suddenly realized I hadn't seen that man again. He had
died – 70 per cent burns and the lung-destroying smoke
had proved too much.

Into casualty at University College Hospital just around
the corner. My clothes were cut off and after that it became

a blur of injections, soothing voices, indistinct faces, tubes. I remember the plastic surgeon telling the nurse to cut all my hair off. I drifted in and out of consciousness – once I opened my eyes and saw a bishop at the end of my bed. Then my wife, Sian, was there. Fortunately she had been warned what I looked like. My face had ballooned to the size of a football. Mrs Thatcher arrived. Sian told me later she'd said some very kind words.

The operation followed, slicing a layer of skin off my left thigh and laying it on both hands. The burned skin was peeled off my face layer by layer. There followed five weeks in the burns ward where I received wonderful care from everyone, from plastic surgeon Michael Brough to the tea lady. Sian's mother arrived to look after the kids.

Friends rallied round, helping to bathe me and feed me and doing what they could for Sian who came to the hospital 35 exhausting nights in a row. There were the cards and messages; from children in schools all over the country, from strangers, from old friends, from Manchester United, from the Queen.

I shrank away from newspapers, radio and television in case the fire was mentioned. I told myself I would sooner or later have to accept what had happened but that it was more important to channel my energies and thoughts into physical recovery. Then one night I inadvertently discovered how many people had died. This was so upsetting I asked to see psychiatrist David Sturgeon the next morning.

All I can say from a patient's point of view is that those early sessions were vital in reducing the trauma. Our conversations over the last year have helped me come to terms with what happened and have got me used to the realization that my life will never quite be the same.

I have never felt grief or guilt – both apparently common emotions experienced by those who survive disasters. No grief because, thank God, I never lost anyone that night. No guilt, either – my actions had in no way influenced anyone else; those people who walked past me to their death had made their own decision on how to escape. I feel desperately sorry for those who lost loved ones, but the dead are people I do not know and whose names I recognize only from television or newspaper stories.

I came home three days before Christmas. Timothy and Lucy had strung a banner across the wall saying Welcome Home Daddy. Christmas was a rather muted affair but I was aware just how lucky I was to be seeing it.

I had to go to hospital every day for physiotherapy. I still go twice a week and sometimes I see the others who were burned there. I remember Ron Lipsius, a guitarist whose hands were so badly burned they had to be inserted into his side so the flesh would grow, laughingly telling physio Elaine Mason how he had seen a sign saying Alight Here for King's Cross.

Then there's Rosalind whose friend died but whose strong, unshakable faith in God has carried her through the ordeal; Damon, the young Scot who had only been in London for a few days and was on his way to see the Christmas lights in Oxford Street; Mariella, whose boyfriend died and who only survived after weeks of battling in intensive care; Steve, the tough Guardsman turned policeman, who is still deeply affected by what he saw and heard that night.

King's Cross is never far away from my thoughts; there are reminders of some kind every day. There are the special gloves I have to wear for two years to flatten and protect the grafted skin. People stare but you get used to it.

Going back on the Tube is harder to get used to. Shortly after coming home I went with Sian, going through King's Cross. The next time I decided to get out and just stand inside the burned and blackened ticket hall. I stepped off that escalator and to my horror saw groups of policemen and firemen. All I could think of was getting out and went straight down to the platform. A train arrived and I sat there willing it to leave but it didn't. A policeman rushed on to the platform and shouted that no one was to get off.

Surely the horror couldn't be happening again? For the

next few minutes I sat there rigid, holding Sian's hand and forcing myself to think of something, anything. Eventually we got going; I found out later that a workman's welding torch had started a small blaze among some rubbish near an escalator.

I have a strong sense of vulnerability. After all, an accident is no longer something that happens to other people. I avoid risks of any kind. Immediately after leaving hospital I found myself hugging the inside of the pavements, keeping close to buildings. I do not dodge through traffic to cross the road; I wait for the green man to flash, aware of quizzical stares sometimes as I stand stubbornly alone on the pavement.

When I visit a restaurant, a cinema or concert hall I make sure I know where the exit is. I try to sit on the end of the row. I remain uneasy in confined spaces, such as aeroplanes, from where there is no immediate way out.

It's almost a year since the disaster. I am keen to put it behind me and to get on with living my life, although the requests for interviews intensified with the publication of the inquiry report looming. It is only right to say here that the press, much maligned and often deservedly, have been very good. With only one exception all those seeking interviews and pictures have been considerate, courteous and understanding, even though they've gone back to their newsdesks empty-handed.

A legal battle with London Transport may lie ahead. My feelings towards those in charge are perhaps best saved for a court of law if that is what the claim for compensation comes to.

But I believe King's Cross was a disaster that need not have happened, and that 31 people died because those entrusted with the safety of London's public transport system abrogated that responsibility in the over-zealous pursuit of cash savings, in an eagerness to please political masters.

Worryingly, I see no evidence that those same people have the commitment or the competence to make the Tube any safer in future. It takes more than the putting up of a few No Smoking signs to run a railroad.

Money has to be spent, not on automatic ticket barriers that actually make stations even more difficult to escape from in the event of a fire, but on extra staff, equipment and trains. But investment on the scale that's needed will need Government sanction and that is the crunch. It's all very well for Mrs Thatcher to turn up at disaster after disaster with kind words but what we really need is for the Prime Minister for once to put people before pounds. Otherwise the next disaster is just around the corner.

Undercover knowledge

JUDY RUMBOLD
14 November 1988

Lingerie is a more lyrical word for it, but in the trade they call it Intimate Apparel. Knickers are a serious business in the male-dominated world of women's underwear – babyish abbreviations like undies and panties are left to the sniggering consumer who, according to Marks & Spencer, is buying more of them than ever.

Whether the customers wear lingerie or not is a different matter – unlike the Americans and the French who, says Next, have wardrobes heaving with serious sports bras and a different set of underwear for every outfit. A quintessentially English trait is to wear the solitary greying bra and user-friendly knickers from five years ago, while the scratchy new lacy things remain untouched in the recesses of a drawer.

They may yet be shamed into different habits. The deliberate visibility of underwear in recent years has elevated it from a position alongside cosmetics as a heavily marketed though essentially useless commodity ('underwear is to clothes what ice-cream is to food', said the novelist Angela

Carter) to something that is a valid reflecton of changing styles of dress. As high-fashion items, corsets, tight Lycra bodices and new Thirties styles have succeeded in stripping underwear of some of its tedious mystique, relieving it of the pressure to titillate with superfluous lace and bows, and rendered it an ambiguous subscriber to both dress and undress.

Marks & Spencer realizes that its underwear reflects changing fashion trends much more accurately than the clothes; the new range of silk and satin lingerie incorporates a camisole top and tap-pants after Josephine Baker, langorous bias-cut nightdresses, and Garboesque satin wrap gowns – styles which complement the looser, more fluid lines of the fashionable silhouette.

Films began to influence tastes in underwear in the mid-Twenties when motion pictures began to bear such titles as *Sinners in Silk*. Undressing scenes were frequently shown, and had the effect of greatly improving women's underwear in real life. Linen was abandoned and real or artificial silk substituted.

Despite its departure into slinky lingeries, Marks & Spencer's enduring image is still that of the sensible knicker; the Marble Arch store shifts 19,000 pairs a week; about one every three seconds, and as many as Next sell in a whole year. 'We're more than happy with our image,' says a spokeswoman, not in the least bit anxious to relinquish cotton interlock knickers so high they hug the armpits for a bit of slinky nothingness. 'If we reject the knickers, we're in big trouble.'

Not so much interested in the nuances of fashion as the frothy rudeness of it all are the increasing number of men who will surreptitiously weave their way through the slippers and rubber plants to the women's lingerie department during the run up to Christmas. Gratefully fingering all that lace with blessed impunity, they go for the camisoles and the french knickers, and avoid like the plague anything that looks as if it might serve a vaguely practical or thermal purpose, or is the colour of cold semolina. Consequently, the post-Christmas period sees hordes of female recipients clamouring to swap scraps of red lace wispiness for something more functional.

Apart from the underwear that seasonally adapts to accommodate the clothes that go on top, there will always be a corner of the market given over to the stuff perpetuating the camp crudity and parodied style of 'French Lingerie' in the form of suspender belts and stockings and various corset-type arrangements assembled around a complex network of lace and underwiring. 'Glamorous', stereotypically titillating underwear made a dramatic reappearance in the 1970s, when Janet Reger's camisoles, camiknickers, french knickers and suspender belts were widely copied and adapted for sale in every chain store.

'However informal, these garments are obviously public dress,' says Angela Carter of the Janet Reger catalogue, and they were often worn as such, but in a more overtly sexual way than recent underwear-as-outerwear trends for long-johns, Lycra bodysuits and corsets worn on the outside.

A popular marketing ploy with underwear manufacturers is to sell women the idea that under cover of the power suit it is desirable, in order to retain some semblance of feminiity, to keep a frothy inferno of sexuality simmering away. It will be her own delicious secret, they say; it will enhance her performance in the boardroom.

It is more likely, of course, that if she's gone to all that trouble and discomfort with the shoulder pads, the short skirt and the heels, she will allow herself the small concession of those old M & S armpit-huggers with the baggy legs and perished elastic. It is a popular misconception that women subconsciously choose the kind of underwear that will accommodate an impromptu strip or road accident.

For most women, ideal underwear minds its own business and pretends it isn't there. It doesn't involve great crusts of lace that itch like hell and dinky pink bows that make a lump on the outside.

Amazingly, no miracle ridgeless knicker materialized during the clingy, body-hugging jersey phase inspired by the clothes of Azzedine Alaia. Women instead chose the body, big sister of the teddy; a tight fitting all-in-one that has become a best-selling item, bought as much for outer as underwear, at both Marks & Spencer and Next. The comfortable knicker's finest hour came when underwear was simplified and stripped of embellishment to complement the keep-fit trend of the early 1980s. Calvin Klein's completely different style of underwear for women was modelled on Y-fronts, boxer shorts and boys' vests, and made the welcome point that women's underwear requirements aren't that different from men's in terms of comfort and fit.

'We've moved away from that androgynous look now,' says Marks & Spencer. 'Women want to look more romantic, in blush colours like champagne and rose.' Do we? At least all this loose satin languor offers brief respite from the corset, the restriction and the boning, and gives the ribcage time to reassemble before the next desirable body shape is casually dictated. The next big thing, says M & S, is cleavage. 'Cleavage is back, busts are back, bras are back.' As in the case of its sensible knickers, M & S packages its enthusiasm in sets of three.

Screwed up

ANDREW MONCUR
16 November 1988

Jiffi, the condom people, have run into a ticklish problem with an extremely sensitive registrar of trade marks. This arises over their application to register in the UK an inoffensive device accompanied by – oh, dear – a Latin phrase. And he won't have it. The registrar, who clearly has a classical education, feels that the words will have to go. What can they possibly be? Well, since you ask, Futue Mundum. The company has been told: 'Objection has been raised to the registration of the mark in the form as submitted because it contains the Latin phrase which means "screw the world".'

A glimpse of hell fire

RICHARD BOSTON
19 November 1988

The highest holder of office in the land is not the Prime Minister but the Lord Chancellor. That lofty post is at present held by Lord Mackay of Clashfern who is not just a member but an Elder of the Free Presbyterian Church of Scotland. He is its former legal adviser and part author of the *History of the Free Presbyterian Church of Scotland, 1893–1970.*

Though there are a mere 6000 Free Presbyterians in Scotland they've got the Lord Chancellor up against the ropes. He has been suspended as an Elder. What he did (if you've missed the story so far) was to attend a Requiem Mass for his Roman Catholic friend, Lord Wheatley.

This was simply not on, since the doctrine laid down by the Westminster Confession of Faith makes it perfectly clear that the Roman Catholic Mass is idolatrous, that the RC church is the Whore of Babylon, and that the Pope is antichrist, a man of sin and the Son of Perdition.

There are certain misconceptions that have been spread by press reports of the affair. Many of these give the impression that Lord Mackay's kirk is the Free Church of Scotland (the Wee Frees) which sometime or other, and for some reason or other, split off from the Church of Scotland and now has about 19,000 members in Scotland.

Lord Mackay's lot is the Wee Wee Frees, the Free Presbyterians who in the 1890s split off from the Wee Frees for reasons best known to themselves. They now have about 6000 members, 80 churches, and 28 ministers. This means that they are outnumbered in Scotland by Sikhs and Hindus (10,000 each) and the Muslims who with 28,000 are more than four times the number of the FPs.

On the other hand, few though they are, the FPs have loads of money. Most churches in Scotland are facing bankruptcy. The Wee Wee Frees are sitting on a cool £2 million, the result of a bequest from a draper called Forsyth who left them his fortune, although he wasn't even a member.

Their beliefs make a bizarre cocktail (teetotal). They are pro-monarchist, pro-nuclear, and pro-capital punishment. They are against almost everything else, especially television. In 1965 their Synod was alerted to 'the grave danger to the life and morals of the nation which is constituted by the present character of many television programmes'. To view them was to risk 'incurring God's righteous anger as well as the censure of the Church'. Those words were spoken by Mr J. P. H. Mackay, now Lord Mackay.

The idea seems to have got around that the FPs are exceptionally strict observers of the Sabbath. Yet again the meejah have got it wrong. It is true that the FPs cook on a Saturday in order to avoid doing so on a Sunday. For the same reason the men shave on Saturday evening. No radio or television, of course. Not long ago a member was expelled for belonging to a golf club that is open on Sundays, although he had himself never played on the Sabbath. The only permitted reading on a Sunday is the Bible. Lord Mackay himself refuses to give interviews not just on Sundays but also to newspapers that are published on a Sunday.

So what *can* they do on the Sabbath? Well, for one thing they are allowed to go to church and listen to sermons that last for three-quarters of an hour. And that's not all they can do on the Sabbath. They can physically assault a *Guardian* photographer.

Though the FPs have places of worship in Australia, Canada, New Zealand and Zimbabwe, most are in the Highlands and Islands of Scotland. But their power-house is Glasgow, at St Jude's in Woodlands Road. This is where the Lord Chancellor had to go for trial. (Incidentally St

Jude is the patron saint of those in dire straits, and a defender of hopeless causes. I'm still working on a rhyme, the first two lines of which run: 'As I was going to St Jude's I met an awful lot of prudes . . .')

I was advised to dress for my expedition as though I was going to a funeral. I have a very dark suit, acquired years ago and only worn about twice. Black waistcoat – 20p at the village jumble sale. Black tie borrowed from my next-door neighbour.

The day I arrived in Scotland, last Saturday, was an exciting one for Scotland, and for Glasgow in particular. Not only had the astounding results of the Govan by-election just come in but also there was a Celtic versus Rangers match on. But these were not for me. My goal was the church of St Jude.

I put on a sombre expression and entered the FP bookshop next to the church. There was only one other customer and he was dressed exactly like me. As we passed one another he gave a slight nod, as though of recognition, and summoned to his mouth something that nearly approached a smile.

It's a very interesting bookshop. I acquired the *History of the Church* to which Lord Mackay was a contributor; also the *Free Presbyterian Magazine*, and three pamphlets. These were: one, *A Warning Against the Anabaptists*, by John Knox; two, *Christmas: an Historical Survey Regarding Its Origins and Opposition to It*; three, *Forbidden Alliances: Concerning Associations and Confederacies with Idolaters, Infidels, Heretics, or Any Other Known Enemies of Truth and Godliness*, originally published by George Gillespie in 1649 and still selling well. I bought a copy in spite of the fact that it has been 'edited to bring it into greater conformity with contemporary spelling, punctuation, grammatical usage', which sounds like back-sliding to me.

While making my purchase I learned that not only were there two services on Sunday but also one that very Saturday afternoon. This gave me plenty of time for refreshment, which I took on nearby licensed premises. Here I struck up a conversation with two young men.

One was a skinhead who was about to go to the Celtic and Rangers match. Since he was a Catholic he was a Celtic supporter. His brother wore thick glasses, had abundant black hair, and his name was Michael. Since he had no ticket for the match and nothing to do that afternoon, I suggested that he should come to the church with me.

This seemed quite safe since he looked suitably sombre, dressed in a black shirt and a black jacket. It was only when we got up to leave that I found he was wearing a pair of blue jeans that had seen better days. We entered the church in plenty of time. Michael led the way, which was unfortunate because he went straight to one of the pews at the very front. This was because he's a Catholic: if you're at the front you are among the first to take Communion and if you're the first to take Communion, you're the first to leave.

As I took my place with my back to the congregation I began to wish that I hadn't brought Michael. And it was a pretty full congregation, mostly middle-aged: grim-faced men dressed like me, and grim-faced women wearing amazing pudding-bowl hats. The Wee Wee Frees keep women firmly in the background.

A dozen men dressed as undertakers came up the aisle and formed ranks facing one another. Naturally there was nothing like an altar. Instead, high above, there was a pulpit and looking down from it and looking at us with an air of total disapproval was the most terrifying man in the world.

I couldn't see his eyes because the light reflected from his glasses, but the rest of his face was highly visible. It was roughly the shape and colour of a tombstone. He wore a fixed smile. The worrying thing about this smile was that it was upside down. His grimness went right off the Richter scale of grimness.

He started to speak in a nasal sing-song voice which was hypnotically monotonous. My first thought was that he must have got this voice and intonation second-hand from an American evangelical revivalist preacher. My second thought was that the traffic was probably in the other direction.

I was so mesmerized that I didn't take in much of the content. I do remember that he pronounced God as in the first syllable of *Guardian*, except at the end of a sentence when it became two syllables: Ga-arrd.

He seemed to be talking to me personally, and he was telling me that if I didn't let the Word of Gard enter my heart, my immortal soul was destined to an eternity of perdition in Hell in the company of Hindus, Hebrew, Muslim, Buddhists, Roman Catholics, and everyone else. It sounded as though even if I did let Gard into my heart my chances of escaping everlasting hell-fire were practically nil. I can assure you that he could go the distance with Dr Ian Paisley any day.

And then the congregation sang a psalm. There was no accompaniment because musical instruments are the work of the devil. The Lowland Scots have a contemptuous term for Gaelic-speaking Highlanders and Islanders, which is Teuchters, but even the Lowlanders concede that the Teuchters can sing. They certainly can. They sang *a cappella* in unison with those sudden swoops as in *Amazing Grace*. It was extraordinarily beautiful and powerfully moving.

Then it was old Stoneface's turn again. He took the opportunity to spend another ten minutes talking about how sinful we all were. Michael was beginning to get quite fidgety by now and kept whispering to me. He even giggled once. I remembered Byron's description of a Methodist preacher who 'on perceiving a profane grin' on the faces of part of his congregation, exclaimed: 'No hopes for them as laughs.'

It needed only the briefest consultation with wee Michael to decide that it was time to do a runner. We had just got into the vestibule when Michael realized that he had left a book under the pew. If it had been me, and if the book had been a Gutenberg Bible, I might have gone back to retrieve it, but Michael is made of tougher material. In his blue jeans he went alone, with Stoneface preaching damnation in front of him and a congregation of about 300 glaring at him from behind. He came back triumphantly holding a paperback novel. A brave man.

We had probably both lost our eternal souls, but at least we escaped unscathed physically. Ian Campbell (name changed to protect the innocent) was not so lucky the next day. He wanted to take some photographs of the congregation leaving the church after the 11 o'clock service. For four hours he waited patiently on the pavement before the FPs came out.

He was attacked. In fairness, he says it was his camera they were after but he's not clear whether his offence was taking pictures of the FPs or using a camera on a Sunday. In his time he has had bottles and bricks thrown at him at such events as the miners' strike and football riots. What made this so different was the element of surprise. He simply didn't expect to be assaulted by people who had just spent four hours in church. He wasn't injured but he was handled with force and his camera's light-meter was smashed.

Now, I must admit that I had had some scruples about this assignment. Was I not being fraudulent in attending the service in what was effectively a disguise? Wasn't Ian behaving like the paparazzi who with long-focus lenses take snaps of celebrities? What were we doing that the *Sun* wouldn't do?

Well, there are differences. For one thing St Jude's is a public place of worship. For another, the evidence being used against Lord Mackay consists of a photograph of him entering a Catholic church. And Ian wasn't using a long-distance lens. He was standing on the pavement, going about his business quite openly.

At any rate, the assault on Ian didn't just smash his light-meter. It also demolished any scruples I might have had about writing about the bigots of the Free Presbyterian Church of Scotland.

Incidentally Celtic beat Rangers three goals to one. I gather that there was very little violence. And here's a date to mark in your diary: 14 December. The Synod of the Free Presbyterian Church has declared it a Day of Humiliation.

The eagle has landed

SHYAMA PERERA
23 November 1988

The Duke of Devonshire's gamekeeper will today explain to a London court how a stuffed and mounted golden eagle called Eric came into his possession.

His evidence is an important link in a chain which started with the mysterious death of the bird on the Outer Hebridean island of North Uist and finished in the West End showrooms of the auctioneers, Bonhams.

The gamekeeper, Mr Robert Law, swapped Eric for four volumes of Kirman and Jourdain's *British Bird Book*, because his wife disliked the creature. The book-dealer in turn sold the eagle to Mr Malcolm Everett of Two Hoots Taxidermy, Truro, Cornwall, because he felt uneasy in a home filled with stuffed wildlife.

But when Mr Everett remounted the bird and submitted it to a natural history sale at Bonhams, the eagle landed with a vengeance, a magistrate heard yesterday.

Inspectors from the Royal Society for the Protection of Birds discovered that the bird was incorrectly registered and, after inquiries, they seized Eric on the suspicion that he had been unlawfully killed.

At Wells Street magistrates court, west London, Mr Everett and Mr Bonhams both denied unlawful possession and control of the golden eagle in July 1986, on the grounds that they believed the bird died after flying into power lines.

However, the RSPB, which is bringing the prosecution,

suspects the eagle was shot down, possibly by crofters who say the birds ate their sheep. It is up to the defendants to prove that the bird was not unlawfully killed.

Mr Mark Love, prosecuting, said: 'At the end of the day, it cannot be resolved how the bird died, whether it was killed by an act of man or it was killed by accident.'

The bookseller, Mr James Whitaker of Leeds, who called the bird Eric, said he had been told the bird died after flying into cables.

(1) A civil servant writes

7 December 1988

It is all very well for Mrs Thatcher to inveigh against the Belgians and the Irish with such self-righteous invective [over the extradition from Belgium of Father Patrick Ryan]. Naturally, she would not care to admit it but in the not too distant past her allegations of being soft on terrorism and allowing political considerations to override the due legal process could have been levelled at Mrs Thatcher herself.

Remember the Coventry Four? These were the four (white) South Africans brought before Coventry magistrates in March 1984 and remanded in custody on arms embargo charges. Rumour has it that Mrs Thatcher was rather annoyed with the over-zealous officials who caused the four military personnel to be arrested in Britain. Rightly, she refused to accede to the South African Embassy's demand for the case to be dropped, but she was keen for the Embassy to know precisely how the legal hurdles governing their release and the return of their passports could be swiftly overcome. Thus the First Secretary at the Embassy stood bail for the Coventry Four, having declared in Court that he was waiving his diplomatic immunity. (The Embassy did not, however, formally confirm the waiver.) Then a petition to an English Judge in Chambers secured the repatriation of the four accused.

Clearly, Mrs Thatcher wanted the four high-profile detainees safely out of UK jurisdiction, back in South Africa and off the agenda well before her June 1984 talks at Chequers with the two visiting Bothas. Strange that Pik Botha, the Foreign Minister, was able to find an excuse for not allowing the Coventry Four to stand trial in the autumn of 1984.

Stranger still that Mrs Thatcher failed to denounce Mr Botha's refusal to surrender the four 'terrorists' (cf the declaration by US Governor Dukakis that South Africa is a 'terrorist state').

P. J. Haseldine

Information Department,
Foreign and Commonwealth Office,
London SW1.

(2) From a former civil servant

9 December 1988

The letter in your columns (*Guardian*, 7 December) from Mr Patrick Haseldine of the FCO illustrates a growing feeling among civil servants – dislike, verging on nausea – at having to support the mendacity and hypocrisy of politicians. It is particularly true of information officers who are in the front line of putting across government propaganda and half-truths to the public, although some of the senior members of the group seem to have stronger stomachs for the job. One disillusioned Central Office of Information official recently publicly described his job as being 'to expound untruths on behalf of government, produce dodgy material, or leak documents in the Government's interest'.

The British civil service has long taken the view that a

breach of confidentiality is an unforgivable and inexcusable thing. What it has failed to acknowledge is that 'official trust' is not the only moral imperative. Yet ministers refuse to contemplate a code of ethics for the civil service let alone an Act to protect civil servants who reveal wrong-doing (and worse) in government, as is the case in the United States. They need to recognize that not everyone will feel able to repress their qualms or be prepared, in the immortal words of Sir Robert Armstrong, to 'pass on the burden of conscience' to their superiors.

In this climate, before ministers criticize the actions of civil servants, they might like to reflect on the ethical standards they set as an example. They should remember that civil servants are individuals with their own moral standards and that people in glass houses should not throw stones.

I fear that once the new Official Secrets Act is on the statute book, we shall see a further tightening of the screws on the civil service to compensate for the withdrawal of the threat of criminal prosecution in some areas.

Clive Ponting

Capel Isaac,
Llandeilo, Dyfed.

Gorbachev at the UN

HELLA PICK
9 December 1988

Mikhail Gorbachev's abrupt departure from New York has only served to enhance the drama of his virtuoso performance at the United Nations. His speech to the General Assembly remains as a monumental challenge to the international community, especially to the Nato allies, that goes far beyond his unilateral pledge to cut Soviet forces by half a million men – and to restructure them from an offensive to a defensive posture.

For the Soviet leader has sought to drive a bulldozer through the assumptions of the institutionalized East–West and North–South confrontations, and to end the military, political and ideological divide that has governed the conduct of East–West relations since the Russian revolution – and particularly since the end of the second world war.

He insists that it is not beyond the wit of statesmen to construct a system of international relations on something better than the deterrent power of military stength. In a changing world, intimidation and political blackmail must be cast aside, and the politics of partnership, of interdependence and of cooperation, should provide a basis for the civilized conduct of international relations.

From past performances by the Soviet leader, the United States and its allies had of course anticipated that Mr Gorbachev's 'Christmas present' would include surprises. But they had not expected such substantial military cuts, nor ones made without strings attached. Still less had they imagined that Mr Gorbachev would set out to convince sceptics of his commitment to change, or meet so many of their concerns about human rights.

For perhaps the first time, even with Mr Gorbachev, there was not a trace of traditional Soviet rhetoric. He assumed the moral highpoint which Western governments until now had always claimed as their own. First reactions here suggest that these governments deeply resent the fact that he has upstaged them yet again. As they see it, he has administered a new version of the Reykjavik cure-all approach. Just as President Reagan's instinct at Reykjavik had been to welcome the sweeping proposals for the elimination of nuclear weapons, so public opinion at the grassroots is now reacting with great warmth to the Gorbachev vision of a world that turns swords into ploughshares.

After Reykjavik, West European governments feared that President Reagan had almost been tempted by

Gorbachev into leaving them semi-naked and exposed to the Red Menace. The parallel today is only marginally different. This time, the US administration stands together with its European allies in fearing that the Gorbachev message will deprive them of public support for their defence programmes, which they consider as necessary today as they were before the Soviet leader made his speech.

The Nato allies do not wish to conceal the fact that Mr Gorbachev is genuinely committed to making dramatic changes in international relations. But they are not sure what the effect will be on their electorates.

Western governments, in their first (acutely defensive) reactions to Gorbachev's promise of troop cuts, have claimed that his statements are the result of the West's steadfastness and its commitment to the twin-pronged policy of strong defences and tough negotiations. The same vigilance must be maintained. To relax now could be the West's undoing. That is the argument.

But even a sceptical Dr Kissinger recognizes that the Soviet leader may not just be pursuing narrow goals, directed at weakening the West, but is, in reality, seeking to shake up the international system in ways that require new Western thinking and new Western responses.

President Reagan and Mrs Thatcher, and Nato's secretary-general, are for the time being concentrating on the Soviet troop withdrawals and extending a cautious welcome. Such a unilateral undertaking to make substantial cuts in manpower and to restructure Soviet forces will, they believe, help to get the new East–West conventional force negotiations off to a promising beginning in the new year.

The message from Nato governments is that the Soviet threat remains, with or without those 500,000 Soviet troops. But they have to admit that the Soviet leader's offer will impress the Western public rather more than the convoluted proposal for negotiating conventional force reductions with the Warsaw Pact that Nato finally managed to put out yesterday after many months of internal alliance wrangles.

The Gorbachev move is bound to make it harder for George Bush to obtain Congressional support to increase defence spending to match inflation. The Congressional pressure on Western Europe to take a greater share of the Nato defence burden is also likely to increase. Yet West European governments, especially the Federal Republic, are already greatly reluctant to maintain existing defence expenditures, let alone to increase them.

Indeed Nato governments may come under growing moral pressure from public opinion to match Mr Gorbachev by offering some unilateral troop reductions of their own.

Do Western leaders have the imagination and the courage to look beyond these immediate concerns into the crystal ball of Mr Gorbachev's new world? Can they imagine an international system free from East–West confrontation?

Before they set about trying to answer these questions, they will still insist on knowing whether Mikhail Gorbachev can 'succeed' and remain in power. They remain convinced that his foreign and defence policies are both deeply controversial within the Kremlin, and are unlikely to survive without Gorbachev at the helm.

General Akromeyev's retirement is interpreted as a sign of powerful discord within the military over the decision to cut Soviet forces and move towards a strategy of 'sufficiency'. And even though the earthquake explanation of Gorbachev's decision to cut short his visit to America, Cuba, and Britain is taken at its face value, there is a lingering question mark on whether another military establishment upheaval has also convinced him of the need to go back home. Yet the breadth and vision of Mr Gorbachev's goals is such that Western leaders cannot indefinitely insist that the West must hold its fire until Gorbachev, perestroika and glasnost are set in cement. The old shibboleths sound tired against Mikhail Gorbachev's self-confessed 'romanticism'.

Fantasy Island plc? Britain in the 1980s

PHILIP NORMAN
10 December 1988

Britain in the 1980s, for me, is summed up by what has happened to the pubs. It is the process which a great English novelist, Patrick Hamilton, called 'ye olde-ing'. In Hamilton's time, the disguise was mock-Tudor; today it is mock imperial Victorian. The style is uniform to every brewing conglomerate: a dark green, scarlet or black facade, covered with gold copperplate phrases intended to suggest Dickensian comfort and plenitude. *Choice Old Ales in Keg & Bottle . . . Rare Imported Wines & Brandies . . . Splendid Home-Cooked Dishes . . . Sumptuous Cold Collations Always Available.*

Not that Britain's drinkers seriously imagine themselves transported en masse back to the era of Pickwick, stagecoaches and post-horn gallops. A weary common faculty automatically translates the flowery 19th century promise into late 20th century fact. The Fine Old Ales will more likely be brand-new lagers. The Splendid Home-Cooked Dishes swelter as usual under Gestapo interrogation-lights next to a Cold Collation far from Sumptuous, never mind Always Available. The whole tariff of ludicrous make-believe is swallowed without protest or dissent.

For this is the Age of Parody. In British life at the decade's end, little remains that does not wear the cosmetic mask of something else thought happier, more desirable, romantic or glamorous. The country through the Eighties has increasingly reminded me of the never-never land in that old American TV show, where people could live out their dreams, however absurd, babyish or perversely unsuited to the environment. Britain truly has turned into Fantasy Island.

The Eighties were never forecast as such. Difficult though it be to remember now, their original profile was of chaste realism. Science, mocked for 10 post-hippy years, suddenly glowed with alluring chic. 'High Tech' became the fashionable rage. Computers ceased to be the butt of ill-natured jokes and transformed themselves into 'user-friendly' household pets. On New Year's Eve 1979, one felt palpable impatience to cross over into that bright new vista of soft-bumpered cars, house-trained robots and cosy red indicator-lights.

Who could have dreamed that in two years the 1980s would have leapt back to the 1880s, with Britain embroiled in a gunboat war containing as much jingoistic pantomime as the 'Grand Tableau' which used to conclude Victorian Music Hall? Who could have imagined all reasonable argument, all pertinent inquiry overwhelmed by a Prime Minister whose sole master-stroke was to rifle the dressing-up box for cast-offs from Churchill, Boadicea and Good Queen Bess? Who, at the height of burlesque, could have conceived a military communiqué beginning 'Be pleased to inform Her Majesty . . .' or the sky over St Paul's screaming with jet fighters as if Hitler, Boney and the Armada had been trounced together? From the Falklands on, we knew what the Eighties *really* were to be. It was Kate Carney's Circus all the way.

Six years later, 'Falklands Spirit', as first bottled by Messrs Saatchi & Saatchi, is confirmed as the decade's major merchandizing force. *Campaign*, the admen's magazine, recently announced that the quickest way to sell anything in Britain nowadays is to link it – however implausibly – with our regained imperial apotheosis. Hence 'Mrs Bridges' jams and chutneys, after 'original' recipes of a Victorian cook who never was, in a kitchen never more real than a TV drama-set. Hence the 'Lark Rise to Candleford' range of toiletries, purveying talc and soap-on-a-rope in the name of villagers who for their ablutions used tin baths and garden privies. *Campaign* subsequently devoted a long, admiring feature to the trouble taken by one soft drinks manufacturer to put its ginger beer into bottles parodying the brown earthenware of old-fashioned 'stone ginger'. Each mass-produced container was to be given a specially 'aged' look as if it had just been unearthed in an E. Nesbit attic. One musical piece has dominated the psyche of the decade. It is Vangelis's theme for *Chariots of Fire*, a film about heroic 1920s athletes, widely interpreted as a parable of Mrs Thatcher's heroism over the Falklands. Its machine-made chords could, indeed, be a Saatchi & Saatchi slogan rendered into melody – dramatic, portentous, muzzily suggestive of green fields and great deeds; of limitless victory forged by a single indomitable will. Hence the patriotism which, after pot noodles, must rank as the Eighties' great synthetic triumph. You can shut your eyes, think of *Chariots of Fire* and feel proud you're British, no matter what beastly things you may happen to be doing. Even the football thugs who smash up Europe carry Union Jacks and evidently believe, in some addled part of their brains, that they are 'an army . . . doin' it like Maggie done it in the Falklands'.

Britain's Age of Parody works on two separate, schizophrenic levels. First, and most obvious, there is *self*-parody – the officially-sanctioned drive to earn money from tourists by presenting ourselves in every possible ridiculous historical cliché and stereotype. Then there is parody as escapism, the device of a people increasingly unsure about their own place in the world and afraid of the present, let alone the future.

The best guide to current mass fantasy is the lengthy advertising films which unscrupulous cinema-chains now show instead of a second feature. Whether the product on offer be shampoo, beer, banks or employment agencies, two dream worlds tend to predominate. One is Fifties America, with drape suits, pink Cadillacs, drive-ins and *a cappella* singing. The other is downtown New York loft life, with stripped wood floors, industrial walls, Venetian blinds and giant ceiling fans (though, naturally, not muggers, rotting garbage or all-night police-sirens). Thus are young Britons most easily persuaded to engage as temps in solicitors' offices with one-bar electric fires, or deposit savings with what used to be the cosy old Woolwich.

Though America has always fed its idylls and illusions to Britain, this used to be at second hand, via Hollywood or pop music. In the Eighties, cut-price transatlantic air fares allow millions to visit every dream landscape ever pined for over a choc-ice in the one-and-nines. Even for stay-at-homes, the American dream can be instantly assembled complete, with baseball on TV, American fast food, American six-packs, popcorn and '57 Flavor' ice cream. There is apparently no Briton too incongruous or mis-shapen to sport a T-shirt proclaiming allegiance to Harvard, Yale or the Miami Dolphins. I even once saw a down-and-out under Charing Cross arches in baseball cap bearing the elegantly intertwined initials of the New York Yacht Club. (Wholesale imitation of a culture founded on wholesale imitation naturally produces some paradox. The 'Yuppie' style favoured by young bankers and brokers in Mrs Thatcher's economic Wonderland is believed the epitome of hard-nosed, thrusting, fingerpopping New York. It is actually New York's rather confused parody of English 'classic elegance'.)

As America's runway-in-the-Atlantic, we have lived under the thrall of a President himself unarguably the greatest concatenation of parody, burlesque and outright slapstick ever seen on the world stage. This is the President who, after what even his own administration concedes was a 'show' invasion, of territory even more inconsequential than the Falklands, awarded 1,000 decorations for bravery. Against Ronald Reagan, even Margaret Thatcher is reduced to the role of bespangled assistant, performing obedient bunny-dips and shouting 'Houpla!'

The terrible power of both has lain in their mutual in-ability to decry any element of the ludicrous, fatuous or fantastic in the constantly changing charades their image-machines devise for them. They simply read the script, whatever it may say, however it may promise to make the collective sphincter of future generations cringe in embarrassment. Presidential pseudo-folksiness will never surpass that quavery post-surgical voice over the world's networks, saying 'Nancy . . . are ya doin' anything tonight?' Mock-Swiftian parliamentary epigram will never again, thank God, descend to the nadir of 'The Lady's not for turning'.

The two leaders present an interesting contrast in the evolution of utter bogusness. While Reagan's matured over long years in Hollywood, Mrs Thatcher stumbled on hers quite by accident. She began the decade as a shrilling harridan, a Tory Kinnock in fact, stressing all the wrong syllables like a badly dubbed foreign film. An attack of laryngitis forced her to drop her voice on television one night, while attempting to explain away something messy in Belfast. The inadvertent result was 'gentle and low . . . an excellent thing in women.' In the general enchanted surprise, that messy something in Belfast just seemed to melt away.

Since then we have watched the Prime Minister put on ad hoc burlesques and discard them with the fretful insensibility of a suburban housewife trying on hats at C & A. There was our Falklands Britannia ('Rejoice!') and the Lady with the Lamp, dabbing Kleenex for poor boys maimed by designer war. There has been, at election-time, the Friend of Little Children (as someone said, 'like Dr Mengele on the board of Mothercare'). With no inkling of incongruity or amazing volte-face, there has been the Earth Mother guardian of the environment and the Cossack-hatted champion of union freedom in Poland.

Most stupendous of all, both in propagation and acceptance, is the defence most frequently offered for a Prime Minister whose grooming, hyping and cosmeticization make the Barbie Doll, by contrast, seem wild and untrammelled. Whatever you think of Mrs Thatcher – the axiom goes – at least she is always herself.

She has, indeed, had the profoundest effect on British

politics, prompting all of every party to the same mad
scramble for tricks out of the same plastic cylinder. Thus
did Labour use its vast electoral opportunity in designing
itself a tatty Dickins & Jones rose. Thus did the SDP deploy
its massed intellects in coming up with yellow for the
rosettes.

Neil Kinnock is the saddest case in his eternal confusion
about which parody his followers wish him to be. Latterly,
not even President Reagan has looked so bewildered by the
contradictory promptings of cue cards. Least fortunate was
the parody chosen for Kinnock's 1987 election campaign
– Kinnock walking with wife amid wild, honest coastal
scenery, like that famous picture of J. F. Kennedy and
Jackie at Hyannis Port. There is a crucial difference, of
course. Kennedy walked beside the surf. He didn't fall
headlong into it.

It might be thought that, with such a motley of fakers,
poseurs and cack-handed card-tricksters thronging public
life, the Eighties would have seen ordinary British people
become steadily more worldly, knowing, perspicacious and
cynical. How is it that, on the contrary, we seem to have
grown – and be manifestly still growing – more gullible,
suggestible and infantile?

Basic evidence of this comes from a source that should
know. In the early Sixties, the advertising industry decided
there must be an end to the little cartoon brand-emblems
with which old-fashioned manufacturers like Tate & Lyle
sugar had built up recognition and goodwill since Victorian
times. It was goodbye to Tate & Lyle's 'Mr Cube', the Bisto
Kids, the Guinness toucan, the Bird's Custard chicks et al.
Twenty years on, what do we find? Mr Cube is back as
genial and villainously bare-legged as ever, so are the Bisto
Kids, albeit redrawn in sub-punk pastels like cast-offs from
Wham. Television ads are swamped with talking, singing
and dancing potato crisps, detergent bottles, bread-knives,
butter-pats and gravyboats. Not only food manufacturers
but faceless public utilities employ Disneyesque little animals and birds to communicate their essential whimsy and

warmth of heart. A world of predatory commerce addresses us in the idiom of prewar nursery walls. I see there is even a condom-by-post firm which warns against Aids with a humanoid sheath, one hand upraised in the stern attitude of a spermicidal Mr Plod.

The fecklessness and irresponsibility that was youth's perquisite in the Sixties has spread to all age-groups in the Eighties. For this, above all, has been the decade of Leisure – pale, spirit-sinking Eighties word! – and its concomitant mass self-delusion, Lifestyle.

Everyone on Fantasy Island, whether employed or not, claims a right to limitless and continually expanding Leisure. Everyone has a Lifestyle, modelled in most essentials on the silvery-haired, soft-focused, barely animate beings who inhabit American TV soap operas. Lifestyle is what turns every High Street into useless labyrinths of video-game shops and every pub not Pickwickized into a pseudo cocktail bar named 'Bogart's' or 'Visions'. It is what has put virtually the entire population into the same perpetual weekend attire of stone-washed denim and sickly pastel turquoise, yellow and pink.

Work, of whatever kind, is seen as no more than a short, painful vigil between pleasure and partying. Postmen make their rounds dressed as postmen no longer, but *Miami Vice* gigolos. Dustmen empty our bins in shades and Bermuda shorts. The very building sites are scaffolded discos where tattooed Travoltas disport themselves in garments one would think too perversely tight for the simplest lifting work. A minor Eighties environmental curse is that macho Monday Morning Fever display of low-rise denim trouser-seat and high-rising anal crack.

Our leaders have been nothing if not skilful in recognizing and exploiting this sybaritic myopia. Alongside real, troubled, neurotic and divided Britain there has come to exist a parallel Leisure 'n' Lifestyle Britain, suffused with all the lip-glossed hyper-reality of the American soaps. This is the Britain shown in Government pre-privatization TV ads, where men, women and children gather in naive wonder to witness mass share-ownership descend from above in the form of an irradiant Stephen Spielberg spacecraft. It is the Britain where services that are every taxpayer's normal right, like post and telephones, are reinvented as soul-stirring dramas of impossible privilege and good fortune. It is the Britain where – also for pre-privatization purposes – the discovery has just been made that electricity is a marvellous thing, used for illuminating homes, factories and cities all over the place.

Lifestyle Britain might alternatively be called Telecom Britain after its most active exponent. It is characterized by relentless substitution of the cosmetic for the material, the superfluous for the desperately needful, and by almost maniacal expenditure on what is not advertising so much as masturbation. Deprived of an efficient telephone system we may none the less call up any number of Lifestyle lines to hear a pop tune, receive a betting tip or engage in sub-pornographic party talk. At Piccadilly Underground station the traveller can now watch continuous pop videos and commercials on giant TV monitors slung above the platform. Near by is the station clock, broken these many months. Journalists – all but for a subversive and threatened handful – follow the official line of make-believe. It has become normal to see banner headlines in mass-circulation dailies, announcing some imminent plot change in *Dallas* or *EastEnders*. With the parody news comes parody sentiment, pumping up public indignation at the minuscule and inconsequential, while most true, aching matters about Kate Carney's Britain are determinedly ignored. In an epoch unparalleled for human suffering, what have been the great issues of British tabloid journalism? There was Who Shot J. R.? There was the mercy dash to Blackie the Spanish donkey. There was the drawn-out agonizing suspense over the naming of Anne Diamond's baby.

The decline of half our national papers to a cross between TV company handout, bingo-card and masturbation-aid is generally agreed to have started with Rupert Murdoch's

Sun. Yet this at its birth – or, rather rebirth – was no more than parody, consciously aping the populist clout of Hugh Cudlipp's *Daily Mirror* at its apogee in the Forties and Fifties.

In almost all its garish Eighties forms, British tabloid journalism parodies earlier times. The breathless, empty gossip columns of *Mail* and *Express* burlesque a form considered redundant and discontinued 20 years ago. Coverage of Royalty reaches back even further, being for the most part couched in glutinous sloppiness that would make Nannie Crawford turn in her grave. My front-page headline of the decade occurred after the 'fairy tale' Princess of Wales attended her first Royal Film Premiere. It was in the once-proud, irreverent *Daily Mirror*: DI WEEPS FOR E. T.

To watch television is to be reassured that nothing in this whole, unspeakable car-bombing, hostage-taking, child-slaughtering world *really* need be taken seriously. Main news bulletins are now presented as light entertainment with disco beat, shiny logos spinning like Star Wars craft, reference pictures, even of the most ghastly things, unpeeling and cheerily floating away, just to show what graphics can do. On Domesday itself, no doubt, the last item on the very last bulletin will be such as to allow the newscaster to put away his pen with an ingratiating smirk.

Television's chief contribution to Eighties culture has been a proliferation of game shows, each one more technologically elaborate and flashingly futile, palliating a vast, unseen audience of have-nots much as Hollywood musicals did in the slumps of 50 years ago. Out of the game show subcontinent have developed spectacular displays of mass ego and exhibitionism, when thousands in pale pink and turquoise receive their Warhol-prescribed five minutes' fame by 'doing crazy things for charity'. What profit might accrue from doing sensible things for charity is a notion which has yet to strike the telethon industry.

The most spaced-out fantasist could scarcely have conceived Royal *It's a Knockout*, wherein Royals dressed as jerks mingled with jerks dressed as Royals in democratic tomfoolery. The subsequent decision of the Queen's third son to quit the Royal Marines and work for Andrew Lloyd-Webber seemed a natural, if not inevitable step. For what else is our Princess of Wales but living testimony to the magic of *Phantom of the Opera*. And how utterly that huge, empty symphonic meringue expressed Fantasy Island. Each spellbound West End night, hundreds stream forth, convinced that what they have just seen was a musical, and trying to remember a tune.

Least affected by Fantasy Island are the young of what can no longer be accurately termed the 'working' class. Born into vistas of unemployment and decay, what basis can they have for self-blinding nostalgia? From them has come the healthy backlash of 'street' culture and 'anti-fashion', crying scorn on parental *Dynasty* shoulder-pads and senescent teenage. The virtue they set most store by is authenticity, re-named Street-Cred. Their whole generation's message might be summed up as Cut the Crap.

Not so the young of what is once more unabashedly termed the 'upper' class, licensed by Kate Carney's Circus to a millennium of born-again snobbery, elitism and braying noise. To open *Tatler* or *Harper's & Queen* magazine is to enter a world of parody debs and chinless wonders barely surpassed in Wodehouse or Waugh. Sense literally boggles at the futile puns; the brutishly witless writing, on subjects like 'sexy people with facial scars' or 'sexy gynaecologists'; the frenzied sucking up to any nob, however tedious or inert.

A curious by-product of stripe-shirted Hoorays in the ascendant is a music-hall Cockney voice, assumed – one can only suppose – as a last two fingers to East End communities obliterated by Dockland 'redevelopment'. Cries of 'Gorbli-mey!' and 'Leave it aht!' ring through the winebars and money-pits as if all therein truly are as honest and plain-spoken as Pearly Kings on Ampstead Eath. Stage Cockney is increasingly becoming the pink-socked adman's nervous tic. Following God knows what managerial brainstorm, the

Victoria and Albert Museum lately advertised itself as 'An ace caff with quite a nice museum attached'.

Sex itself is turning into parody, and likely to continue so as Aids Phobia takes hold. The great male sex object of the Eighties is Rambo, a musclebound half-wit beyond all macho burlesque. The great sex goddess is Joan Collins, a parody vamp who would have been laughed out of even the silent-screen Twenties. The girls who began the decade in parody Princess Di hacking jackets end it in parody Alexis frills, flounces and naughty little hats with veils. Most of the Seventies' hard-won notions about female dignity and equality are – with Kate Carney's strong approval – thrown back into the closet again.

Here and there, the national trance has been disturbed. The ash-haired, blandly smiling waxwork show has wobbled with unforseen movement. A voice has defied every convention and profit-incentive by stubbornly ringing true. There was the voice of Bob Geldof as he rubbed Fleet Street's nose in some truth. There was the voice of Terry Waite, God help him, a true old-fashioned hero as compared with the Eighties Richard Branson million-dollar power-boat kind.

There was the voice of Doctor Cutting from the Beirut refugee camp and of the man whose daughter was blown up at Enniskillen. There were the voices of the parents whose children were so disgracefully abducted by 'social workers'. Latterly, there has been the voice of Mikhail Gorbachev, more forceful and inspiriting than the entire cue-carded, back-lit, photo-opportunistic White House Medicine Show.

I myself gave an inward cheer to an anonymous Sussex clergyman who was present on the day when the Prime Minister – outdoing parody yet again – demonstrated her government's 'Christian' principles by signing the Channel Tunnel deal in the Chapter House at Canterbury Cathedral. The feisty voice of that clergyman deserves to ring down the ages. 'One can only think of Christ casting the moneychangers from the temple. But He didn't say "On your way out, stop off in the Chapter House and ruin the economy."'

Nor let us forget a figure whom the Eighties have mocked for his earnest efforts to grapple with non-*Dallas* matters like inner-city decay and hospice-care, and to evolve a genuine thought before speaking. To hear Prince Charles is to feel a glimmer of hope, if not for the Nineties, then perhaps the Two-Thousands. The future King of Fantasy Island – against all odds – is for real.

Armenia's quake: out in the open

JONATHAN STEELE
12 December 1988

One body lies unmourned and unlamented under the tragic rubble of the Armenian earthquake. The timid, self-serving and ultimately mendacious media tradition which blacked out all accidents and disasters in the Soviet press in the past is finally no more. Unlike the Chernobyl catastrophe which was covered up for two days and then reported in the most tight-lipped way, this tragedy has been reported almost as fully and honestly as anyone could wish.

Eyewitness accounts by survivors, graphic descriptions of the rescue efforts, tough questions about the authorities' lack of preparedness and incompetence, accusations of shoddy design and building work, and astonishingly self-critical comments about the way Britain and France were able to send specialist disaster teams while the Soviet Union apparently has none – all this has already been published in the Soviet press. More is bound to come.

The distance between the cover-up in the first days after Chernobyl and the way the Armenian catastrophe has been reported now is one more measure of the distance President Gorbachev has taken this country in the last 30 months.

Along with honesty about problems and misfortunes,

compassion and sensitivity to individual grief have not been the norm of public discourse here for decades. The old slogan that 'a single death is a tragedy, the death of thousands is a statistic' used to be drummed home here every time a disaster happened. If it was covered at all, it was done in a remote and clumsy fashion. Now the papers have shown front-page pictures of women weeping over child-sized coffins.

The government newspaper, *Izvestia*, has been one of the best. 'I was sitting in my office when everything started collapsing,' it quoted Znehya Saakyan the day after the full extent of the tragedy was known. 'I lost consciousness before realizing it was an earthquake and that I was buried. Everything felt like a dream, though there was practically no air to breathe. My son David saved me.

'He had been working near by and when it all started he rushed to the ruins, which were all that was left of our office. My left hand was sticking out. It seems he recognized me because of a ring on my finger. I remember him crying, "Mummy, give me your hands." He saved me and I am alive now. But my elder son vanished with his family. My other son is injured and in some hospital. Can't you help me find out where he is?'

Komsomolskaya Pravda was already raising questions on Friday morning about the slowness of the rescue operation, and the possibly faulty design of the buildings which may have made the disaster worse. Where were the seismologists, and the architects when they were put up, it asked?

Izvestia asked why so much of the rescue work was being done by hand, and why more cranes and lifting equipment were not available. It praised the thousands of volunteers who had given help and driven or flown to Armenia to assist in the rescue effort. But why was so much equipment standing round at the airport, and why were planes not unloaded faster? These are the sort of questions which disasters always produce. Help never comes as fast as it is needed. It is too soon to know whether all the criticisms are justified, but the fact that the press is willing to echo what everyone is saying is a major step forward.

One criticism already seems valid. The Soviet Union's civil defence and disaster preparedness has been shown to be poor, giving the lie, incidentally, to Cold War propaganda in the West about Soviet superiority in this field.

Television has shown in great detail the arrival of international rescue teams, including the French and British, with their sniffer dogs and special equipment for locating survivors and digging them out. Mr Gorbachev was shown thanking a French expert. The coverage surprised many Soviet viewers. They had not appreciated how massive the international help has been.

It has helped to increase that already palpable sense of gratitude and pleasure here that the Soviet Union is accepted as part of the community of nations (which is one of the many Gorbachev achievements). But is has also alerted people to the deficiencies of the Soviet system. 'Why don't we have specialist rescue teams,' *Izvestia* asked. 'Our system of civil defence is weak and slow,' complained *Komsomolskaya Pravda*. Armenians have noted that France and Britain are not even countries which are prone to earthquakes, yet they have experts.

In astonishing scenes Soviet television last night showed Mr Gorbachev surrounded by anxious and angry people. Why hadn't the earthquake been predicted, someone shouted? What about the likelihood of epidemics, another man yelled. How often do Mrs Thatcher and Mr Reagan put themselves in situations where people would speak to them as openly, equally, and democratically?

The disaster coverage has not been a smooth process, and along with the new journalism, traces of the old are still visible. Bad habits die hard. Soviet television has been slower to open up than the newspapers, and indeed some papers have been better than others. But then variations in quality are a sign of a press which is already, or at least becoming, out of government control.

One aspect has been common to all coverage, a clear

effort to present the response to the tragedy as an all-round effort in which people of all republics and nationalities have rallied round to help Armenia.

After all the emphasis on nationalism during the recent Supreme Soviet debates on the constitution, it is as though a general press advisory has gone out in order to try to counteract it. Stress the multi-national solidarity. Show that we are all one Soviet family, or as an eight-column headline in *Komsomolskaya Pravda* put it, 'There is no such thing as someone else's grief.'

As a result of this coverage, reports of something less than solidarity in Azerbaijan have been suppressed. Armenian sources report that the earthquake was greeted with black humour and celebration drinks in some parts of the Azerbaijani capital, Baku. 'We threw the Armenians out just in time' – that kind of comment.

Foreign journalists are still barred from Azerbaijan, so it is hard to tell whether the reports are true or just a product of Armenian ethnic hatred in reverse.

Comment on Mr Gorbachev's visit to the area has also not been faultless. The good thing is that he bothered to go to the area at all, and that on the whole coverage has been low-key. On Friday night Kremlin-watchers were amazed to see no pictures of his plane touching down from New York. Apparently the aim was not to take up valuable time with the usual boring pictures of an airport receiving line.

At least Mr Gorbachev turned up, though there are some Armenians who wonder why he did not come rather earlier, when the hundreds of thousands poured out of Azerbaijan into Armenia two weeks ago. Was that not also an unprecedented tragedy for the Soviet Union? Did compassion not call for a direct appearance on the spot, and a greater sense of urgency about the unfolding ethnic disaster in the Caucasus?

To report such questions is still the exclusive privilege of the foreign correspondent. If glasnost advances at the speed we have seen this week, next time round it may be Soviet journalists who do it.

Arafat sees the future

DAVID HIRST
16 December 1988

There are occasions when people cannot see history unfolding before their eyes. This was surely one of them. 'Well, that's it,' said one Palestinian who did, 'but none of you seem to have noticed.' It was after the press conference which the PLO chairman, Yasser Arafat, held on Wednesday night with ostensibly nothing more momentous in mind than his desire, as he put it, 'to highlight my views before you'.

In essence, it did not sound very different from what had gone before – the resolutions of the Palestine National Council in Algiers, Arafat's Stockholm declaration recognizing the existence of Israel, and his solemn peroration, the day before, to the UN General Assembly. All of that had been designed to meet long-standing US requirements for the PLO's admission to the 'peace process' and, in the opinion not merely of Palestinians and Arabs but even of such serious respectable European pillars of the international community as Sweden and Austria, it incontrovertibly did so.

It was the conditioning of years that contributed to this blindness, the feeling that whatever the Palestinians did, the Americans, on Israel's behalf, would find yet more for them to do. For surely no candidate for Washington's approval has ever had to perform such tricks, to jump so many hoops, as Arafat and the PLO. And after all, asked one Palestinian almost as surprised as everyone else, how could anyone have seriously expected such a *coup de théâtre*, when this had been preceded, in the space of a month, by three such resounding American Noes – No to the PNC, No to the Stockholm declaration, and No to Arafat in New York?

Yet, though the substance of Arafat's declaration remained essentially the same, the wording was different, and, in Middle East peace-seeking diplomacy, great breakthroughs are apt to be measured in phraseology which, even to those who know, is obscure and Talmudic.

In that clinching statement Arafat had bunched his three main operative clauses – concerning Israel's right to exist, UN resolution 242, and terrorism – all together in a neat little package. The apparent caveats and reservations which the Americans, almost alone in the world, had persisted in finding objectionable, he left out altogether (as is the case of his 1985 Cairo declaration on the legitimacy of resistance inside Israel and the occupied territories) or inserted in a different part of the statement (as in the case of the Palestinians' right to self-determination and statehood).

This was the incantation, the magic formula salable to a potentially hostile American opinion, which the Administration needed. So thus, almost unnoticed until the confirmation of it from Washington, was history made.

And though their satisfaction or undisguised delight is tempered with the anxiety which the unknown always brings with it, this – for once and for all Palestinians – is a truly historic event. 'It is not just our entry to the peace process,' said the PLO spokesman, Ahmed Abdul Raman, 'it is our passport to the world.'

For the Palestinians, the ostracism which they suffered went back further than Henry Kissinger's 1975 Israel-inspired American refusal to talk to the PLO until it recognized Israel. It went back all the way to the original calamity of 1948, the rise of the state of Israel on the debris of their own community, their dispersal into exile, and their subsequent down-grading, in a diplomatic environment shaped and dominated by the United States, from a people deserving of resurrected nationhood, into mere refugees entitled to no more than humanitarian concern, charity and eventual resettlement in their Arab hinterland.

Whatever, by a strict, arithmetical calculation of

diplomatic profit and loss, the PLO may have lost by the immense concession which it made to secure US recognition, it is, for the foreseeable future at least, outweighed in Palestinian minds by the much greater gains of which it holds promise.

For an entirely new process, a new dynamic, has now been set in motion, and though, of course, the Americans are very far from saying it, for the Palestinians the end of that process must, and can only be, the creation of an independent state in a portion of their original homeland – the 23 per cent of it constituted by the additonal territories Israel conquered in 1967 – that state which the overwhelming majority of Israelis, be they Labour or right-wing Likud, have always portrayed as a mortal danger to the very existence of their own state.

There is more, however, to the forthcoming meeting in Tunis between the US ambassador, Robert Pelletreau, and a PLO delegation than Arafat's entry to Washington on a potentially equal footing with Shamir or Perez. There is another earthquake closer to home in an Arab world which, since the calamity, has sought to preserve its tutelage over the political will of the Palestinian people. In the past 40 years much of the history of the Middle East has, often more surreptitiously than publicly, revolved round the competition of Arab states – chiefly but by no means exclusively the 'front line' states of Egypt, Jordan, Syria and even little Lebanon – to monopolize, dominate or resist that will.

To begin with, in their immediate, prostrate aftermath of the calamity, it was in good measure a voluntary subservience which the Palestinians granted to their Arab brethren, and in particular to the Egypt of President Nasser. In him they vested their hopes for the 'liberation' of Palestine in its entirety. And yet, even before the shattering Arab defeat in the 1967 war and the immense blow it dealt to the prestige of that greatest of modern Arab champions, the Palestinians, in the shape of a still clandestine and much reviled Arafat and his embryonic Fatah guerrilla movement, began that process of self-assertion which achieved yesterday's apotheosis in Geneva.

Between then and now Arafat had struggled to preserve his sacrosanct 'independence of decision', both by diplomacy and sometimes – against Syria and Jordan – by conflict as bloody and brutal as any against the Israelis, and emotionally far more damaging. In the darkest days, and especially since the Israelis and the Syrians in virtual concert drove him from his last, Lebanese 'state within a state', he seemed just about on the point of forfeiting it altogether.

But if there is now universal amazement at the US volte-face, one can also discern, with hindsight, an instructive precedent for it. Last summer, in a move that astonished too, King Hussein repudiated the habits of a political lifetime and formally abdicated his juridical and administrative stake in that part of his former kingdom, the West Bank, which, with the dramatic decline in Arafat's fortunes, he had formally been trying to restore, with Israeli and American connivance.

'It was the decision of a mature leader,' said one Palestinian, a tribute which very few would be inclined to bestow on President Assad of Syria, who has of late been so desperately, but so unsuccessfully, trying to retain at least a partial grip on the all-important Palestinian card. He is the Arab leader, more than any other, under whose feet this earthquake will cause the ground to shake.

It is, of course, the intifada which has made this historic breakthrough possible. The immense concession Arafat made to achieve it could only have grown out of the sense of strength, pride and purpose which it has lent Palestinians everywhere, not just to the inhabitants of the occupied territories.

And it is the intifada that will ensure, if anything can, that in the long and gruelling struggle that undoubtedly lies ahead, this concession will eventually yield the fruit of independent statehood.

Rumours had it that, in addition to their long-standing requirements, the Americans were also demanding something more: that Arafat call upon the West Bankers and the Gazans to end the uprising. But that, he said, was something that 'neither Arafat nor anyone for that matter can stop'. It would only end, he said, with 'practical and tangible steps' towards the 'establishment of our independent Palestinian state'. For him the intifada is the basically non-violent, but far more effective, alternative to the 'armed struggle' – or terrorism, as the Americans have it, which on Wednesday he so finally and fully 'renounced'.

The intifada, plus the moral force of world opinion, are the two key instruments on which he will explicitly rely if he possibly can. For no Palestinians have any illusions that this is a triumph of which both 'friend' and enemy, Arab and Israeli, will not seek to rob them. The friends cannot of course advertize such a malign intent; officially, for them, one has to be Arab as well as Palestinian.

The enemy has no such inhibitions, and the Palestinians have little doubt as to where will begin his campaign to portray Arafat as wholly unworthy of the new respectability which Washington has conferred upon him: the hint lies in the prompt assertion by Israel's Labour foreign minister Peres that 'a single petrol bomb thrown today in the territories' would undermine the credibility of Arafat's undertaking that Palestinian terrorism is no more. If a Labour minister thinks like that, the Palestinians ask, to what desperate lengths, in their bid to preserve a climate of Arab–Israeli hatred and violence that has served them so well, would Likud ministers, or even more extreme than they, be prepared to go?

The importance of being earnest

DAVID HARE
17 December 1988

I saw Cecil Parkinson across a room the other day. It was the first time I'd ever seen him and the effect was as irresistibly comic as I'd always hoped. It was like seeing Max Miller in the flesh. When a girl in a spectacularly short skirt walked by him, he angled his eyes down further towards the floor and redoubled the intensity with which he was talking to his friends.

He always makes me laugh on television because he has to pretend to be so desperately serious. It must be exhausting. His only way of clawing back into power has been to try and establish that he's not at all the kind of person we all take him to be. His brows furrow more deeply than any man alive. Every interviewer's question is answered with a numbing earnestness which is intended to convey a single message: 'I am a political heavyweight. Don't think for one moment I am interested in girls.'

The whole effect is ridiculous because he's missing the point. The charge against him is not that he had an affair, but that this affair illuminated aspects of his character. It's not until you read Sarah Keays' own book, *A Question of Judgement*, that you begin to understand what actions were the mainspring of the story. While he was still going out with her, he secretly tried to block her advancement in the Tory Party. He used his influence to make sure she was not selected as a parliamentary candidate. This was at the same time that he was telling her he was going to marry her. If he now wishes to appear as a reformed character, then he wastes his time trying so hard to look sober. What we want him to look is honest. Unfortunately his present policy for the privatization of electricity precludes this.

It is usually at this point alleged that it is unfair to pass comment on the personalities or private lives of politicians. But are we meant to say nothing about a man who is currently appearing on every television channel, torturing the English language in order to find a weasel-worded formulation which doesn't quite say what the entire electorate knows to be true? The privatization programme will involve both immediate and long-term rises in the cost of electricty. It's a fact. Among observers of all political persuasions, it is a fact so universally *acknowledged* that you do begin to look very hard at the face of the one man in the country who is wriggling about denying it.

Parkinson is introducing into the system a wholly unnecessary layer of people whose duty will be to make large profits for their shareholders. It will no longer be a priority to provide the cheapest possible service to the entire community. Parkinson will steal from everyone something which is theirs, and for which they have paid with their taxes. He will then hand it – against the owners' will – to a group whose interests will be in conflict with our own. In opinion polls, 85 per cent of people declare themselves opposed to his actions.

Politicians love the idea of rehabilitation. It is important that anyone can get back. It confirms a view of the world in which a belief in *realpolitik* is sauced with sentimentality. That is why you hear the phrase about Parkinson 'suffering enough'. But the lion's share of suffering has been done by Miss Keays and her daughter. For them, there are no signs of rehabilitation. Miss Keays has committed a crime for which there is no forgiveness, and which was, in terms of *realpolitik*, inept. Powerless, she attacked the powerful. Still, Parkinson will no doubt prosper in this Government. He has one priceless asset for a politician, which only John Selwyn Gummer has in such abundance. He does have the ability to make us laugh.

Thatcherism itself has only one joke, which is how grotesquely inefficient it has become. Selling off water and electricity from the back of a lorry doesn't even make economic sense. Those of us who have watched groups on the Left become prisoners of dogma now stand in awe as the Right self-destructs in the same way. Take transport. In any sensible capitalist country, the government spends a fortune making sure that people get to work on time. Japan and France have fast, efficient public transport systems. It's only common sense. After all, you do want the workers to get to work.

In southern England, for the last six weeks, we've all been locked in one enormous traffic jam of the Government's making. We sit there, victims of the theory that it would be politically improper to give the rail, bus and underground networks the massive injections of cash they so plainly need. The M25 has become the perfect symbol of the age: free, unregulated, ideologically pure, foul-tempered and at a near-permanent standstill.

Aftermath of Lockerbie

DAVID SHARROCK
23 December 1988

The milkman was out on his rounds as usual at 5 a.m. weaving his float through the crush of fire brigade, police and army vehicles.

Milk bottles were left in tidy queues outside houses which looked as if they had just been hit by a hurricane. The smell of smoke and fuel hung in the air. The streets crunched under foot with the sound of fuselage fragments and masonry debris.

The baker, Mr Hunter Wilson, was busy making loaves for the emergency services, volunteers for families forced to evacuate their homes and for the media people who descended upon the town before dawn broke.

Police kept Sherwood Crescent, where the Pan Am jet finally came to rest, closed all day. They had worked through the night by arc lights to clear the crash site and managed to reopen the A74 by-pass round the town by 10 a.m. Heavy machinery was brought in to sweep away the carpet of fragments which coated the dual carriageway. Near by stood the charred remains of several houses, all but demolished, only gable ends and chimneys left intact.

Debris from the aircraft was all over the town, from heavy twisted sections resembling modern sculptures to alloy fragments as small as 10 pence pieces. A foam rubber piece of seating flapped forlornly in a tree top.

The petrol station on Carlisle Road, originally thought to have exploded during the impact, was charred around the roof, but solid.

In a green fenced-off area in the heart of the town, Mr Ted Argo was checking for damage to the United Meat Packer's abattoir. He examined the still-smoking battered jet engines embedded in a six foot crater. The engine cowling had come to earth 20 yards away in the back yard of Nether Hill Farm. It resembled a smashed silver egg.

Above the abattoir on a gentle hill in Rose Bank Crescent was a scene of total devastation. The side of a semi-detached house had been torn away, its contents spilled out and scattered amongst the aircraft's debris. Inside the house furniture still stood like stage scenery. A door was ajar, a wardrobe leaned against the surviving wall. A table lamp rested on a chest of drawers. A white sock appeared to be trapped in the broken roof joints, hanging from a body on the roof, hastily covered with a tarpaulin.

Other bodies lay similarly covered in the crescent. Beneath the debris, police believed the bodies of 44 passengers were buried. The fallout was spread about the back gardens. A brown leather attaché case lay tangled in the remains of a shredded inflatable life-raft.

Telegraph poles which had snapped like matches and hundreds of grey airline meal trays, their contents smeared across concrete tarmac, added to the chaos.

A single running shoe sat in a freshly dug garden. A seat

was jammed through an upstairs window. An unused life jacket, still neatly folded in its plastic sleeve, lay in a gutter. Other personal items were strewn around: a yellow baseball cap bearing the slogan 'Croker College' with a serpent design, and a Louis Vuitton make-up bag.

House of Windsor plc

DANIEL JOHN
29 December 1988

The latest opinion poll about the Royal Family would have given Her Majesty something more than the turkey to chew over this Christmas.

Just over 80 per cent of the 918 people questioned in yesterday's *Daily Telegraph*/Gallup poll favoured keeping the monarchy in its present form, while two in three felt the country received value for money from the Queen.

But the one statistic which would have given something more than food for thought at Sandringham – and set brains whirring at the right-wing privatization think tank, the Adam Smith Institute – was that 40 per cent of those polled believed the Royal Family cost too much to support.

If there is one thing which stirs up a lot of debate in Mrs Thatcher's cost-conscious Cabinet it is money – or more to the point, how to save it.

Not that £5.2 million, which is the official sum set aside for the Civil List (the annual 'family benefit' to the monarchy), is much to be quibbling about, you might think.

However, if you consider that the Queen's personal fortune – consisting of land, properties, investments and the like – is estimated to be in the region of £5 billion, then there will be some people who say Her Majesty could support herself and her relatives more than comfortably.

And what is the solution much preferred by the present government for state-owned bodies which would be better off running their own affairs? Yes, you've got it. Privatization.

Unthinkable, perhaps; heresy, almost certainly; but impossible – not in the least. Of the remaining publicly held assets in the UK, the Queen's vast portfolio could, with a little bit of tinkering, lend itself to an offer for sale to the great British public – leaving past female high fliers, Sophie Mirman of Sock Shop and Body Shop's Anita Roddick, trailing in Her Majesty's wake. Not surprisingly, the properties, estates and businesses which are associated with Her Majesty are spread between her own private interests and several government agencies. But given the work undertaken in the last two years to make bodies like the Crown Estate more commercially-minded, the company which would own such assets and be privatized already has a definable shape.

'Monarchy plc' could be split into three divisions: property, transport and investment. As an initial step, the new company would take over responsibility for the Crown Estate, one of the largest property organizations in the country, from the Commissioners appointed by the Queen who run its 270,000-acre portfolio on her behalf.

Currently valued at £1.68 billion, the estate – which was handed over to the Exchequer in 1760 in return for the Civil List – is rich in quality and quantity and generates net income of £33 million a year.

From Glenlivet, Scotland, in the north to Dell Quay Wharf, Southampton, in the south and from the gold mine of Clogau St David's, Gwynedd, Wales, in the west to Croxton, Norfolk, in the east, the portfolio includes some of the most sought-after land and buildings in the country. In London alone, its commercial property takes in the whole of Regent Street, much of Pall Mall and St James, Carlton House Terrace and the Regent's Park Estate.

Perhaps the most unusual and little-known element of the estate, is the Crown's ownership of half of the land lying between high and low water marks within the UK and nearly all of the territorial sea-bed for 12 miles out. This also gives the estate the right of mineral extraction (except coal) on the Continental shelf.

If that is not enough, Monarchy's property division would also include the Queen's private estates which currently come under the responsibility of the Duchy of Lancaster and would add a further 35,000 acres of land to the portfolio. The Duchy takes in part of the Manor of Savoy around the famous hotel and provides the Queen with revenues of £1.95 million a year.

Together, and after a further revaluation, the two estates are likely to be worth in excess of £2.5 billion. And then, of course, there are the royal palace and residences.

Putting a value on them is certainly difficult, but if Bracken House, the headquarters of the *Financial Times*, can go for £140 million, Buckingham Palace with its 600 rooms has to be worth at least twice that – history and all.

Add to that Windsor Castle standing in 4,800 acres, Sandringham with its fields of blackcurrants, stud and royal pigeon loft, Balmoral, home of the Queen's herd of Highland Cattle, Kensington Palace and Clarence House, the Queen Mother's residence, and you have the jewel in the property crown.

A conservative estimate then would add another £750 million to the total value since any buyer should expect to pay a hefty premium given the reputation of the current occupiers.

No less tangible would be the transport division of Monarchy plc. It includes the luxury yacht Britannia, currently part of the Royal Navy but operating under independent command, the re-vamped Royal Train whose costs are met by the Department of Transport, the Queen's Flight of two British Aerospace 146 jets, a twin-prop Andover and two Wessex helicopters which are the responsibility of the Ministry of Defence and five Rolls-Royces, paid for out of the Civil List. Recent investment in up-dating the fleet has totalled more than £55 million.

Flogging off the family silver takes on a different

meaning altogether when it comes to valuing the investment division of Monarchy – the Queen's art collection, antiques and, above all, jewellery.

Priceless is a word that is often used when talking about the Crown Jewels and with a list that ranges from the Imperial State Crown to the Cullinan Diamond it is little wonder that no definitive value exists. But it is safe to say we are looking at hundreds of millions of pounds – and probably at least a billion.

So we have a company which has assets of up to £4.5 billion alone, but on published figures produces income of only £86 million – made up of £35 million from the two estates, after a £35 million payment to the Exchequer, plus a further annual donation of £16 million from the Queen's private income.

The task for the management of Monarchy would be to make those assets 'sweat' as City jargon goes. As a straightforward property and investment business, its turnover (tiny in proportion to its net asset worth) is largely meaningless.

Revenue is the key to covering costs like the Royal Household (which takes up three-quarters of the £5 million the Queen and her family receives from the Civil List). But all told, the total cost of keeping the Windsors every year is estimated to be at least £30 million. Crucial decisions then would have to be taken at the outset to make Monarchy a much more attractive proposition to the City.

For a start, given the Queen and her family's importance to the tourist industry, the sell-off would include a Government 'royalty' for Monarchy's contribution in bringing in the £7 billion-plus spent by visitors every year. A similar charge would also be made by the Queen for carrying out her duties as Head of State at home and abroad.

Closer to home, the Royal palaces could be offloaded on a 'sale and lease back' with an arrangement to allow the Family to maintain a residence within Buck House. A large chunk though could be rented out as prime office space to companies with an up-market image – Liberty's, Rolls-

Royce and Savills the estate agents to name but three. The
remainder would become a museum to house the art and
antique collection. Visitors would, of course, be charged an
entry fee.

Only Balmoral, reputed to be the Queen's favourite residence, would be maintained as a family home. Since
Windsor is in need of more luxury hotels, the castle could
be refurbished to provide five star accommodation for American and Japanese tourists.

Sandringham would be turned into an exclusive nursing
home, possibly under the BUPA label, while Kensington
and Clarence are well-suited to become the headquarters
of a couple of international business conglomerates, say
Hanson and Unilever.

The Crown Estates have already felt the winds of change
in the Government's money-making drive and this would
be continued with under-exploited assets like the foreshore
and sea-bed being developed into marinas or used for mineral extraction and dredging.

In terms of size, transport would have to be expanded
rapidly to be competitive through the acquisition of say,
British Airways, British Rail (London Midland and
Scottish-to-be in Monarchy's case) or the Royal Navy. When
privatized, Monarchy would be debt-free and with its strong
asset-backing should at least be able to buy one of the three
comfortably. And if the commercial paper market picks up,
perhaps all three.

But a more business-like decision would be to sell off the
division as a whole and hire a plane or a yacht when
need-be. Staff costs would be cut quite dramatically too if
the Royal Household was sold to its management to provide
a contract service.

The net result then would be a cash-rich, property-driven
operation which would command a place among the Han-
sons, GECs and ICIs of this world in the FT index of the
top 30 UK companies.

But, as the Queen and her family would retain a control-
ling stake in the business in perpetuity, Monarchy would

almost certainly become a sleeping, paternalistic giant with a low investment profile.

Given the nature of the financial world at present, what odds would you give on a management buy-out being launched by the Queen's successor within a few years of its float?

For Prince Charles – 'voted' the favourite member of the Family above the Queen herself in yesterday's poll – the choice would be simple: a kingdom or a bourse. The decision would never be in doubt when you consider the reputation of the Queen's heir. And the name of the buy-out company? How about Restoration plc.

Hot stuff in Sodom

ALEX HAMILTON
31 December 1988

Sodom is no place to go looking for sin. Hoteliers in the smart places near by on the Dead Sea say there is plenty – perhaps it is gluttony they are thinking of, and they encourage it by organizing mountain ranges of sweet cakes, with cream-capped peaks. But Sodom itself is unbounded virtue, nothing but a factory dedicated to extracting health-giving minerals from the Dead Sea.

This vast sprawling mesh of girders and cables and cranes has a bleak and wintry look due to the salt that has enveloped and whitened it. Actually we are here at one of the hottest places on earth and, at 1292 feet below sea level, certainly the lowest. The director, Schloma Drori, is very proud of his dreadful establishment, proclaiming that without it the Israeli economy would collapse.

Stepping out to take pictures of the weird scene, with salt floes and rings and ribs of salt like ice in a background of eau-de-nil liquid, with no animal or bird life in sight but crows on the sandstone bluffs and Mack trucks powering along the narrow shore, I inhaled deeply and my trachea was immediately furred like Victorian plumbing with layers of potash, bromines, sulphur, salts and fertilizers.

Behind the salt pans lay the Negev, scenario of Ben Gurion's dream of settlement, partially realized. On the way from Eilat was Timna Park, 60 square miles that include the Pillars of Solomon, an awesome pre-Cambrian formation that gives the feeling Israel arrived 500 million years ahead of the rest of the planet. And not so far away was a new 'safari reserve' planned for animals of the biblical kind. To date, there are ostriches.

But here we are in No Birds Land. Among a ghost town of tin sheds, statuesque lumps of salt rear out of the escarpment. This one is said to be Lot's wife. So is that. That one too. Take your pick. Whichever she was, she was evidently a very large woman.

More interesting, I thought, were the Arubotayim, or chimney caves, which few tourists see. They can be found down a narrow defile, through a rock arch, into the cliff. Two caverns, connected by a tunnel, have patches like marble in the walls, where water polished the salt. In this world, on the crystal shores of the Dead Sea, the Moriah Spa shows up like a mirage. There are flowers in beds around it, each plant attached to a hose with its own water jet. They treat flowers like children here, and get up in the night to give them a drink.

But that sea is no place for real children, no place for splashing about. A few drops of the glutinous stuff in the eyes or lips sting cruelly; abrasions burn. Pictures of pert minxes reading books and waving a cocktail as they float like beach balls are not wholly mendacious – Peter the Fisherman could have walked on this one – but they give little hint of the real ethos.

Visitors at the Spa are mainly fubsy matrons and fussy old chaps from the dumpling countries, taking mud treatment and wading out with hot sulphur squelching round the toes to marinate in the brine. They teeter forth gingerly, using a salt-encrusted handrail to keep their balance.

They dare not paddle, nor go on their fronts to swim, but stand or bob gently in their separate spaces, the more venturous interlaced in pairs to compose a kind of human cradle. Everybody is thrilled by the novelty of water in which it is impossible to sink, but soon they are subdued in the strange scene. Medically, it may be life enhancing, but I could not escape my idea it was embalming fluid.

Another fine place to pickle silversides is Ein Gedi, a spa run by a kibbutz, very nearly lively at times, on the northern of the two halves of the Dead Sea. It is highly organized and efficient. Everything is labelled with graphics – I've never seen so many signs to instruct simple-minded foreigners. The only Hebrew notices not translated are those telling people not to make such a noise – apparently an Israeli habit.

The mud is different at Ein Gedi – for a start it's free and everybody helps themselves from huge tubs on the strand, and daubs themselves blacker than tar. They seem not to mind how they look and positively welcome being photographed. Perhaps they figure everything in the landscape is bizarre.

I took the full hot mud treatment, encased like *boeuf en croute* to make sure I was not just medium rare. The mud MDs were a jovial crowd. 'We have the best mud in the world,' one said to me. 'Of course,' I said, 'but where is the second best?' 'Romania,' he answered promptly, 'so people come from all over the world for treatment on the Dead Sea, and the Israelis go to Romania.'

Sun-rise *Times*?

LEADER
6 January 1989

Page four of yesterday's *Sun* contained a prominent news story chronicling how eager viewers had 'besieged' High

Military ceremonials: the old and the new

ABOVE: A runaway horse scene-steals at the state opening of Parliament. November 1988.
(Photo **Martyn Hayhow**).
BELOW: A Red Arrow relaxes with fellow pilots of the RAF stunt team. May 1989.
(Photo **Sean Smith**)

Trying the communication thing
ABOVE: Geoffrey Mulcahy of Woolworth Holdings shows off his company's new corporate identity. February 1989. (Photo **David Sillitoe**)
RIGHT: President Bush strains to express himself. February 1989. (Photo **Don McPhee**)
BELOW: The Archbishop of Canterbury extends his horizons at a meeting in Ashfield. (Photo: **Denis Thorpe**)

Sporting life

ABOVE: Athletics at Wimbledon 1988. A recumbent Pat Cash watches Boris Becker in retreat. (Photo **Ken Saunders**)

RIGHT: A Rugby fan rises above it all at the Leicester versus Barbarians match. December 1988. (Photo **Frank Baron**)

BELOW: Michael Carter seizes the ball at Crystal Palace. December 1988. (Photo **Frank Baron**)

Cocklefishermen from King's Lynn working in the Wash. One of a series on the fishermen for which **Denis Thorpe** was awarded the title of Photographer of the Year in the annual competition run by Ilford. August 1988.

Man in his environment
ABOVE: Pylons near Blackstone Edge, Yorkshire. April 1989. (Photo **Denis Thorpe**)
BELOW: A 1903 cutter, out on Southampton Water in 1989. (Photo **Frank Martin**)

ABOVE: Basingstoke Canal – fresh perspectives, December 1988. (Photo **Martin Argles**)
BELOW: Cambridge trains for the Boat Race. February 1989. (Photo **Frank Baron**)

Signs of protest
ABOVE: Out on the roof at Risley. May 1989. (Photo **Don McPhee**)
LEFT: A Palestinian fighter, Nablus, West Bank. October 1988. (Photo **Sean Smith**)
BELOW: Top floor, Kelvin Estate, Sheffield, all through 1988. (Photo **Denis Thorpe**)

Tragedy

ABOVE: The Clapham rail crash. February 1989. (Photo **Frank Baron**)
BELOW: Prince Charles visits Liverpool's ground at Anfield to pay respects to those who died at Hillsborough. May 1989. (Photo **Denis Thorpe**)

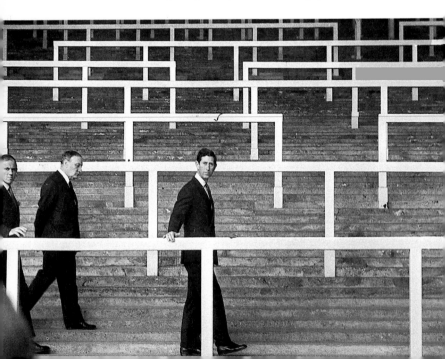

Street stores with orders for satellite dishes boosted by 'the growing programme range of market leaders, Sky Channel'. Dixons were reported to be snowed under with orders thanks to the 'fantastic range' of programmes being offered by the Sky station. One thing these reports omitted to mention was that Sky Channel is owned by Mr Rupert Murdoch who also owns the *Sun*. Nor was any mention made of Mr Murdoch's main rival, British Satellite Broadcasting, which asked the Director General of Fair Trading to prosecute Sky for misleading information contained in an advert placed by Sky in *The Times* (also owned by Mr Murdoch).

It is worth mentioning this as Mr Murdoch comes close to victory in his bid to buy the William Collins publishing group, because although at one level the deal is about book publishing, it is also part of a world-wide corporate strategy in which newspapers, printing works, film libraries, data bases, books, satellite television and magazines converge on one another yielding global economies of scale for the company with unknown consequences for the consumer. Many of Collins's authors are, rightly, worried about a loss of editorial freedom if they get drawn into Mr Murdoch's debt-financed media chess game. They don't know yet what the publishing equivalent of pushing satellite television through the *Sun* will be. Alas for them, their views may not prevail, as shareholder resistance to the increased offer of £403 million fades.

In cruel corporate terms it is difficult to object to a multi-national company like News International taking over an established Scottish publisher in view of the huge number of take-overs which British firms were involved in last year in the US, including Mr Robert Maxwell's $2.6 billion acquisition of Macmillan Inc. Companies which exist by selling shares to the public always know they are vulnerable to take-over. Publishers wanting to ensure independence may have to think of alternatives to the joint stock company.

If the offer is successful, Collins's authors still have power to vote with their feet by leaving to join smaller companies, as some are now threatening to do, thereby cutting off the flow of income to a Murdoch-owned Collins from future books. But against this the more successful authors must weigh the advantages which the US end of the Murdoch empire might bring to their American sales. The economics of publishing are exploding globally (in terms of distribution and marketing) but shrinking in terms of production, as desk-top publishing brings about a dramatic cut in costs which ought to spawn a new wave of small firms.

Meanwhile Mr Murdoch and his rivals are creating multi-media empires capable of linking world-wide book syndications with satellite television serials, while their newspapers reveal the private lives of the actors involved amid advertisements dressed up as new stories. If you want to complain about what happens here you can go to the Press Council. You may or may not be happy with the outcome. But who can you complain to about a satellite programme beamed from the United States involving an Australian soap and French book rights? The new global media empires are escaping from national sovereignty. Some form of international surveillance is badly needed to fill the gap.

Boom-time for British rats

MAEV KENNEDY
14 January 1989

One day the tools of Mr Ray Bloomfield's trade will undoubtedly turn up at an auction of rural antiques: handsome brass and iron ratting spoon, mid-Suffolk, property of a rodent operative; rat grave-digger's shovel, ditto.

When Mr Bloomfield became a rodent operative – 'but I don't mind being called the rat man' – 25 years ago, he made the spoon out of part of an electric light and an old serving spoon. With it he doles out rat poison and wheatmeal, and the odd mercy killing blow to the skull.

Mr Bloomfield and his spoon have never been busier. Rats are popping out in unprecedented numbers in suburban back gardens as well as sewer tunnels, village hall playgroups and rubbish dumps. The Institute of Environmental Health Officers confirms the problem is national, and suppliers of rat poison ran out of stocks several times this winter.

Mr Norman Foster, the health officer for Mid-Suffolk council, could not find time to watch *The Pied Piper of Hamelin* over Christmas, but he felt a keen professional interest. Mid-Suffolk is one of many authorities forced to bring in contractors to supplement their pest control staff. The rat calls start in late autumn, when they come in from the fields seeking warm winter quarters. In 1986–87 Mid-Suffolk had 687 complaints. In 1987 it shot up to 1,323. This winter, there were 1,416 cases by 31 December. Rats in houses get priority, because of the danger to children and risk of disease. In the past, Mid-Suffolk always got to them the same day. This winter they have a delay of several days even in urgent cases.

The institute is most worried about the increase in rats in urban areas, where they are finding it easier to reach the surface through the crumbling brick of many inner-city sewers in London, Manchester, Liverpool and parts of Bristol. It blames water authorities' cutting back on sewer-baiting programmes and is acutely worried about the implications of privatization. Health officers will be lobbying parliament with their suggested safeguards next week.

In Suffolk they blame the weather. 'It's perfect for rats,' said Mr Bloomfield. 'They hate heat and they hate cold. These bad summers and warm winters suit them just fine.'

Mr Foster, who keeps a gnawed-through lead pipe as a souvenir of his time as an environmental health officer in York, agrees. Rats usually live about a year, but his Suffolk rats are surviving into a ripe old age, joined by the five litters of six babies each that a healthy female can bear each year. Apart from disease, the damage is vast. Mr Foster has just closed down a playgroup in a village hall where rats had destroyed toys and equipment. Anything salvageable will have to be scrubbed and disinfected; the most sinister of the rat diseases, Weil's, is carried through urine and is a killer.

Last week, Mr Bloomfield was paying his third visit to a haulier's yard. It takes several visits to be sure of clearing a site and he calculates that a pound of poison only kills four adult rats. A tarpaulin pulled aside revealed a warren of shallow tunnels, and a dying rat. 'He's an ugly one,' Mr Bloomfield said. 'Beautiful, some of them are, beautiful thick glossy coats.'

He hates killing field mice, but feels no sympathy for the dying creature. He will not touch a rat, alive or dead, even with his gloved hand. 'If they get you, even a scratch, you're ruined for life. Sorry my friend.' The spoon cracked down on the rat's skull, and Mr Bloomfield went off to fetch the shovel.

Gun law rules USA

MARTIN WALKER
19 January 1989

In California, 10 bullets a second spraying across a yard full of schoolkids playing. Six dead. In Florida, the police shoot an unarmed suspect fleeing on a motorbike, and the smouldering ghetto starts shooting back. Three dead so far. But put this in perspective. On average, over 60 Americans die by shooting in the US daily.

And last Friday, in the country where the Constitution guarantees its free citizens the right to bear arms, Bernhard Goetz was finally being sentenced in a New York court. Four years ago, Goetz shot four young blacks he thought were planning to rob him on a subway train. They were 'armed' with a screwdriver.

As Darell Cabey lay squirming and bleeding at his feet, Goetz said 'You don't look so bad – here's another', and shot him once more in the spine, crippling the boy for life. Goetz was acquitted of assault by a New York jury, but was finally sentenced last week to one year for possessing an unlicensed gun. He could be out in 51 days.

The city of Washington DC has one of the toughest gun control laws in the nation, and yet is still the murder capital of the United States, with 372 murders this year.

I can walk into a shop called Metro Pawn in Virginia, about ten minutes from the *Guardian* office, show a driving licence and hand over $255 in cash. And I then walk out quite legally armed with a MAC-11 9 millimetre submachine gun. It has a clip of 50 rounds, which it fires in one long four-second burst. One best-seller is the chrome-plated Raven .25 semi-automatic, 'a popular ladies' gun' that is easy to conceal and costs only $59.95.

'In 1968, the police in Orlando, Florida, were faced with an epidemic of rape. A total of 2,500 women were trained to use guns, and the next year rape fell by 88 per cent, and burglary by 25 per cent,' says the National Rifle Association, the most effective political lobby in the country.

'According to a National Crime Survey study, carried out in 1979–85, when a robbery victim does not defend himself, the robbery succeeds four times out of five, and one in four of the victims is injured. When the victim resists with a gun, the robbery success rate falls to 30 per cent, and the victim injury rate falls to 17 per cent,' argues David Kopel, a former district attorney in Manhattan and a prominent opponent of gun control.

Statistics are tossed back and forth like grenades. The NRA says that of an average 92,000 accidental deaths a year, about 300 are from handguns. Take out the car accidents, and throw in other kinds of gun, and the figures look different. In 1984, the last year for which the National Center for Health Statistics has a detailed analysis, there were 1,668 'unintentional firearms deaths in the US', of which 287 were children under the age of 15.

The NRA has an income of over $70 million a year, mostly from its 3 million membership dues and donations, but over $10 million from gun manufacturers for ads in the NRA publications. This money is pledged to fight all forms of gun control, and in recent years the NRA has even fought attempts to ban the new plastic guns which would let a hijacker take a weapon past metal detectors.

This week, Ronald Reagan leaves office, seven years after taking an assassin's bullet, and still quoting the old gun lobby dictum: 'When guns are made criminal, only criminals will have guns.' He is replaced by George Bush, who celebrated Christmas with a little quail-hunting, and who fought the election on a platform that said: 'Republicans will continue to defend the constitutional right to keep and bear arms.'

Catching the spycatcher

ANDREW RAWNSLEY
24 January 1989

I would like to offer Douglas Hurd, who in his spare time writes political thrillers, what I think is a pretty gripping idea for his next book. The plot came to me last night as he was making his speech on the Security Service Bill.

Brilliant in its simplicity, it will be a best-seller, particularly if the Government cooperates by attempting to ban it. The book's provisional title is: *The Home Secretary is a Spy*.

The central character is a deceptively emollient, senior figure in a Conservative Government who has always secretly hated the British people and will do anything to hurt them. To that end he has already drawn up a broadcasting white paper designed to put the country's television entirely in the hands of a malevolent foreign power, Rupert Murdoch.

He has also enthusiastically cooperated in the Chancellor of the Exchequer's programme of long-term sabotage of the British economy, though he sometimes wonders if the Chancellor isn't being a bit too obvious about it. The Home Secretary, though undetected for years, harbours an understandable fear that he might eventually be exposed. He introduces new legislation, let's call it the Security Service Bill.

This law, unique among English-speaking democracies, makes it impossible for anybody but the Home Secretary to have control over the security services. In his speech presenting his bill, this Home Secretary, let's call him Douglas Hurd, refuses to accept the need for any independent parliamentary or public supervision. He suggests it would be too risky to allow a select committee of MPs or even of Privy Councillors, however distinguished or patriotic, to supervise the security services. Even former Cabinet ministers, even former Home Secretaries, so he suggests, could not be trusted. But what is the difference between a former and a present Home Secretary? Only this – that a Home Secretary in office would be a great deal more use to an enemy power as a spy.

Hurd is aware of the complete inconsistency of his argument, but he gambles that years of careful recruitment by MI5 from only the most stupid applicants to the intelligence services have ensured that there will be nobody bright enough to notice.

Slowly but surely, beginning with his power to appoint the director-generals of MI5 and MI6 without any reference to Parliament, Hurd begins to fill the intelligence services with fellow agents.

Now, one of the few remaining members of the security services still loyal to Britain might yet discover the truth. This loyal MI5 man might long have wondered why the Government allowed the security service to waste nearly all its time and resources bugging and burgling innocent and harmless trade unionists and civil libertarians. It made no sense at all, except as a calculated distraction.

But who could the MI5 man go to with his suspicions? He could tell the new commissioner for the security services, lauded by Hurd in his speech as a guarantee of independent oversight of their operations. But that, of course, is the most brilliant deceit of all. For the commissioner is appointed by and reports in secret only to – by now you're ahead of me – the Home Secretary.

Well, there it is, Mr Hurd. You may think the idea is wildly improbable, if not utterly ridiculous. Couldn't conceivably happen in a mature democracy.

But then I would have said the same about your bill, and it's already in print.

War wounds

JOHN VIDAL
30 January 1989

War came to Private Frank Gilchrist, 2nd Battalion Scots Guards, as he and a mate stepped out one night to have a smoke on the deck of the QE2. They'd sailed all 7000 miles hardly knowing where the Falklands were, why they were going or what was expected of them. Of course the politicians would sort it out and home they'd all come, laughing, friends together, chums for life.

Like hell. The pair of them sat down on some boxes on deck. Frank lit up and they chatted away in the dark. A naval rating came and joined them: 'Do you know what you're sitting on, lads?'

'No.'

'Coffins. Black rubber bloody coffins. There's bodies in there.'

'Christ,' thought Frank. 'Bloody Christ.'

From then on things happened quickly. They transferred

to a destroyer, then landing craft. They walked past dead men thinking they were alive and live men thinking they were dead. He remembers thinking the politicians should be down there with them, clearing up the limbs and flesh.

They shot at aircraft and young Argentines. They smelled death and sickness and pain. They fought on Tumbledown. It was all very, very messy.

And then Frank was shot. In the leg.

So they put him on the Uganda hospital ship and gave him morphine. Frank got a taste for it. He played up his pain to get more, to drift off and forget the images of war. Back in London he found a dealer and in no time he was really hooked. He told the army and after a week of close arrest he was out on Civvy Street without so much as a thank you or a counselling session.

He went up to Liverpool where there were 15-year-olds selling heroin on street corners. He stole to get it. He injected it. He dealt in soft drugs and he was caught with an ounce of hash, given 18 months and sent to Walton and Risley where he kicked the habit. One of the wardens was an old sergeant from the Falklands.

When he was released he asked to go home to Edinburgh rather than back to Liverpool. He started having dizzy spells and getting sick. He was told he had Aids.

'God,' he thought, 'I'm going to die.' And he went out on the tiles for a week.

It's a story of our time, a harrowing tale of an individual caught up in some of the more dramatic events of the last 10 years, some would say a young man with a profound ability to be in the wrong place at the wrong time. Of course Frank's story could be told tragically, politically, or socially, with self-righteous anger or justifiable bitterness, but the soft-spoken Scot tells it straightforwardly with something akin to fatalism.

His life, he says, had been one of continually having to adjust and adapt. He wouldn't change it and he doesn't regret it. He doesn't blame the army, or his parents or friends or Mrs Thatcher or anyone else. They've been his decisions, it's his problem and it's his life and dammit he's still living it fully. Aye, there's a tragedy there, but there's also humour and warmth, new friendships and interests to celebrate.

The story doesn't end there. A year and a half ago Frank dropped in on his actor brother at the Edinburgh Festival to borrow a few quid. He ended up telling his story to Philip Hedley of the Theatre Royal, Stratford East, who asked if he'd be interested in turning it into a drama.

Now Frank had never been to the theatre before. He hesitated and went to see *The Normal Heart*, a much-praised American Aids play. He hated it because it was full of coffins and wheelchairs, and didn't show that people with Aids could be normal, be bastards, be funny. It was a celebration of death and it was out of date.

So he agreed and over the next year he talked at length to Vince Foxall, Stratford East's writer in residence. What has emerged is *Just Frank*, his life story, from the schoolboy always causing problems on the Gaza strip (as he calls Pilton in Edinburgh where he was brought up), to the milkman he became and the army he signed on with to get away from a stupid, going-nowhere life.

There's bits of the story he doesn't like but they all happened and he says he's not there to pick and choose what should be seen. There's bits that bring a lump to his throat, bits that make him laugh yet others find too moving to watch. He doesn't like the costumes because they're too good. He finds it weird seeing his friends up there on the stage.

'It's not an Aids play,' he insists. 'It's not a Falklands play, either. It's a play about one person. I think a lot of people with Aids will hate it. The characters in the play tell anti-Aids jokes, there are anti-gay scenes.'

Frank is heterosexual, though most of his friends are now gay. He remembers going to a counselling session and finding he was the only 'straight' and being in the minority for the first time. It came as a shock and so did the reactions of other Aids sufferers who treated him with caution. He found his friends couldn't accept him. The stereotypical image of an Aids sufferer being gay or a junkie was rife.

'People expect people with Aids to all get on. In reality it's not like that. You're still you. There's no use in me sitting down and worrying because I'd just be wasting time.'

His total involvement with the production has been valuable occupational therapy for him. Between it and Scottish Aids Monitor (who have treated him wonderfully, 'like a human'), he's now getting fed up living his life through Aids. Now he's ready to move on, perhaps into theatre as a stage hand ('but I've got no O-levels'), perhaps into photography, certainly something new.

It won't be without a sense of fun or dignity or a new appreciation of beauty. 'I used to go to bars and discos and come out drunk,' he says. 'Now I go up on Arthur's seat with my Doberman. I love the rain.'

He hands over the lyrics for a song Tom Robinson has written about him for the play:

> I'd wish I'd seen it all before
> I wish I'd wondered how
> to smell the rain and see the trees,
> I'm glad I have it now
>
> Hey, hey, I can't stay,
> I'm gonna go on my own sweet way,
> Living life from day to day,
> No matter what you do or say
> Hey, hey, my own sweet way.

There's much more of it but he says cheerio and turns back to writing his first night good-luck cards to the cast. He laughs and slips a condom into each.

Myth Baker

LEADER
30 January 1989

Earlier this month Mr Kenneth Baker described a vision. He unveiled a 25-year blueprint for the universities. This was the Government's first long-term look at what should happen to higher education since the Conservatives came to power 10 years ago. Some of Mr Baker's goals, such as doubling the proportion of teenagers going on to college from one in seven to almost one in three, were both ambitious and welcome. But there was one huge hole in his plan: the means by which the system was to reach its higher plateau. The first test of Mr Baker's dream comes this week with the request from the vice chancellors for a partial restoration of the cuts which have led to 19 per cent of lectureships and 36 per cent of professorial posts remaining unfilled.

Mr Baker's mass higher education plan has been built on a myth. He indicated that his model was America, which he purported to believe was market-led and privately financed. Both assumptions are wrong. More than nine million US college students, some 80 per cent of the total, are in public institutions. True, some of the most famous names in American higher education are private institutions but even the private sector depends on student grants and guaranteed loans. More than 90 per cent of community colleges are publicly financed as are impressive state universities like Michigan, Wisconsin and California. Higher education in the US is not market-led. Outside elite Ivy League colleges, much of the private sector struggles to survive.

Britain has suffered from a poverty of ambition. Far too few school leavers go to college: a mere eight per cent to university and some 14 per cent into higher education all told. Compare this to 20 per cent plus in France, West Germany and the Netherlands – or 45 per cent in the US. Is it surprising that low skills and inadequate qualifications are two chief causes of our economic ills? The problem starts earlier than college. Only one out of three 16-year-olds stays on at school and a mere one in five among 17-year-olds.

Mr Baker wants to widen access and to raise the proportion going to college to 30 per cent by 2014. This is much more ambitious than his predecessors, who cut universities' budgets by almost 20 per cent and forced them to lay off 6000 staff. But Mr Baker's vision will remain a mere dream if he thinks the funds for his expansion can be raised in the private sector. The Government has let sixth form maintenance grants, the one programme which did help persuade more pupils to stay on at school, to wither on the vine. Worse still, it is now proposing a loan system for university students which can only narrow rather than widen access.

University pay is an even more immediate issue. The universities and the Association of University Teachers agree about the erosion of their status. Academic salaries have declined by 20 per cent relative to average earnings since 1979. The vice chancellors have mishandled this year's negotiations, delaying giving any offer until the exam boycott began. But the real villain is in Whitehall. University funds for this year are being squeezed again. The universities are only able to offer pay rises of just over three per cent in a year in which price and earnings rises are running far higher. The campus exodus tells its own story.

The universities want another £64 million not just to raise the basic offer but also to bring in two Thatcherite principles: merit awards and discretionary supplements in shortage subjects. Neither can be introduced without more cash. If Mr Baker believes what he said this month, the extra has to be found. It was not a £9000-a-year academic lecturer who described the Government's approach to universities as 'illiterate, innumerate, miserable, negative and philistine'. That was from an eminent Conservative back-bencher, Robert Rhodes James. Time to repair the damage.

Toad into lark

2 February 1989

TERRY HANDS, the RSC's artistic director, reviews *Guardian* theatre critic Michael Billington's directorial debut at the Barbican

Some say the lark and loathed toad change eyes,
O, now I would they had chang'd voices too . . .

Romeo and Juliet III, v

Well, actors do it – playwrights do it – I've even known producers do it. Let's all do it. Let's direct a play. The latest recruit to a much, abused and more misunderstood profession is a critic, Michael Billington. It is an odd choice. Critics are soloists – directors, teamsters. I should have expected a desire to act, like Jack Tinker, or to write, like Irving Wardle. But no, Mr Billington, perceiving directors as auteurs or interpreters, has plumped for power.

His 'disarming apologia' in Friday's *Guardian* before the first night (would we all could) shows how much he now qualifies that perception. In fact a director is much more teacher than tyrant. He coordinates.

The play is *The Will* by Pierre Marivaux, to be performed by the RSC on the Conservatory Terrace at the Barbican. In my adopted role of critic, for the first time at an RSC first night I feel unapprehensive.

The Terrace is an appropriate setting for the play – a greenhouse jungle, ideal for Marivaux's predators. In *The Will* – a technically brilliant one-act – the Marquis and the Countess love each other but he has been bequeathed

600,000 francs provided he marries Hortense. If he doesn't, he loses 200,000 francs. Nobody wants him to marry Hortense – not even Hortense – and the play is the conspiracy of all the other characters to persuade him that the path of true love is worth 200,000 francs. In fact, by the end he has both Countess and cash – but then it *is* a comedy.

The play has all the difficulties of our own Restoration period. Nobody does anything – they simply talk, and activity of any kind has to be invented. Mr Billington's production is at its best in the confrontations between the Marquis and the Countess when he trusts the language and Jane Leonard expertly relates her growing exasperation to increasing assaults upon her garden. Here, word and action cohere to tell several stories.

But he fails to relate the servants to the main theme – their cunning and bloody-mindedness reflecting and underpinning their more mannered masters and mistresses. It is partly focus – which in a French play means control of every word, every gesture, and does not include two musicians centre stage who don't play; it's partly stage mechanics. The movement of a Marivaux is as precise as a Swiss chronometer. Mr Billington gives us a sundial in an English summer.

It is not really his fault. He has simply responded to the translation, though that too is a director's responsibility. Michael Sadler has freely adapted the original into a text at once speakable and funny, but it has none of Marivaux's glitter and danger. Thirties costumes add to the Anglicization, together with English diffidence, archness and self-consciousness.

These are assertive, greedy people. At one point a bird trilled in the Conservatory – it should have been an alligator. The characters talk of war, aggression, anger – we are given Parisian hanky-panky. The company achieve a surface of sorts but not a meaning. And there is no sex. From Marivaux's high style we descend to what is at best suburban Labiche.

I accept that directors should not go to rehearsals with

all the answers. On the other hand, they should go with the right questions. And the first of these must be what is the difference between a French play and an English.

But the performance is fun. The actors flourish in the comfortable security of Billington's vision and if that reduces a sinister jungle to a genteel garden, at least it is a party to which we are all invited. It was full house on Friday night. I hope it will not be Mr Billington's last outing as a director. He brought the best out of his actors, held his audience, and successfully assaulted a traditional theatre barrier. For me, it will be the last time. It is hard to criticize. I'd rather appreciate. It requires enormous experience to surrender to a performance and yet retain a pencil in hand, or head.

At the end of the performance I went over to congratulate Michael Billington. 'No, no,' he said hurriedly. 'You can't talk to me. You're a critic.'

Princess Diana finds small worm in the Big Apple

MARTIN WALKER
3 February 1989

The Princess of Wales wiped her hand on her skirt in New York yesterday morning, and probably lost whatever chance she had of taking this hard and cynical, but deeply sentimental, city by storm.

She had just made a brief and evidently token foray into the small crowd of poor people from the lower East Side housing estates, had smiled and chatted and pressed a little New York flesh – which was almost deep-frozen after awaiting her arrival for over an hour in the chill wind.

As she turned away, the Princess wiped her hand none too discreetly on her skirt. She then marched past the massed lenses of the city's press and television corps and replied to their beseeching questions about whether she liked the Big Apple with a brisk: 'Morning.'

'That lady sure don't take no prisoners,' the chap from the *Daily News* muttered.

Later about 100 supporters of Noraid, an organization accused of channelling funds to the IRA, demonstrated outside the Brooklyn Academy of Music where the Princess was attending a gala performance by the Welsh National Opera. In the city's tabloid newspapers yesterday, the royal family's superstar had to share the front-page billing with a shock-horror story about a three-year-old tot used as a human shield in a drugs-deal shoot-out.

The *New York Times* reported the Princess's arrival with an extremely cool and brief caption beneath a photograph tucked away on a page inside. *Newsday* raged on its front page at the way city employees were scraping chewing gum off the pavement where the Princess might step, when the city had so many better things to do.

Mr Pete Hamill, who has made his soft-hearted, tough-guy column in the *Daily News* into a minor art form, greeted her as 'the most famous welfare mother in the world, a permanent recipient of British dole.

'She does no work, has no known talents and derives her celebrity entirely from the man she married.'

All that is true, and fair comment, but it started considerable quivering among the stiff upper lips of the royal-image controllers yesterday. They are so accustomed to the easy successes of public relations from the practised servility of the British, the politeness of the Commonwealth, and the snobbish sycophancy of the Reagan White House that the hardboiled curiosity of New York has come as a surprise.

This city knows about real celebrities. It gave its heart to President Gorbachev in December, even though he strangled their traffic in 'Gorby-lock' and had all police leave cancelled as 6000 officers cleared the streets for the only news-media superstar with the power to blow New York off the face of the earth.

By contrast, the police department assigned a mere 400 to the Princess. It will take a lot of retouching and careful camera angles to make this visit anything like a success. But then the image is all.

Mr Rupert Murdoch's Channel Five television filled its screens with a cockney pearly king serenading the Princess at 7 a.m., while the winner of a Princess of Wales lookalike contest handed out samples of shepherd's pie.

China no Dada

JASPER BECKER
6 February 1989

The artists wore French berets and the police arrived in a Citroën. China's biggest exhibition of art in the Dada mode opened and closed yesterday in a flurry of moral outrage from both sides. The aesthetic tolerance of the police finally snapped during yesterday's private viewing, when one artist shot at her reflection in a mirror with an air pistol.

They seized the pistol and the artist who dreamed up this particular happening, and made it the excuse to halt the China Avant-garde Exhibition at Beijing's National Gallery.

'We are very angry. This took years of preparation but the police don't understand art,' said one frustrated painter from Tibet, sporting long hair, three-day-old stubble and insisting on speaking in broken French to complete the image.

Beijing's bohemians and the French ambassador had turned up to view the 150 works of art staged by more than 100 artists from all over China.

Having had to wait since 1986 to hold the show, they featured the full repertoire of surreal works, including a giant vagina with a zip, a large plastic breast suspended from the ceiling above a matching phallus, a dead winter cabbage, plastic gloves, obscure mechanical contraptions, images of drooping clocks, and sheets of paper hung along the ceiling.

The Ministry of Public Security inspected the exhibition before it opened, and objected to a triptych of Chairman Mao portraits over which a metal grid had been painted. But the artists refused to allow the show to go on without all the paintings.

The authorities gave way – but apparently were not informed that there would also be some live happenings. Two artists showered art lovers with condoms and money, others dressed themselves up in fancy dress 'statements', including three who were evicted for appearing in white sheets à la Ku Klux Klan.

A report that someone acted out a suicide in the nude on a bed of soft-boiled eggs was, perhaps unfortunately, inaccurate; but some artists were planning to perform the Last Supper.

It was the pistol which provided the police with the excuse to close the exhibition, as this could be said to contravene public order. The painter who provided the air pistol was the only one still being held yesterday afternoon.

Viewers were invited to make their own interpretation of the happening, but the artists said there was no political meaning. After being evicted, a large number of people gathered outside the art gallery, scuffles broke out, and at one point they threatened to hold a sit-in.

Police toting Uzi sub-machine guns and tin hats then appeared. Soon afterwards, the artists rolled up giant canvases on the forecourt bearing the exhibition's logo: a road sign indicating no left U-turns.

After negotiations between artists' representatives and police, it was agreed that the show may reopen tomorrow provided the ground floor, containing the most shocking works, remains closed. The exhibition had the backing of the Ministry of Culture, which has pursued liberal policies recently, after last year halting preparations during an anti-bourgeois liberalization campaign.

The national art gallery is now open for hire. Last month

it featured China's first exhibition devoted to nudes, and drew huge crowds. Existentialism and experimental art first became the rage in 1985 and 1986, with a group proclaiming 'Dada is dead'.

The brochure for yesterday's show says 'goodbye to ideas of art meant to please human senses or instruct people with dogmas'.

The Sky's the limit

MICHAEL WHITE
6 February 1989

The state of Britain cannot be all bad when Mr Rupert Murdoch has to turn up on a chaotic west London building site early on Sunday morning in order to solicit financial assistance from the rest of us.

Normally he contracts out this kind of work to newsagents around the planet. But yesterday's launch of Sky Television (Why Sky incidentally? True Blue or just close to the Sun?) was a gamble even by Digger standards. Experts not yet employed by News International say it may cost him £500 million before showing a profit – if he's lucky.

The *Sunday Sky Times* supremo, Andrew Neil, faithful Tonto to the Aussie Kemo Sabe, was at the mid-day Isleworth HQ press briefing to do the introductions and get a word in edgeways. 'The timetable is working out perfectly,' he insisted edgeways (several times). That was to say they have time to get the product right before anyone tunes in.

Half last night's potential audience of 600,000 homes are in the rich advertising markets of rural Ireland and 100,000 would-be British punters must await what Mr Murdoch called 'the night-shift in Japan' to deliver their £199 dishes. Currently it is easier to buy a cruise missile and certainly easier to make it work.

So the good news is that Sky is costing Mr Murdoch a

packet, which means that dozy British publishers, sleepy US TV stations and Turkish kidney-sellers are safe from his restless genius for a while. The bad news is that he went ahead anyway, with all four channels: Wapping II. Ours is now a nation of four-lane traffic jams but eight-channel TV. Aren't you proud?

At Isleworth last night, guests of Mr Murdoch's bank manager, we watched history made. In fairness there were no visible nipples, only Dolly Parton, though there are rumours that the Sky teletext service includes a Page 103 Girl. But the drive for sensationalism guaranteed early appearances by Frank Bough, Roy Hattersley and Mozart, not to mention Rupert Murdoch who found his way on to two channels, not to mention last night's films – *The Colour of Money* followed by *Ruthless People*.

For a man whose global overdraft is four billion quid, this Murdoch was remarkably cheerful as Sky's rocket lifted off on a solid fuel of Digger pound notes; this despite being forced to sit through 20 minutes of promotional film whose hyperactive graphics and hyperbolic verbals included the gem: 'If Gorbachev coughs we'll know about it.' (Astra is evidently a CIA satellite.)

That was not one of yesterday's many technical questions which Mr Murdoch, always an engaging rascal, fielded gracefully. Hands in blazer pockets, his battered smile occasionally reinforced by a dry joke, he was as unpretentious as a Sydney estate agent. When Mexican TV respectfully asked if the tycoon was 'very proud to be bringing immediacy to Britain and Europe' even he sensed that was going too far.

Later he unblushingly denied planning to sell any assets to stop Sky pushing him into the red and said it was impossible to define the percentage of American programme content. Downhill skiing from the US might involve 'British skiers, British cameramen, how do you define it?'

Mr Neil bravely blamed the BBC, ITV and their unions for not letting Sky buy their products – which were often inferior to American ones anyway.

As for the 'more means worse' argument, in the 30-channel US market it was 'total nonsense' the Tycoon told a whingeing pinko questioner from the *Guardian* (myself). 'I don't know what you mean by down-market and up-market,' he subsequently explained. 'That is so English, class-ridden, snobbery-ridden. I'm an Australian. I believe in equality.'

Upper-class Australian renegade he may be. But in his funny way, bless him, he probably believes it: the media tycoon as provincial outsider with a chip on his shoulder (Mr Neil). As such he is the perfect Thatcherite instrument to do to British telly what she did last month to British law and health care.

But only if we all buy enough dishes to impress the advertisers. In return he promises not to charge for yesterday's new channels for at least three years – and then only 10p or so. 'Practically nothing.'

Despite Mr Neil's nerves ('Keep your fingers crossed. I have my legs crossed as well'), the actual launch went off perfectly. The assembled news-media moguls, politicians and Australian bouncers at the Sky party actually stopped talking and chanted: 'Ten – nine – eight – seven . . .' and watched for a full minute before resuming their conversations. Television to them is not a medium for watching but for appearing on or owning. The first news item was a spinechilling tale of British kidney sales which, in the time-honoured tradition of news-media launches, was duly pronounced to be at least a fortnight old.

The V&A's new blitz

JOHN EZARD
10 February 1989

Inscribed in the shrapnel-scarred wall of the side entrance into what used to be the peace of the Victoria and Albert

Museum in London are the proud words: 'Damage to these walls is the result of bombing during the blitz. It is left as a memorial to the enduring value of this great museum at a time of conflict.'

This week the conflict has gone on inside the South Kensington building; and doubts have begun coursing round the international art world about how long, at this tempo of self-inflicted wounding, the V&A's acknowledgedly pre-eminent value can endure.

In seven days of what one of the institution's internationally famous scholars calls 'shock-horror', two events unprecedented in the courteous annals of museums have happened. Last weekend five of the V&A's nine top curatorial keepers were called in by their director and offered voluntary redundancy, one of them at an interview lasting three minutes. Four other high-graded curatorial staff were similarly made offers they were not intended to refuse. In just over two hours of briskness, professionals with a total of 130 years high-level experience in the museum were pointed towards the scrap heap.

And today the director, Ms Elizabeth Esteve-Coll – the V&A's former librarian, admiringly labelled 'a bit of an Edwina Currie' by a *Guardian* interviewer in the pre-salmonella days of her appointment in January 1988 – is contemplating a vote of no confidence and demands for her resignation by most of her senior-graded staff. These include not only the victims but the young Turks who could expect to inherit their jobs.

Their union, the First Division Association, asked yesterday for an urgent meeting with Lord Armstrong, chairman of the V&A trustees. Other Civil Service unions fear lower-tier redundancies which would bite deep into the museum's 700 staff. But what has particularly aroused concern about the V&A restructuring plan in the art worlds of London, New York, Paris, Vienna, and West Berlin is its abolition of the 81-year-old role of keeper as a specialist with lifelong knowledge of, control over and daily contact with the five million artefacts in the world's first, and still foremost, arts and crafts museum. The role has been duplicated throughout Europe and the United States.

Restructuring would merge five departments into two new mega-departments, with more lowly qualified specialists in a 'research' role and administrators responsible for day-to-day control of objects of art. The ceramics department, for instance, acknowledged as the best in the world with 80,000 objects in its care, would lose its keeper, Mr John Mallett, and its deputy keeper, Mr Michael Archer, and be reduced to two D grade research assistants.

West Berlin's director-general for museums, Professor Wolfdieter Dube, said yesterday that he had been 'absolutely shocked' at news of the redundancies. 'What is happening at the Victoria and Albert is very important for all the leading museums of the world,' he said. 'Frankly one has to ask questions about the cultural understanding of the British Government.

'If they can't house objects properly in museums, why don't they give back the Elgin marbles? Because at this rate nobody qualified to look after them is going to be left in your museums. This restructuring is such a stupid, crazy way to run a museum. The curatorial tradition works successfully in all the museums of the world.

'Museums are institutions which collect objects, conserve them and display them for the education of the public. You can only do these things with knowledge of the objects. No administrator can have that. It isn't their function.'

Restructuring was first urged by Mr Richard Wilding, head of the Government's Office of Arts and Libraries until last year. But staff regard a talk given to them last year by a woman from the OAL as the real omen. She said the OAL was 'in close contact' with the museum. One curator was heard to say that in nearly 20 years service he had never met anyone from the OAL, so who was it in contact with? The answer was: 'Mainly with the director.' A few days afterwards a committee to discuss restructuring was announced.

On 27 January, Ms Esteve-Coll called senior staff

together and handed them a five-page document on restructuring to be implemented 'straight away'. She said no redundancies were being contemplated. The announcement of redundancies a week later is understood to be due to a sudden Whitehall offer to fund these, without loss to the V&A's annual £12.9 million grant, if they were finalized before the financial year ended.

Staff chosen for redundancy included a number opposed to restructuring. They have been given until next Friday to decide. Fear of use of the Official Secret Acts against them has prevented them speaking identifiably, but one said yesterday: 'What has united everybody is the proposal to divide knowledge from control of objects.'

The V&A's spokesman, Mr Graham Wiffen, said: 'The loss of individuals is always sad. But many, many scholars have come and gone and it has not weakened this institution. There is a potential in the new structure for people to do more academic work than ever before. Everyone will know how to handle objects.'

Memories of Afghanistan

JONATHAN STEELE
13 February 1989

'You remember that mother who lost her son. She kept repeating "He fulfilled his duty to the end. He fulfilled his duty to the end." That's the most tragic thing. What duty? I suppose that's what saves her, her notion of duty. She hasn't yet realized that it was all a ridiculous mistake. I'm putting it mildly. If she realized, if she opened her eyes to our whole Afghan thing, she'd probably find it hard to hold out.'

Igor has been back from the war for more than three years now, but like many other survivors he hangs out mostly with other Afghan vets. He lives in the industrial town of Lyubertsi, on the outer edge of Moscow, a shapeless collection of high-rise blocks of flats and building sites, distinguished by nothing but the reflected glory of an authentic hero, the first man in space, Yuri Gagarin, who once studied at the local technical institute. A small monument stands by the door.

Igor and his friends want to build their own monument in Lyubertsi. They formed a club last May which now has about 25 members, plus another 40 who sympathize. One aim is to persuade the local authorities to put up something in the town's park which will commemorate the boys who served and died in Afghanistan. Another is to put on pressure for better veterans' benefits, proper psychiatric help and artificial limbs for those who were wounded for life.

I first met Igor, who is training to be a journalist, at a weird encounter between his group and a party of American Vietnam veterans which was hosted by an archbishop of the Russian Orthodox church. The Americans had come to Moscow with offers of help in supplying prostheses. The Vietnam vets were fifteen years older. Not many on either side spoke each other's language. Yet they all said they felt an immediate wordless rapport. The sense of having fought a remote, pointless war, which those who were not there could never understand, brought them together.

That was last September. Since then I have seen the Afghan vets twice more. One evening they came round and watched a video of Peter Kuzminski's documentary on Afghan vets for Yorkshire television, which was shown in Britain last year. It was by far the best thing they have seen on the war, they said, fuller, more human, less sensational than an Italian documentary which someone showed them and the few things that have appeared on Soviet TV.

They all feel the war was a mistake, if not a disaster. Yet as the last Soviet troops pull out of Afghanistan to the relief and delight of everyone you meet here, the view that the war was pointless is not as widely shared as you might believe. 'Thank God our boys are safe,' is as far as many

Soviet citizens want to think. Not everyone wants to reflect on why they were there.

Yuri is training to be a sociologist. He agrees with Igor that it's only later, after the war, that you fully realize what it was all about. 'The first feeling while you were there is that you start to get fed up. You get fed up with the shooting. But you don't think about it. You don't want to. Slowly, very slowly, after the war, you begin to think, to imagine, to remember what happened, the ruined villages, the expressions on people's faces. Not all the Afghan vets understand. Many of them, a substantial proportion, think that what they did was necessary and right.'

Leonid agrees. He is a professional army officer. He stayed in the service in spite of his views on the war in Afghanistan. 'While you're there, you think you're fulfilling your duty. Your motherland sent you. Many people stay like that. Actually, you still feel that, but over and above it you wonder what the point was.'

Some of the Afghantsy, as the veterans are called, say their first glimmerings came when they realized how little contact they had with real Afghans, the people they were supposed to be helping. Yuri explains: 'Mainly our contact was with kids in the villages we went through. They were always running some kind of little business. Swapping stuff, selling stuff. Sometimes drugs. It was very cheap. You felt the aim was to get us hooked. There was not much contact with Afghan adults, except with the *sarandoy*, the police.'

They admit they were very green when they arrived in Afghanistan. 'The first thing which surprised me was the countryside, the Asian moon, the stars. I felt like a tourist with wide-open eyes. We don't have the same chance to travel like you. It was exciting,' says Igor.

The simplest things were not explained. 'The army is huge. Labour is cheap. They do what they like,' Igor goes on. 'Many eighteen-year-olds lost their fingers. They were not told properly about grenades. They never trained us properly. They just said the Afghans were different people and had a different climate. They gave us a small bit of paper, telling us what not to do, and a little dictionary. That was it. "Don't fraternise. Don't look at women. Don't go into cemeteries. Don't go into mosques."'

They may not have known much, but many had an inkling that it was not going to be fun. 'I remember one paradoxical thing,' Leonid recalls. 'Everyone knew I was in Afghanistan except my mother. My father, my brother, cousins, everyone. I wrote to a friend who passed my news on to them. I wrote a separate latter to my mother, telling her I was in Mongolia. Mongolians are very nice people, I told her. The countryside is lovely. Everything is fine.' Other people tried to avoid being posted to the war. 'Just like in America, people with connections did the best for their sons.'

The Afghantsy say they knew less about the war in the beginning than the Vietnam vets. It was local, and the rest of the country had no idea what was going on. It was not like the Second World War. 'I suppose the Vietnam vets felt the same. But they had publicity about it from the first day, unlike us.'

Soldiers who died could not have 'Afghanistan' mentioned on their tombstones at the beginning. The special decree which Brezhnev's successor, Yuri Andropov, brought in, in 1983, to give veterans benefits and special housing rights, was not published, which is why the local authorities often ignore it. Glasnost on the war came very slowly, and is still not complete.

There was no real chance of opposing conscription or demonstrating publicly against the war. Igor remembers hearing of one case in the Western Ukraine in 1983 or 1984, four or five years after the war began. 'Some mothers went into an army office when they heard their sons were going to Afghanistan. They just refused to let them take their kids away. I don't know what happened after that.'

Leonid believes the Soviet troops in Afghanistan were less cruel than the Americans in Vietnam. His image is made up perhaps of stories of the My Lai massacre, or of films like *Apocalypse Now*. 'The Americans didn't hold back. They shot. We were not able to. You could be walking along. You knew a man you saw was an enemy, but you couldn't fire unless he fired first. What kind of war is it when I have to wait? It was a ridiculous paradox.'

'It wasn't a paradox,' another veteran interrupted. 'It was policy, and it was right.' They have no knowledge of the booby-trapped toys which the Mojahedin claim the Soviet side dropped on villages. They say they did not bomb indiscriminately, and only fired artillery rounds when it was clear the Mojahedin were in a particular village. Loudspeaker warnings were given to civilians to come out. There was no systematic bombing, no chemical warfare, no napalm.

The Afghantsy often have a heightened sense of justice, and a feeling that they have taken risks with their lives, which gives them a right to expect more from other people. They reject the notion that they are all misfits in civilian life now, or have chips on their shoulders, and are easily prone to aggression. That is just the image of the vet which the media play up. But they concede that they get annoyed with any bureaucrat or factory foreman who treats them like dirt. 'People spit in our faces, instead of into the faces of the government which sent us to Afghanistan. We were soldiers. We obeyed orders. But you get this first primitive reaction from people. We don't have a developed public opinion here yet.'

Igor and his friends have no doubt the Soviet troops had to leave Afghanistan. What will happen now that the Soviet troops have left? Two think the Afghan government will collapse. Another disagrees. People were tired of fighting.

The Afghantsy call the Mojahedin *dushmans*, shortened usually to *dukhy*, which means 'spirits' or 'ghosts'. The ghosts knew they could not capture a major town. On the other hand, the vets' respect for the Afghan government forces is not high. 'Many are cowards. If the ghosts shoot, the army runs away,' says Igor. He asked one soldier what he would do after his conscription period was over. 'He said he would join the ghosts. They pay better.' Yuri remembers being in Herat in February 1985 when Soviet troops captured a group of 48 Mojahedin. Later, they got hold of the government newspaper, *Izvestiya*, which said the Afghan army had captured them. Another time they found a cache of rebel weapons. Army photographers came in and posed Afghan troops in front of them.

They are suspicious of the official Soviet death toll of close to 15,000 dead. Lyubertsi, with a population of 180,000, lost 23 boys. As a proportion of the total Soviet population that should produce a total of 27,000 dead. But they do not consider the Afghan war to have been a defeat. 'You see the proportion of casualties,' Yuri said. 'Fifteen thousand of ours dead, or 17,000, and one million Afghans. It's hard to understand. Najibullah said last autumn that 248,000 people had died on the government side, I think. That means 700,000 on the other. It wasn't a Soviet–Afghan war. It is a civil war. A powerful country like ours cannot be defeated. If we had sent more men in, it would have been outright occupation or genocide. We thought it was better to leave.'

Food warnings to be taken with a pinch of salt

ANDREW RAWNSLEY
15 February 1989

To clear up public confusion about food poisoning, this column's medical advisers have issued the following guidelines on which Government statements are now safe to consume. The short advice is: none of them. The longer advice is inevitably rather more complicated.

In general, the risk to the healthy adult from ministerial statements on the safety or otherwise of eggs, cheese or other dairy products is quite small, providing anything said by ministers on radio or television is taken only as part of a normal balanced diet of light entertainment and comedy.

The elderly, the sick, babies, pregnant women, cheese producers, egg farmers and other vulnerable groups should not be fed any ministerial statements, which carry an unacceptably high risk of spreading panic and confusion.

Everybody should avoid anything produced by John Mac-Gregor or Kenneth Clarke, where the Whitehall foot-in-mouth outbreak is at its worst. According to the agriculture minister: 'There is no question of banning sales of cheese made from unpasteurized milk.' According to the health secretary: 'John has said he is considering banning cheese made from non-pasteurized milk.'

All further statements by Mr MacGregor or Mr Clarke should be regarded as unfit for human consumption until further notice or they are told to hand in their notice, whichever is the sooner. The column's Chief Medical Officer has also issued the following advice about anything said by the Prime Minister. For healthy people there is the usual level of risk associated with believing anything said by the Prime Minister, whether hardboiled or scrambled. Everyone should avoid listening to answers to questions made out of raw or chilled Thatcher. She is best served – as she was in Question Time yesterday by Mr Kinnock – thoroughly roasted.

Answers made up of mouldy statistics or stale scorn – 'I really had expected better of you' to Mr Kinnock – are a reliable sign that she is in trouble, that he has asked an excellent question and she knows it.

The Government's latest statement on cheese – read by Mrs Thatcher at Question Time – must be regarded as unsafe. Preliminary tests suggest it, too, is badly infected with the fatal mixture of confusion, panic and complacency which is sweeping Whitehall.

'The position,' Mrs Thatcher said, 'is that in Scotland there is already a ban on sales of unpasteurized liquid milk and cream to the general public . . .' Yes, but read on. '. . . the Ministry of Agriculture is considering whether unpasteurized liquid milk and cream for sale to the public should also be banned in England and Wales . . .' Notice the first symptoms of confusion.

Are the Scots more easily poisoned than the English or Welsh, or is their milk and cream more poisonous? Confusion is usually followed by a severe outbreak of consultation documents. '. . . a consultation document will be issued shortly . . .'

After a while they will develop into a Code of Practice. '. . . A Code of Practice for major manufacturers has already been issued . . .' Told you so. 'A Code of Practice for smaller cheese-makers is in draft.' By now confusion is epidemic. Why less urgency about smaller cheese producers? Are they less likely to be poisonous than taller ones?

Until further clarification is available, only buy cheese from Welsh dwarfs. In the meantime, take all Government advice about food only with a large pinch of salt.

Poisoned utopia

AZIZ AZMEH
17 February 1989

Like all religions, Islam is neither above nor beyond history. For 1400 years it has taken a bewildering variety of forms, each of which has proclaimed itself the most authentic. Without this protean quality, no religion can become universal or span a diversity of times, places, societies and cultures and be the religion of medieval Kurdish tribesmen, 18th-century Moroccan peasants, Cairo scholars, Malaysian traders, Saudi monarchs and Iranian revolutionaries.

This elementary fact seems to be fast receding from the public consciousness with the spectacle of self-appointed inquisitors, judges and executioners in the name of a definitive Islamic monolith. In the name of this monolith, we are witnessing the fostering of a deliberate archaism, the call for the restoration of a putative utopia.

In this utopia, nothing protrudes over the surface of uniformity in ritual, obscurantism, piety, or interpretation of the Koran. Nothing disturbs the authority of the elders, nor the seclusion and subordination of women reduced, in the prurient imagination, to causes for temptation or saved by relegation to motherhood.

Not unnaturally, this call for the absolute introversion of the single voice can only thrive on adversity. It must generate tokens of evil, and can only conceive the difference in terms of triumph or annihilation. Salman Rushdie has found himself caught up in the midst of this fantastical frenzy, and has become a token by means of which the authors and purveyors of this particular brand of recent Islam can project their demonology, and foist upon the various Muslim communities in this country a uniformity that has no justification in their histories or traditions.

Muslims generally, including British Muslims, belong to many nationalities, cultures, classes, and are divided, like everybody else, by different and contradictory ideological and political directions. The denial of this great diversity of Islamic traditions and of the reality of history does not convince the observer that a monolithic Islam is forming a society according to a pre-established model, but rather confirms the fact that religions do not constitute societies or histories, but are rather constituted by them.

Two particular histories have formed a particular form of Islam in Saudi Arabia, and another, extremely right wing, sectarian and marginal Islam in Pakistan. The two have fused ideologically and entwined organizationally to attempt the imposition of a uniformity on the multifarious mass of Muslims in Britain. Presided over by a number of Muslim organizations, the goodwill of ordinary pious Muslims throughout the country has been appropriated and injected with the twin analgesics of uniformity and a sense of transcendental narcissism. The distinction between piety and segregationism disappears, as does that between imagination and reality. The instrument is demonology. Salman Rushdie thus becomes the exorcist's instrument for exhibiting magical efficacy, as Moses did with the miracle of his stave and Abraham with Nimrod.

Over the past century, several Muslim intellectuals in the Arab world and elsewhere have tackled matters held sacred. Sixty-five years ago Taha Hussein lost his job due to a passage considered suspect by the religious authorities of Egypt. He came back afterwards to take up more senior positions and rose to a stature unparalleled in Arabic letters this century. Other offenders were 'defrocked', yet others unsuccessfully prosecuted and others threatened by mob violence or silence. One of the major novels of Naguib Mahfouz, this year's Nobel prize laureat, is still unavailable in his native Egypt because Al-Azhar does not like it, but it is readily available on street stalls in Beirut, Damascus and Tunis. The dispute between the demands of religious groups and the cultural life of the Arab world is not unique to Islam, nor to today's Britain. It is a continuing one, and is co-extensive with religion. It will not abate, and will remain inconclusive for a long time.

But the notion of a heresy punishable by death, and the refusal to countenance difference and dissent, and the construing of all difference from within as demonic, is of another nature altogether. It involves the vitalist logic of opposition between annihilation and triumph, which lies at the base of all Fascist movements.

Its refusal to acknowledge history or the reality of difference is a matter that modern Islam has ejected from its practical dealings with life and relegated to the museum of unused history, much as Britain still retains an archaic law on blasphemy. That efforts are made to resurrect and even to transcend the procedures of Islamic law towards incitement to murder bespeaks nothing but the acute sense of unreality of groups who pretend to represent a unitary Truth that exists nowhere and must therefore be made.

It is now evident that some Muslim leaders in Britain have been genuinely alarmed by the excesses of the past three days. It is hoped that this alarm will enhance the sense of reality which is inseparable from any sense of responsibility. Fundamental to this reality is the reality of difference, as of the distinction between outrage and the desire to annihilate books by banning them or authors by murdering them.

Scott's last outpost, frozen in history

PAUL BROWN
20 February 1989

The seal steaks are stacked neatly in the lean-to ready for feeding the huskies, but the last dog, still chained outside in the bitter cold, has been dead for 76 years.

Inside, Captain Robert Falcon Scott's sleeping bag lies on his bunk just as he left it before setting out on his last journey – an attempt to be the first man to reach the South Pole. On Cape Evans, in the Ross Sea, Antarctica, nothing rots, and the hut which housed Scott's last expedition from January 1911 to January 1913 remains.

The combination of Scott's failure to reach the pole first and the story of his death on the return journey, only a short distance from safety, made the British turn him into national hero. Cape Evans was so remote that once the great age of exploration was over, the hut was abandoned to fill up with snow, which surprisingly left its contents perfectly preserved in the dry cold.

When, in 1947, the American explorer Richard Byrd visited the hut, the lone husky was 'still standing on its legs outside looking still alive'. Twenty years later, a New Zealand team painstakingly chipped out the ice from inside the hut and found to their astonishment its contents as Scott's party must have left it.

Yesterday, on the dining table, it was possible to read in an edition of the *Field* (the country gentleman's newspaper) dated 30 May 1908, that 'There has been more rain than is suitable for the time of year' and an article on how to improve milk yields.

By Scott's bunk was *The Green Flag and other stories of war and sport* by A. Conan Doyle, labelled inside the fly-leaf 'British Antarctic Expedition 1910'. Underneath was *Stalky and Co* by Rudyard Kipling.

Scott's spare boots, gloves, a shirt and coat are neatly arranged as befitted a naval officer. The whole hut is stacked with an amazing variety of food, medicines, scientific equipment, sledges, skis, and even snowshoes for the ponies that never proved any use in the Antarctic.

It was still possible to smell the Fry's cocoa powder which has spilled from one of the few damaged tins. There were unopened bottles of India Relish, tins of pickled herring, a box of bloater paste 'guaranteed free of chemical preservative' and a half used bottle of Heinz tomato ketchup, looking slightly pale after 70 years frozen solid.

Gone was one feature of Scott's expedition: the line of Huntley & Palmer biscuit tins which marked the boundary between the wardroom, occupied by Scott and his 15 fellow officers and scientists, and the messdeck for the nine seamen. Another great polar explorer, Sir Ernest Shackleton, took it down when he visited and occupied the hut two years after Scott's death. He had different ideas on how to lead men.

Otherwise, out of respect for the dead hero with whom he had made the first unsuccessful attack on the pole, Shackleton left the hut undisturbed. At the messdeck end are the stove, the cooking utensils, most of the stores, unidentified board games with counters, and a compendium edition of *Tit-bits* from 23 September 1905 to 17 March 1906.

The wardroom contains the dark room used by the expedition's photographer, Herbert Ponting, with its bottled chemicals needed for making the glass-plate negatives. In Dr Edward Wilson's corner is a perfectly preserved stuffed Emperor penguin and many medicines provided by

Harrods, including an unopened bottle of chloroform, some refined camphor flowers and some tablets made from the thyroid gland of sheep. Judging by the quantity left, these had not been needed.

The pile of lemon peel, squeezed to the last drop, was probably an attempt to stave off the scurvy which plagued the expedition. Outside the hut is a notice set up by the restoration party from New Zealand, which is still digging out the stables, asking people not to remove items from 'this shrine'.

Apart from restoring Captain 'Titus' Oates's bunk and replacing the window panes, everything has been put where it was originally found under the ice. Closing the door on the dim interior and walking out into the twenty-four-hour daylight, the husky was still on guard outside, next to the unused bales of hay for the ponies.

Looking over my shoulder it was not hard to imagine the ghost of Captain Scott, the intrusion over, resuming his seat at the wardroom table, to smoke a quiet pipe.

Prince Philip pays homage to Private Trout

MICHAEL WHITE
27 February 1989

Everyone knew why Prince Philip had to visit the local Commonwealth War Cemetery, to balance that nod before the Imperial coffin. What Private R. Trout of the Royal Army Ordnance Corps would have made of it no one will ever know. On this weekend's evidence he might want to call it a day.

Private Trout died a prisoner of war, probably as a malnourished slave labourer in a Japanese factory, on 24 February 1943 – 45 years to the day before Emperor Hirohito was buried with full international honours.

The Emperor was 87. Private Trout was 22. Lieutenant Philip Mountbatten RN, also serving in the Far East, went on to marry the daughter of King George VI who ceased to be Emperor of India that same year, 1947, a direct consequence of the war Japan had just lost. It is an unjust world.

Private Trout's share of victory was to become one of 1738 British, Dominion and Empire troops whose remains lie under rows of neat bronze plaques, interspaced with roses and azaleas. The spot has been lovingly tended for nearly 40 years by Lieut-Colonel Len Harrop, aged 73, who started the war on an anti-aircraft battery defending Rochdale from the Luftwaffe and ended it sorting out war graves. He got hooked. Quiet cemeteries like this one exist in 123 countries.

On Saturday, Hodogaya Cemetery, a green oasis in the Yokohama–Tokyo sprawl, was far from quiet. The Duke arrived with ten cars. Local British expatriates were out to greet him, including a few old soldiers.

Only one, Wilfred Haw, aged 77, had actually fought the Japanese directly – unless we count the *Sun*, which was represented by a dogged Royal-watcher, Harry Arnold of 'We are not amused' fame.

Accompanied by Sir Geoffrey Howe, Prince Philip, brisk, tanned and looking more than ever like a Royal Rex Harrison, laid his wreath 'In Memory of the Glorious Dead' on behalf of himself and Elizabeth R.

It was cold, wet and increasingly a shambles. The Prince spoke to the locals, inspected the graves and reproached the nearest of the media scrummage whom he spotted showing disrespect. 'That's right, jump about on the graves,' he snapped.

It is the thought that counts. But what thoughts remain appropriate here except the personal memories of widows, like next month's British Legion party, who finally make the trip?

The *Sun* is right in one sense. Official Japan regards the Great East Asia War as an unfortunate calamity, which was no one's fault. Or as much the fault of the feeble Chinese, Koreans or the white imperialist powers as her own. Silence and euphemistic text books are the best policy.

The emperor was, how shall we say, an accessory before a lot of nasty and premeditated facts in 1931–45, not the Rape of Nanking but certainly Pearl Harbor. His personal inaction also prolonged the war in its bloodiest final phase, which is all Mayor Motoshima of Nagasaki was pointing out.

It would have been asking a lot of a sheltered young god to resist the aggressors around him, but a lot was to be asked of young men including Private Trout. 'The Emperor obviously did not feel he was responsible,' a Japanese woman told me. 'He did not kill himself.'

Quite. It is sometimes pointed out that the war guilt question has been best tackled by Japanese Christians, including Mayor Motoshima, who was harrassed as such in pre-war Japan.

Spurred by a Christian sense of responsibility, individual Germans did resist Nazism, did acknowledge war guilt and did de-Nazify later. Compare that with Japan, where in 1989 individual leaders do not acknowledge fault for taking bribes, let alone war guilt.

Against the majority

MELANIE PHILLIPS
3 March 1989

Should the Bible be banned? As a Jew, I find the New Testament deeply offensive. The notion that God actually had a son, or that He comes in three parts, is a gross blasphemy to members of the Jewish faith who believe in one indivisible Creator. It is therefore extremely peculiar that the Archbishop of Canterbury and other Church of England bishops should have called for the current blasphemy law to be replaced with a new offence of insulting or outraging the religious feelings of any group in the community. Were this to happen, the New Testament would immediately find itself in some difficulty. Dr Runcie's suggestion, made last year after a special committee of bishops considered the subject, arises from a desire not to cause offence to people of different faiths than Christianity, the only religion covered by the existing common law offence of blasphemy. And indeed, one of the reasons why British Muslims are so enraged by the Rushdie affair is that the blasphemy law discriminates against them. If it is wrong to insult Christianity, they say, why isn't it equally wrong to insult Islam? Yesterday, the Bishop of Stepney became the latest voice from within the Church of England to suggest, as a result, that the blasphemy law should be extended to other faiths.

This is a terribly muddled and dangerous attitude. Muddled because since every great faith believes itself to be the one true faith, it will by definition give offence to subscribers to the others. Dangerous because curtailing free expression on the grounds that it might cause offence is an unacceptable curtailment on liberty. I am hugely offended by Easter, when I am besieged by the message that the Jews killed the Son of God. I don't picket the Home Office demanding that Easter should therefore be abolished. The Prime Minister decided that the public should not be offended by Sinn Fein making capital out of IRA atrocities, and that got us the wholly unacceptable television ban which further dented our free society. There is a significant difference between curtailing free expression so as not to give offence and doing so to protect the civil rights or physical safety of minority communities. That's why the blasphemy law is wrong but the Race Relations Act or Public Order Act are right. Discrimination within the law, however, is also unacceptable. All faiths should be treated equally within the law. So the right course must be to abolish the blasphemy law altogether, not extend it.

But blasphemy is not the only area where Muslims are discriminated against. Catholics, Jews and members of the Church of England enjoy voluntary status for their schools under which the state contributes to capital and running expenses. Muslims cannot. The Government and the education authorities shrink from funding Muslim schools because they are frightened of creating racially segregated ghetto schools, and because they are concerned that they would fail to equip Muslim girls in particular to play an equal part in society. But similar qualms could be expressed about certain highly orthodox Jewish schools. Surely, if we believe that it is the right of the Jewish community, or the Catholics or the Anglicans, to educate children separately from the secular majority, then the same right must be extended to Muslims – with the same caveat that if the state is providing much of the funding, then the state has every right to lay down minimum standards that must be met before the cash is handed over.

We are, however, a society which is terrified of pluralism. Much so-called multi-culturalism lightly camouflages a desperate tendency towards homogeneity, towards making everyone the same. In the home secretary's Birmingham speech last weekend, the sub-text was the British horror of separateness. No minority would thrive, he said, if it withdrew itself from the mainstream of British life. Behind this sentiment presumably lies ministerial anxiety about separate Muslim schools. But another current issue threatens minority faiths. New legislation requires schools to provide mainly Christian collective worship and religious assembly. Educationalists and the liberal establishment have condemned this as an attempt to foist Christian beliefs on other faiths. But this week's protest by the National Association of Head Teachers makes instructive reading. Their published complaint was mainly one of administration – it would be difficult to find staff to implement the law, that teachers would opt out of assemblies, that children withdrawing from Christian assemblies would cause chaos. Alternative assemblies, they said, would, moreover, 'militate against the school unity that headteachers and deputies would always wish to foster'.

Well, I was withdrawn from school assemblies and scripture classes, and I don't think that threatened the unity of my school one jot. Multi-cultural assemblies probably sound highly attractive to those liberal members of the majority, Christian-based secular culture who are anxious that their children don't grow up thinking that Jews or Muslims are strange or fearful. To them, assemblies devoted to explanations of Divali or Chanukah are positively desirable elements of their children's education. But among the minority faiths themselves, perspectives are necessarily a little different. They feel under permanent threat by the majority culture which bombards them all the time. An important part of the Jewish experience, for example, is the centuries-old struggle against attempts by Christians to assimilate them into their faith. The desire for separateness is important and should be respected.

All faiths should be treated equally under the law, which at present they are not. But freedoms must be preserved too; the freedom to write things that others find offensive, certainly, but also to remain outside the mainstream rather than be assimilated into one homogeneous group and to be respected, not for one's ability to turn oneself into a majority clone, but for the differences in one's culture of which neither the law nor ministers of the Crown should make one feel ashamed or attempt to suppress.

History without intelligence

RICHARD NORTON-TAYLOR
9 March 1989

A defence minister has a clandestine relationship with a callgirl. A high society consultant with a network of exotic contacts, who knows the girl well, has been introduced by an editor of a national newspaper to a Soviet military attaché. The consultant has been approached by MI5 to lay a honey trap for the attaché.

But things run out of control. The girl with whom the attaché starts an affair is the one who is having an affair with the minister. The story begins to leak out, the minister lies to parliament. There has got to be a scapegoat.

The home secretary summons senior civil servants and police officers and encourages them to look around for a crime with which to prosecute the consultant. At the trial, the consultant explains that he was recruited by MI5 to persuade the attaché to defect. He is greeted by incredulity and the Security Service, relieved, disowns him.

The official report into the scandal, written by a senior judge, makes no reference to the intrigue in Whitehall and the antics of MI5. It is 25 years before the role of MI5 emerges, first in two books, and now in a film where it is lightly touched upon. Phillip Knightley and Caroline Kennedy say in their book, *An Affair of State: The Profumo Case and the Framing of Stephen Ward*, that the MI5 officer, who used the case-name Woods, told them that Ward's version of events at his trial was correct. Asked if MI5 could not have found a way to have confirmed that Ward was working for the Security Service, the officer replied: 'Yes. Ward might have been alive today had that happened.' The second book on the affair, *Honey Trap*, by Anthony Summers and Stephen Dorril, goes further, suggesting, on the basis of claims by an unnamed MI6 officer, that Ward did not commit suicide but was killed on orders from MI5.

Neither of these books, their authors agreed yesterday, could have been published under the Government's new Official Secrets Bill. The Bill, to be debated by the House of Lords for the first time today, imposes an absolute, life-long duty of confidentiality on members of the security and intelligence services and bans authors and journalists from referring to their activities. If the Government gets its way, the truth about a scandal similar to the Profumo affair would be suppressed for ever.

Lord Bethell, the Tory peer and historian, has written to Douglas Hurd, the home secretary, warning him of the dangers of banning the kind of books which 'have benefited our country by teaching us historical lessons which we would do well to remember'.

He referred to one of his own works, *The Great Betrayal*, published in 1984, about attempts by the CIA and MI6 to unseat the communist regime in Albania 40 years ago. That book, he reminded Hurd, was written with the help of 25 intelligence officers, including Sir Dick White, former head of MI5 and MI6, and George Young, former deputy chief of MI6. All of these are silenced by the Government's Bill.

Hurd has now back-tracked from his earlier assurances that the criterion for authorizing books mentioning the past activities of the security and intelligence services would not be whether or not they damaged national security.

Pressed in the Commons last month by Julian Amery, a Tory MP and wartime intelligence officer, to explain how any book relating to intelligence would be allowed in future, Hurd replied that permission would be 'rare and exceptional'.

Lord Bethell, commenting from personal experience, accuses Whitehall of abuse of power by retaining official records 'simply because they might be embarrassing'. The Foreign Office is refusing to disclose papers about Hess's flight to Scotland which could help to unravel the controversy surrounding the death of Hitler's former deputy.

The Government refuses to release documents relating to wartime code-breaking that could shed light on claims, reported in the *Guardian* yesterday, that Britain broke Japanese naval cyphers before the attack on Pearl Harbor.

Even official histories have been caught in this paranoia about the disclosure of past activities in the secret world. Only now has Mrs Thatcher, after ten years, agreed in principle that two books can be published. They were commissioned by the Government, with the blessing of the intelligence establishment, before she was elected in 1979. One – *The History of Strategic Deception in the Second World War*, by Sir Michael Howard, former regius professor of modern history at Oxford University – is an account of how enemy agents captured in Britain were used to send back misleading information to their German masters.

The other – by Anthony Simkins, former deputy head of MI5 – is an account of wartime activities of MI5 and the Special Operations Executive. If these authors are suppressed, what can lesser lights expect?

No safety underground

DAVID SHARROCK
10 March 1989

It is 8.45, Tuesday morning, and the swarm of smartly dressed commuters spilling out of the Jubilee Line already carry that persecuted look on their faces, that defeated slump of the shoulders.

They are stuck in the bowels of Baker Street station; with only one escalator operating, a sea of humanity has to pass through the mouth of a syringe in order to fulfil another eight office hours. At 5.30 they will be trying to perform this miracle once more, in reverse. A placard leaning against the idle escalator reads: 'We're sorry, but one of the escalators at this station is out of service because of a defect', to which a wag has added in felt tip . . . 'of management'.

Half an hour later, two stops away on the Metropolitan Line, a woman London Underground staff member is remonstrating with her superior, who stands shyly in the half-opened door to his office. Behind them straggles a line of people waiting to buy tickets. The blinds are drawn on both ticketing windows. 'You're going to have to get someone to replace him, because they're all waiting here and they're SEETHING,' the woman says.

'The service is terrible, I don't know how they put up with it, I wouldn't use it.' The man who said that is a train driver with more than 20 years' service with London Underground. Morale among the travelling public may be low, but within the network itself it looks as if it could not be lower.

John (which is not his real name – all the drivers and station staff I spoke to only did so on the basis that their identities were not revealed) was having quite a good day. A Jubilee Line train operator with ten years' service, he had started work at 5 a.m. and was taking his daily break, in the Baker Street station canteen.

'Sometimes the break is only forty minutes, before you have to go back down and pick up the train. The queues for food can be so bad, you get ten minutes to eat and that's it,' he says.

He takes a table on his own. You can spot the drivers because they all sit alone, the force of habit from the not too distant days when they buddied up with their guard. One Person Operation, referred to universally as OPO, ended that. OPO is why John is getting out later this year.

'I'm not happy with it. The safety aspects are extremely worrying, especially on the deep level tunnels, like parts of the Jubilee. In an emergency, like a fire, as an operator I might be expected to control three to four hundred people on my own.

'For example, there was a bad fire at Oxford Circus two

or three years ago. Fortunately then they had guards. But you just imagine trying to evacuate that lot on your own.

'But also the quality of the job has gone down the drain. Now it's pretty soulless. A lot of drivers have complained about the isolation, the loneliness. The job has always been boring to a point, but at least before there was the camaraderie. That's gone.'

At the turn around the drivers and guards would always have a few minutes for a quick chat, which helped break the monotony. Now John says he can go the whole day without speaking to anyone.

We headed towards Wembley Park, the train's feeble lamp casting a grey light on the snug intestine walls.

The train rolled slowly through St John's Wood, closed while its wooden escalators are being replaced, 15 months after the King's Cross fire. OPO means the driver is responsible for opening and closing the doors. A driver cannot see the length of the train as well as a guard, who would stick his head out on to the platform. The solution was to put up mirrors and television screens for the driver at the front of the platform.

But even on a dull March day the screen at Kilburn was reduced by the light to an unintelligible dark blur. 'As soon as I move off and past those mirrors I can't see anything behind me. I've been in situations when people run into the train as it's moving.

'There was an occasion when a young man, who was drunk, did that and got his foot caught between the platform and the moving train. It was only through luck that I saw him and stopped. In the past that would have been caught by a guard.'

John recalled the evening of a fracas on his train. 'There were five white guys kicking a black guy. Me and the guard did go and intervene and broke it up, because when there's two of you you have a certain sense of security. On my own I would have just stayed where I was and called on the radio.

'With the new system something might be happening on

the train and the driver might not even be aware of it. Basically your instructions are to stay where you are, call for assistance and wait for someone to come down.'

This is not always successful, thanks to the destaffing of many stations, John believes. 'Sometimes there might be only one person on duty at a so-called lightly used station, so they just stay in the office. If you have a problem you blow the whistle, but maybe they can't hear that. Someone on the train had an epileptic fit at Kingsbury, so I blew the whistle and there was no response. I got in touch with the controller by phone. It was eight minutes before someone came down.'

London Underground Ltd (a subsidiary of London Regional Transport) wants to run all tube trains without a guard, with a loss of around 1600 jobs. At present, the Northern, Bakerloo, and Central lines still operate with guards. LUL is looking at plans to introduce automatic trains on these lines.

Drivers view this as an attack on the safety of the underground system as a whole. They scorn the 'leapfrogging' procedure of evacuation on OPO trains. For instance, if a driver suffers a heart attack, the passengers must wait until the train behind approaches.

The driver of the second train then appoints a 'responsible' person from the passengers to protect the cab while he boards the first train and drives it away. The passengers on the second train must wait until the arrival of a third train. The leapfrogging continues until a relief driver can get into the tunnel.

'There's a genuine feeling of insecurity, which is creating bad morale,' said another driver. 'What's going on right now, the OPO and the destaffing of stations, it's all to do with preparing for privatization. Safety has gone out of the window and has been replaced with a cheque-book mentality. Profit is all they care about. You only need to look at the number of people with fifteen or twenty years' service who are leaving.'

The malaise stretches beyond drivers. Signalmen

complain about the decision to halt preventative maintenance along the lines. Now repairs are carried out on the basis
of failure, one claimed, which 'looks good for cutting costs in
the short run but could take years to take effect, perhaps with
disastrous results'. In May, LUL plans to introduce a pilot
scheme called 'Action Stations' in the upper reaches of the
Metropolitan Line beyond Harrow-on-the-Hill. The old
grades of station foreman and leading railman will be
merged, to create the Station Services Manager. He or she
will be the only staff member at the station.

Ticket machines and automatic barriers play a crucial
role in this destaffing policy. But the new barriers have
already raised an outcry, and months after their introduction most people refuse to use them, preferring to queue for
the ticket collector, who will disappear under the Action
Stations scheme.

Barriers are soon to be abolished on Tyneside. The Metro
there confirmed this week most barriers would be replaced
by open staggered railings. The official reason is incompati-
bility with bus tickets. Local opinion has it that no-nonsense
Tynesiders have even less time for them than Londoners.

One station foreman on the Circle Line described them
as a total disaster. 'Someone got stuck in them this morning
and I had to shut the whole thing down to release them.'

LUL said the barrier system had been through rigorous
safety tests during installation. As a result of the Fennell
Inquiry's recommendation, the viability of installing pas-
senger panic buttons on the gates is being looked at.

London Regional Transport has also commissioned an
independent safety review of the system. If the gates are
unsupervised at any time, they are left open. In the even
of a power failure the gates open automatically.

LUL said the gates, costing £165 million, would help
prevent fare-dodging, which accounted for £25 million lost
income last year. The system would also make station staff
more mobile. The barriers were not linked to any plan to
cut staff.

Raw nerves in the meat market

JAMES ERLICHMAN

10 March 1989

We were, so to speak, flies on the wall – of Smithfield Market. 'Dress shabbily,' he said. 'That way we stand a better chance of not being caught and turfed out.'

I took his advice and wore my worst anorak. Dr Alan Long, pimpernel of the vegetarian movement, knows how to infiltrate abattoirs and meat markets and escape with his hide intact. EEC inspectors think British meat is filthy. We came for a first-hand look.

Smithfield is one of the biggest and oldest (c 1868) meat markets in the industrialized world. The smell greets you first, making a swift descent from nostrils to stomach. Next comes the noise, made mostly by a lot of large and raucous men. These are the Hogarthesque porters, called pullers-back, pitchers and bummarees, who hump the meat.

'Meat markets are mortuaries without temperature control. That's why they smell,' Dr Long says. 'And this one smells the most because it is so archaic and insanitary.'

Uncovered hunks of meat are pitched everywhere on old barrows. Turkeys with slit throats hang upside-down above cardboard boxes of rabbits on the floor, deceased but still in their skins.

We step outside, me for a breather and Dr Long for more inspection. He peers into a plastic bin on the pavement filled to the brim with something wet and brown. 'Is that lung?' he asks of the first man to walk by. 'Yeah, but wadduya want to know for? Are you one of them health people?'

Dr Long, who can charm even a bummaree, smiles sweet innocence, and says no. 'That's OK then,' says the man. 'Besides, it only goes for pet food.'

We pass into the poultry hall – built separately. A man in a shabby anorak reaches into a box of poultry pieces, picks up one or two, rolls them in his hands, and tosses them back. If there are any health inspectors about they challenge neither him nor the porters in filthy aprons who smoke openly. They also seem not to notice that the whole place is open and unprotected from flies. 'I've often seen birds flying around too,' says Dr Long.

Outside we watch the bummarees hook quarters of un-covered beef and sling them on to the none-too-clean floor of an ageing van. 'Raw meat is a better medium for bacteria than cowpat,' says Dr Long. He would, wouldn't he? Vegetarian zealot. Probably made it up, except that his doctorate is in organic chemistry and he worked for years with bacteria, designing antibiotics for Glaxo.

Leading supermarkets, including Sainsbury, Tesco, Safeway and Marks and Spencer, say they *never* buy their meat from Smithfield. So who does buy the £300 million worth of meat it sells each year?

Dr Long sidles over to a stall-holder and asks him. Mostly small butchers and caterers – hotels, restaurants, school kitchens – comes the reply. Business isn't too bad, he says, except for poultry, which has been hit hard by fears over salmonella and listeria poisoning.

This stallholder sells everything from Chinese rabbit to Brazilian beef. But not Botswanan beef. 'Can't trust the quality,' he says.

Glad to see someone has standards? 'Not really,' says Dr Long when we are out of earshot. 'The racial prejudice around here is as fragrant as the carcasses. Botswana's beef isn't handled by many because they call it black man's meat.'

Smithfield has long been an embarrassment to the Labour Party and the Transport and General Workers' Union which organizes the place. Restrictive practices are rife and non-white faces few. The City of London wants to spend £40 million on modern facilities, but is demanding job cuts in return. The lads at Smithfield are not best pleased with this solution. And when riled they have been known to get quite nasty.

'I've seen fights break out quite often during my little early morning visits,' says Dr Long. 'The previous super-intendent of the market used to keep a truncheon.'

Judge caught in the act

MARTIN WAINWRIGHT
15 March 1989

The Yorkshire judge and controversialist James Pickles has often said that he might well have become an actor like his daughter Carolyn and his late uncle, Wilfred of the Wireless.

Instead, he has ended up on the different stage of the Northern crown court circuit; not Stratford, but a decent billet – best costume in the cast and biggest chair on the dais, ideal for blinking over his half-moons, muttering quips and fixing counsel with the occasional spine-chilling scowl.

Yesterday the 63-year-old judge was back at a favourite venue, Leeds Courthouse, scene of last Friday's melodrama, 'The Jailing of Michelle Renshaw'. No punter could expect gold again so soon; and to begin with the proceedings looked dull.

Crown court theatre is deceptive, though. Judge Pickles has been described as the Boycott of the Bench and the analogy with cricket is accurate. Game and legal proceed-ings involve sudden eruptions of drama into a long and little-comprehended snooze. So it proved in Court 12.

Regina was confronting Raphael Japhet York over a matter of £61.45 allegedly nicked from a Leeds sweet shop. A brief prelude saw the judge content himself with a little machine-gunning of Mr York's counsel Jeffrey Lewis.

'What do you want to happen? I'll do whatever you want

to do,' he said at 200 words a minute. 'Just tell me. Have what you want.'

The truth (in this case: 'Just pipe down and I'll tell you what I want') had to be wrapped up in tact and legal verbiage by Mr Lewis; but eventually he explained that new evidence, submitted only five minutes before a trial five months in preparation, required a brief delay.

An hour-long interval followed. The clerk, usher and tape-recorder operator waxed indignant at criticism over the Renshaw case. 'A gentleman,' they all called the judge. 'Much more handsome than he looks on television,' said the tape-recorder lady.

Ten teenagers on a business law course at Wake-field District College, over specially to see the famous Pickles, began to chafe. 'Don't upset the judge when he gets back,' pleaded their course co-ordinator George Holmes. 'If you do and he sends you down, I'm not taking any responsibility.'

Then, in a flurry of wigs, the cast reappeared. An Augean task might be necessary, said Mr Lewis, with a trace of anticipation: combing thousands of microwaved betting slips at William Hill's to fortify Mr York's alibi.

The judge began to growl and his Yorkshire voice started to rise. 'Look, pre-trial review was on February twenty-second,' he said. 'Then or soon after all the decks should have been cleared. This doesn't look good. It's wrong and it's not fair to the defendant who is waiting in custody to be tried.'

Mr York, stuck since October in Leeds' worst address, Armley jail, perked up. Was the Unsackable Pickles, Scourge of Hailsham, going to redeem the whole expensive and largely pointless morning by setting a still-innocent man free on bail?

We all thought he was bound to. No, agreed counsel, there was no danger that Mr York might abscond. Yes, his Mum was in court with £10,000 ready for a bail bond.

'But the difficulty, Your Honour,' said Mr Lewis, explaining why four other judges had refused bail, 'is that it is alleged that a former girlfriend, a central witness in the case, has been threatened.'

The judge's eyebrows went through contortions worthy of Henry Irving. 'I think the less I have to do with this case the better.' A saddened Mr York was stood down.

Dickey problems

DEREK BROWN
20 March 1989

I have got a stepney in my dickey. Should I: (a) seek urgent medical advice, (b) water it daily, or (c) make sure it's hard enough to use? If you chose (c), you passed the entrance test in Hinglish, the glorious jumble of good, bad and ugly English used in the subcontinent.

A stepney, I recently discovered, is a smashing old word for spare wheel or tyre. It is also a white slaver's mistress, which is a useful thing to know. A dickey, I knew all along but had forgotten until coming to India, is the Wodehouse-era slang for a rear-facing spare seat in a car, applied here to the boot. Like most other things here, such words are never discarded. They go on forever, often cherished and sometimes abused, but never thrown away. Instead, they are guarded in the treasure house of archaisms, local words and the mildewed British Raj slang that makes up Indian English.

You don't leave town here, you go out of station. You put up, rather than stay, in a hotel. You don't get offered tiffin any more, but you will almost certainly be invited to take a peg of whisky.

Nothing ever happens three times in India; it happens thrice. An event is not brought forward, but preponed. A politician who would not dream of simply withdrawing a statement might decide on reflection that it was infructuous, and resile from it. If you buy something on HP, the

initials will not stand for hire-purchase, but for hypo-
thecation, which is more or less the same thing. And what
you pay will be a quantum, never an amount, of rupees.

All these later examples underline one of the outstanding
features of Hinglish, especially in the written form – its
extreme pomposity. In newspapers, books, and especially
in official correspondence, writers fall into a ponderous,
aldermanic style incorporating, inter alia, quasi-legal
phraseology, literary clichés (many of them attributable to
the Bard of Avon) and even the odd word of French, sans
translation, to the extent that one can only assume many
a reader, particularly among that overwhelming majority
for whom English is a secondary language, would be at a
loss to follow the thrust of the esteemed scribe's argument,
let alone sustain his or her interest through the obfuscatory
sub-clauses, the mangled syntax, and the brain-crumbling
length of a single sentence such as the one which I have
set before you as a humble attempt at parody, and which,
you will no doubt be glad to learn, is now finished.

But there is much more to Hinglish than the windbaggery
of the newspapers. According to the census, fewer than
250,000 Indians out of 800 million speak English as a first
language. The 20 million or so who have a reasonable
understanding of it are by and large the prosperous, educated, influential ones. English is the language of the legal
system and, to a large extent, of commerce. It is the link
language of government, and of the bourgeoisie. And with
the burgeoning of the Indian middle class, there has come
explosive growth in English-medium education. Or, as I
recently saw on an advertising board, 'English-midium
educati'. For the fact is that demand has far outstripped
supply of qualified teachers. New schools are springing
up everywhere. Tutors tout their names on signs fixed to
tree-trunks. Cheap text books abound in every bazaar.
The English most of them offer is at best a rudimentary
variation of 'babu' office language.

At worst, this level of Hinglish is a kind of pidgin. Cinema
adverts offer prime examples, particularly those for films

which promise, and never deliver, a treat to the sex-starved young men of India. 'Terrific treat for Gayful Youth,' said one recent come-on. And another: 'Lustiest Female Warriors Risk Their Very Lives To Fulfil Their Passions!!!'

For those who can afford it, a 'pukka' education is still heavily biased towards English-English. Lots of Shakespeare and P. G. Wodehouse, with liberal dollops of Keats, Wordsworth, and other modern authors. Inevitably American spellings and words have started to appear, to the distress of older Indians.

The preposterous public schools, on the other hand, with their blazered uniforms, their Latin mottoes, their play-the-game standards, continue to process the offspring of the governing classes, without concession to India, let alone America. Innovation, as we say here, is eschewed, in favour of the quaint but moribund language of another land in another age, when God was in his heaven and there was a stepney in every dickey.

A death in San Salvador

SCOTT WALLACE
21 March 1989

Bill Gentile, a newsweek photographer, Arturo Robles, a Mexican photographer, and I spent the Saturday night before the elections in Usulutan City. Usulutan is one of the most fought-over provinces in El Salvador.

We spent the night there, planning to get up early. We had information there might be some problems around San Agustin and San Francisco Javier. We could hear a helicopter and the droning of a push-pull, as they call them here, a Cessna spotter plane, used to fire phosphorous rockets and to strafe. It's a good little counter-insurgency aircraft.

We bounced up the road towards San Francisco Javier

for about half an hour from the Pan-American highway. Peasants warned us to hold back, telling us it was still going on, which, of course, for a journalist is like a green light. We drove up into the town and saw uniformed men.

It took us about a minute to figure out they were left-wing guerrillas. Then we saw that one guy had an AK-47, and another was wearing a T-shirt. But we weren't even sure then, because sometimes the army makes its people look like guerrillas to trick people.

There had been heavy fighting there since dawn. After five hours the guerrillas drove the army out of the town, and then went to the school and burned the ballot boxes. We stopped and photographed a dead body on the road, a policeman killed in the fighting. Around the corner a dead pig lay in the road.

The guerrillas were just relaxing, buying lemonade, and we were talking to them, when another car-load of journalists arrived.

It was a Dutch crew: Cornel Lagrouw, a cameraman with the Dutch church broadcasting network, Ikon, with his wife, Annelise, who was also his sound person. We all know each other quite well, so it was fun to see them.

We didn't think we were going to see much more. We were just taking pictures of the guerrillas, when all of a sudden gunfire rang out. We were on a hill, right on the edge of town, and several guerrillas were pointing their rifles in the air at a plane. It seemed that the plane was going to swoop down and strafe the town, so we dived for cover.

Then we noticed other guerillas down in the town were firing, not up in the air, but down a side street. They started running up the hill, firing as they ran, and we started running up to the top of the hill, not really knowing where to go.

The guerrillas said: 'The army was coming back, but we've chased them off. They've run away.' And things calmed down again.

But the plane came back and they fired some more shots

at it. The troops moved up again and it looked, this time, as if they took the guerrillas by surprise. All of a sudden they were close to the town, and shooting. The guerrillas started to pull back, and Bill and Arturo chased off down the street to follow them.

We stayed on the hill: I was right next to Cornel. We were standing behind a stone wall and through the foliage you couldn't really see any imminent danger.

But just a moment before he was hit, I had moved away from him and I was about ten or fifteen feet off when he just gave a gasp. He had been hit.

The firing went on. Bill and Arturo came scrambling back at full tilt. All of a sudden the army was coming into the town. The guerrillas had melted away; they were nowhere to be seen, and Bill and Arturo were afraid they were going to be killed.

Cornel was just lying there. We immediately grabbed him and put him in the Jeep and took him down the hill to where his car was, a station wagon. We threw him in.

He was going very fast. His eyes were already going.

We climbed into the vehicles, me into the Jeep, and we burned out of there with white flags flying.

We were pursued, first by a helicopter, strafing us, and then by the plane, which started firing rockets at us. We had to bale out twice and take cover. It was terrifying.

Our vehicles were clearly marked. But who knows what you can see from a helicopter? Maybe they assumed that anyone who was in that area had no business being there and was therefore a target.

The second time we took cover, we ran right into a peasant's yard and dived out of the truck. The helicopter came in closer and the people were terrified, and begged us to leave. As soon as we could, we got out.

But the other guys were pinned down for a while. They had Cornel's body. It's hard for people outside to realize; people in these areas have been living with this daily for eight years now. Neither one side nor the other is in full control.

Sometimes you think this is a low-level, small war, but the magnitude of the fighting for a country like this is tremendous. It's very exciting and kind of interesting, until something like this happens, and then all of a sudden this very exciting and interesting situation becomes a nightmare.

It makes you think twice about what you're doing and what it is all for. Cornel was a beautiful guy, a great mate. I'd known him for four years. It certainly wasn't worth the pictures he shot.

• *Holland said that the cameraman's death was an 'accident' and that it was not considering diplomatic steps against El Salvador.*

Splintering the Russians

MARTIN WOOLLACOTT
21 March 1989

Day in and night out, the flat crack of the tank guns reverberates through the little Bavarian town of Grafenwoehr like a giant fist repeatedly striking the table. The very wurst bounces on the supermarket shelves, and the old houses seem to have their steeply-pitched roofs pulled down around their ears.

The essence of the Atlantic Alliance – the thing without which it would not be Nato – remains an American army in the heart of West Germany, and one of the curious things about the Americans in West Germany is how they seem to fit into a continuity of military history. Wherever they are – and they are usually in old barracks – the ghosts of other soldiers seem to survey their doings. The principal industry of Grafenwoehr, for instance, has been preparation for war since 1907, when the still autonomous kingdom of Bavaria designated the area as a training ground. The

Nazis expanded it in 1936. Afrika Korps battalions trained here. So did the Spanish Blue Division, as well as many other units which went to the Eastern front.

The Americans arrived in 1944. They have been here ever since. Draft after draft of young Americans have shivered on the ranges of Grafenwoehr, one of the US Army's three major training areas in West Germany, and slogged along its forest tracks. Three generations of tanks, guns, and infantry weapons have been driven, hauled, and manhandled through this place, and God knows how many scores of thousands of wooden Russian tank and soldier silhouettes reduced to matchwood. It has been going on for so long, we have to remind ourselves, that some of those who have trained for war with Russia at Grafenwoehr are dead, of natural or at least non-military causes, including Elvis Presley, who was here in 1959.

Nato at the top is a complex international bureaucracy, operating out of old office blocks smelling of floor polish and too much coffee, and dealing in ominous abstractions. Down here at what they call the 'bottom of the stack', you have a Puerto Rican sergeant huffing and puffing as he runs with his squad through the coarse grass of a clearing in the Bavarian forest. Mottled body armour and the new coalscuttle helmets give them the look of agile turtles. It is bitterly cold. Men and weapons hit the ground in a small symphony of thuds, grunts, and clanks, the sergeant shouts 'Enemy personnel to your left!', and the M-16s and the light machine-guns are firing, soon joined by the cannon on the squad's personnel carrier. More plywood Russian soldiers and tanks splinter, and one of the soldiers is laughing and whooping. The lieutenant, watching from behind, is also chuckling and muttering to himself, rubbing his gloved hands together. 'I love it when it's like this,' he says. 'They're so excited, they're out of breath, the adrenalin is really flowing.'

You have to go back to the Thirty Years War, in which, incidentally, Grafenwoehr was burnt to the ground, to find a comparable period of ideological division, foreign intervention, and foreign occupation in Germany. The remote parallel to the United States in those days would be Habsburg Spain. Spain's pikemen were impressive, too, but Spain's international purposes turned out to be over-ambitious and unreal.

The American army in Germany is now a very curious animal. At a moment when fighting with Soviet forces is utterly unlikely, its officers and NCOs are better prepared, in a way, than they have been for years. This is partly thanks to the development, in the United States, of very sophisticated battle training. At Fort Irwin, in California, the US Army has established a wired and computerized manoeuvre area where units up to brigade size can fight almost real engagements with mock Russian units. The spirit of Fort Irwin has penetrated the whole of the officer corps. Another factor is the quality of many of the recruits to the now all-volunteer army. Indeed, the army offers such a good deal on college financing that combat units in particular now have a heavy sprinkling of would-be students, so that riflemen in a foxhole may as well be discussing the best university at which to take a masters degree in International Relations as anything else.

That somehow expresses the unreality of it all. For the truth is that this American army is now operating in an almost hostile environment. Europeans in general, and West Germans in particular, are increasingly uninterested in soldiers and war games. A tide of opinion, set in motion by the deal on intermediate range missiles by Gorbachev's unilateral cuts and concessions, and by the hopeful changes in Eastern Europe, is sweeping through the Continent. It wants nuclear weapons out, foreign soldiers out, and European military establishments cut.

Up at the top of the stack, at Shape (Supreme Head-quarters Allied Powers in Europe) headquarters, that tide is lapping at the desks of senior officers. General John Galvin, the Supreme Allied Commander, Europe, is a mili-tary intellectual who served with the Air Cavalry in Viet-nam and wrote a highly regarded book on air-mobile warfare. Galvin complains irritably that much of European opinion acts as if Gorbachev had already withdrawn half his tank armies from Eastern Europe. But nevertheless the atmosphere at Shape is unmistakably pacific. The Gorbachev cuts are called 'encouraging' not so much because of the actual numbers involved as because they meet the argument that present Soviet deployments are offensive.

There is calculation here. Soldiers and Nato bureaucrats have caught up, after some stumbling, with the general mood, and they realize now that any military proposition has a better chance if accompanied by a pat on the back for Gorbachev. Indeed the favoured approach is to argue that a particular policy – including the contentious one of modernization of battlefield nuclear weapons – is to be commended because by adding to the West's predictability it will help Gorbachev. Much of this is very special pleading indeed.

But one doesn't have to deny to serious men their own kind of honesty. An entire generation of Western professional soldiers has lived with the nightmare of nuclear weapons more intensely than anybody else except peace campaigners because they have had to wrestle weekly and monthly with the question of what it would be like if they were actually used. These are not the academic theologians of deterrence but men who actually had to ask themselves what they would do, as one officer in Heidelberg put it, when 'the battalion next to you, and the goddam hill it was on, just disappear in a nuclear cloud.'

As this nightmare begins to recede somewhat, their relief is tangible. Young men who entered Western armies in 1948, like Galvin, or like his British number two, General Sir John Akehurst, have paralleled in their careers the life of Nato. They joined at a time when the just war against Hitler was the formative experience. Later they fought Communists in peripheral wars whose justness is more than debatable, but in which military force was still a relatively rational instrument of policy. Then, as the prize for success in their profession, the ablest of that generation were allowed to preside over the preparations for nuclear war.

Believe though they did in deterrence, the strain has told, as it would on anyone. The private mood of Shape leaps ahead to consider substantial American, and British, withdrawals from West Germany and equal-sized, defensively organized – and heavily monitored Nato and Warsaw Pact forces on the central front, with few or even no battlefield nuclear weapons, at levels well down from the present size of the Nato armies. It is cautious, professionally suspicious, and it wants even more on the table from the other side. But the instinct is that Gorbachev means what he says and that there must be a full response from the West. The day when the wurst stops bouncing in Grafenwoehr may not be too many years away.

Stud in screw-up sensation

SHELLEY BOVEY
23 March 1989

After months of hoping it might not be true, I have to face it. He's gay. Not that I am any kind of homophobe, you understand, but I have still got to come to terms with it. All 80 quid of it in fact. That was what I had to pay for my male Burmese kitten. For a cat? Yes, but he was no ordinary cat – a handsome, caramel coloured, yellow-eyed stud from the classiest cattery in Richmond.

It all began a couple of years ago when things were getting out of hand. As a cat lover, with true Catholic principles and six randy female Siamese all lusting after the farmyard tom, I decided to introduce a bit of quality, not to mention polygamy, into their breeding habits and buy them a husband of their very own. Not a male Siamese. One doesn't want to be so obvious about these things, but a Burmese and a Siamese liaison produces exquisite and unusual kittens called Tonkinese. The vet admired him immensely. The family loved him, the cats mothered him and somewhere along the way he got named Claude.

When, I asked the vet impatiently, would he become interested in his female companions? Six months onwards, apparently. But by nine months there was no sign; quite the reverse, in fact. Whenever one of the lady felines came on heat, they naturally threw themselves at Claude. Siamese are particularly brazen, and they rolled in front of him, clawed the ground, sniffed excitedly under his tail ... Did I say naturally? Claude was appalled. Whenever he heard the unmistakable raucous call of the Siamese on heat and saw them coming for him, blue eyes blazing, he ran and hid, terrified.

I took him to the vet for a thorough physical check-up when he was a year old. The vet said he'd got the biggest balls he'd ever seen – Claude, I mean. No trouble there – a fine specimen of a stud. Should be siring kittens all over the place. He *might* be a late developer, but it was unusual.

He wasn't a late developer. None of us could fail to notice that he was just developing somewhat differently. Soon it was unmistakable. Claude, at rest, turns his head affectedly to one side. One paw is tucked under his chest. The other droops languidly. Our stud cat is undeniably limp-wristed.

Meanwhile, the faithful black tom who has impregnated so many of the local cats, has been calling far more frequently than is necessary. Previously I could always tell when one of the cats was coming into season by the familiar yowls outside the back door and a large, patient, black cat sitting on the window ledge. Recently he has been turning up when none of the ladies was interested, but the last few weeks have revealed all. While the other cats continued to doze in front of the Aga, Claude is alert at the first call from outside.

One bound through the cat flap and he and Black Tom are greeting each other affectionately, nose to nose. That casual, first kiss is just part of a now familiar ritual. Claude then gets down and rolls enticingly in front of Black Tom.

Then they disappear, but I don't wish to go into that. Afterwards – well everyone knows that a tom cat will try and kill another on its territory. Not these two. They sit on the table outside the kitchen window, close together, exuding contentment, wrists dangling limply over the edge of the table.

Sins of the fathers

4 April 1989

Mr Patten is reported to have said (*Guardian*, 31 March) that parents have a duty to teach their children that it is 'Right to tell the truth ... and to look after those less fortunate than yourself.' Where did the parents of our present Government go wrong?

Rosemary Nash

Danger from the money machine

JEREMY SEABROOK
17 April 1989

Hillsborough has now become yet another place-name to add to those that make up the by-now voluminous gazeteer of wasted human lives. Already there has been talk of 'learning the lessons of Hillsborough'; but if the lessons of Bradford, Heysel, Manchester Airport and the *Herald of Free Enterprise* had been even half absorbed, this most cruel visitation might have been avoided.

What all these have in common is that they arose from the processing of people through time or space for the sake of experiences provided by the entertainment, holiday and sports industries; as such, they touch upon one of the central purposes of the economy in its most benign guise – that of leisure society. This, it turns out, is dedicated to the necessity of making as much money out of people as possible, in this instance, by making them pay – some, alas, with their lives – for the privilege of standing for two hours in what are nothing more than overcrowded cages.

Because these experiences are associated with pleasure, it is easy to disregard the dangers, whether these are the use of unsuitable material in the manufacture of aircraft seats, insecure and overloaded ferry boats, or football grounds that prove to be deathtraps.

It is only when things go wrong that some deep insight is granted us into the true value placed on human life by the purveyors of entertainment, escape and fun to the people.

'We were like animals in a zoo,' said one man afterwards. It was a zoo in which the watchers were primarily electronic: the cameras of the media, the police videos and computers represent a vast investment in the paraphernalia of surveillance, which could monitor every anguished moment but do absolutely nothing to help.

What a contrast this prodigious outlay of money presents with the absence of life-saving equipment. The doctors present testified that there were no defibrillators, and that the oxygen tents were without oxygen; but the presence of all the media hardware ensured that the spectacle of football was swiftly transformed into a spectacle of a quite different genre.

The carnage – how sad that the hyperbole of football writing becomes hideously appropriate – raises intensely political issues. Those who insist upon referring to the incident as though it were an Act of God, a sort of natural tragedy, betray only their interest in concealment. The very public display of their humanitarian concern merely masks its absence in the more fundamental matter of preventing the gratuitous squandering of young lives.

Football is perhaps the only remaining experience in our

social life where passion – and partisan passion at that – is engaged. Nothing could be further removed from the other characteristic crowd scenes in our society: the people shuffling through the shopping malls, for instance, are self-policing, introspectively concerned as they are upon the relationship between individual desire, money and the prize to be purchased; remote too from pop concerts, where the shared focus of cathartic emotion is funnelled on to a single person, and its expression is without conflict.

But football continues to reach something which neither of these possess – the passion of locality, and of places once associated with something more than football teams. That Liverpool should have been connected twice with such unbearable events is perhaps not entirely by chance. For the great maritime city, with its decayed function rooted in an archaic imperial and industrial past, sport now has to bear a freight of symbolism that it can scarcely contain.

The energies of partisan, mainly working-class male crowds remain, as they always have been, the object of great anxiety and suspicion to their betters. These energies are perceived as perhaps the last vestiges of the turbulence of the mob – unruly, defiant and unpredictable – in a society where all other public passions have been tamed.

The forces released by football provide a glimpse of collective power that has been successfully neutralized in the rich Western societies; a suggestion that such passion could possibly be harnessed to social and political endeavour rather than sublimated in sporting conflicts.

Apart from the sight of the inert young bodies stretched out in the sunlight, perhaps the most chilling images were those of the anguished faces pressed against wire fences. They looked as if they had been taken from the iconography of repression of authoritarian states, and they evoke something quite other than the idea of sport. They bore the tormented expression of those in prison camps; indeed, many spoke of 'the terracing that had become a prison', the inevitability of disaster within those reinforced enclosures, where the grisly facts of the quantity of pressure they were calculated to withstand was conveyed with scientific precision.

We can only guess at what unwanted and redundant human powers are being controlled in the use of all this apparatus of containment; what frustrated visions and cancelled dreams are being policed, what doomed alternative use of these energies is being fenced in, sifted through the mechanistic click of the turnstiles. What an irony is the Government's obsession with identity cards in this context, when it is precisely a sense of identity that so many are trying to reclaim in these conflicts between geographic entities that have become, physically, interchangeable. For what now differentiates Sheffield from Nottingham, Manchester from Liverpool, Bradford from Leeds, with their homogeneous housing estates, the sameness of their shopping centres, the identical service sector economy?

There remains also an old class prejudice in the treatment of those who must be systematically humiliated in the pursuit of their afternoon's pleasure. 'We are treated like animals,' some said afterwards; and in their words is an echo of how Government ministers had described them at the time of earlier disasters. The very idea of 'fans' is a humbling social role, a diminishing and partial account of human beings.

Indeed, there could be no greater gulf than that created by the exaggerated adulation that the stars and heroes receive – the inflated transfer fees, the publicity, the column inches and admiring TV interviews – and the abasement and inferiorizing of the fans, punters or consumers. The players are mythicized, whisked upwards into an empyrean of fame and celebrity, in which everything they do or say is reported, no matter how trivial; in the process they become remote from their votaries and followers, who are kept in their place as effectively as they once might have been through the mysteries of breeding or station. Part of the process of erecting the infamous steel barriers is connected with enforcing this separation: the pitch is inviolate, the fans must remain content with the wall poster, the autograph, the fantasy.

Already, the aftermath of these tragic disasters has taken on the aspect of a known ritual: the Prime Minister arrives, prayers are offered up, shrines are set up at the scene of the accident, and a fund is opened. It means that these inadmissable horrors have become part and parcel of our social life; they have become familiar. Once again, the real lessons are likely to be that the public enquiry will be a vast exercise in concealment of the true relationship of these unnecessary tragedies to the necessities of what are no longer amiable Saturday afternoon pastimes but are part of a remorseless machine for making money; how fitting that the advertizing hoardings had to serve in place of absent stretchers.

Bombed out

JULIE FLINT
18 April 1989

Shortly before six o'clock last night, after a month of severe rationing and 36 hours of blackout, the office generator self-destructed.

We lit the candles. As they flared, we were running for the semi-shelter of a back room as shelling enveloped us – anti-aircraft guns and 155mm and 240mm artillery, according to the experts. After the bombardment, which lasted for the better part of five minutes, there was a new noise, equally deafening in its way: the twittering of thousands of birds.

'They're frightened,' a colleague said, nonchalantly slapping down a full house. 'Every time there's a bombardment like that, more birds die than people.' Give or take a few fools and swaggerers, we are all frightened – in East and West Beirut.

Already 265 people have died. More than 1250 have been wounded. This is a terrible war – pitting the might of the Syrian army and its Muslim allies against the joint forces of General Michel Aoun's Christian brigades and, now, the Lebanese Forces militia.

The bombardments, when they are not continuous, come out of nowhere. Forget the friendly old Kalashnikovs and rocket-propelled grenades. These are weapons packing 1000 pounds of explosive, rockets that pierce three or four walls before exploding, whistling like banshees as they pass you.

A 240mm shell, similar to that which killed the Spanish ambassador in East Beirut, was lying yesterday in the office of Mr Selim el Hoss, Gen. Aoun's counterpart in West Beirut.

'We've never seen anything like this one,' said Mr Hoss, a moderate man whose dogged efforts to control his radical ministers collapsed when Gen. Aoun blockaded the admittedly illegal ports of West Beirut – denying, as he continues to do, the very existence of an East–West government split.

In their highly organized, wealthier Christian enclave, radios give second-by-second security reports. West Beirut, predictably, is less organized; the flashes come 10 minutes after your house has twisted and the cats, eyes like saucers and bodies rigid with fear, have crawled into spaces where they cannot be reached. You open the windows . . . glass kills . . . open the refrigerator . . . fridges explode . . . and, in the most awful moments, lie on the floor in a corner.

Sunday, if not the worst bombardment of eight years in the Lebanon, was somehow the most frightening. There were rockets, which go along, and mortars, which go up and down and require a different defence.

For a little more than two hours, they peppered the half-mile between home and office – a half-mile that took two hours to cover, the last part on foot.

Taxi? Forget it. There was nothing on the street. When it was all over, there was a mortally wounded dog, a dead man and a lot of grey – grey smoke, grey cinders, grey rubble, grey faces.

Ten yards down the seafront, on the first leg out, a mortar exploded next to our local petrol station, ripping the backs of the pumps and tearing a man-sized hole in the wall. First stop, to duck into the nearest basement, already full of screaming children. After 45 minutes, we thought the shellstorm had eased a little and a swashbuckling young Shi'ite who runs a coffee wagon cranked it up, brought it round and headed towards the office.

We got 200 yards before a shell fell almost alongside us, forcing us into another basement. Then back to square one, tyres screaming, a little further back from the centre of the storm. An hour later, it appeared to be over. We piled back into the coffee wagon and roared off again.

A hundred yards short of our target, a cluster of shells plopped in front of us, killing one man and turning the street corner by the Cavalier Hotel into mashed potato.

Yesterday, I moved, with the rigid cats, into the Cavalier. It at least had electricity and water which, as of today, will also have run out in West Beirut. Pour the bubbly stuff into the tub, turn on the taps . . . nothing: two mortars on the roof, broken pipes. No water.

Down to the bar, up to bed – dirty and emotional.

Awakened at five a.m. by the sound of plate glass crashing into the street. It continued to crash all day – dozens of picture windows shattered beyond repair and with nowhere to go but down, helped along by an army of boys with brooms.

Yesterday began with the wailing of the funeral processions of the 24 people killed in West Beirut on Sunday. It ended with my friend's Nadim, a five-year-old with a page-boy hair cut and a voice like Eartha Kitt, saying the latest edition of his prayers: 'Please God, make the nasty, nasty men stop the bombing.' Amen to that.

Faith in the farther land

RICHARD GOTT
29 April 1989

In a damp and muddy lane, by a neglected cemetery over-
hung with tropical vegetation, I find – a trifle out of place
– a street sign, much streaked with green. It bears the
name Luisa N. Förster. The N stands for Nietzsche.

To myself I murmur 'Eureka', for after a long journey to
the very heart of rural Paraguay, by train and bus and
lorry, I have found what I came in search of. For this is the
colony of Nueva Germania, New Germany, the place where
Elizabeth Nietzsche (the sister of Friedrich, the philos-
opher) and her husband, Bernhard Förster, tried to start a
utopian settlement based on the racist and socialist
fantasies that were typical of their age. Where better than
Paraguay to demonstrate the superiority of the master
race?

It's election time in Paraguay, but in truth the details of
the campaign matter only to the people of Paraguay (and
perhaps not much to them), so I thought I would take time
off to discover what happened to Luisa and Bernhardo (as
their street names proclaim) and to the descendants of the
14 peasant families from Saxony who were brought out
here just over 100 years ago. It may be, in this postmodern
age, that people are more interested in Nietzsche than in
Paraguay.

According to the public record (well-documented in R. J.
Hollingdale's excellent biography of Nietzsche), the experiment ended in failure and disaster. Förster was accused of
incompetence and corruption. The affair concluded with the
suicide of Förster (100 years ago, in June 1889), and the
unfortunate return to Germany of Elizabeth – who went on
to do untold damage to her brother's reputation. For she

published the contents of his wastepaper basket as though they were great philosophy and pretended that he shared her virulently anti-semitic views. She ended up, suitably, in the embrace of the National Socialists. Hitler himself attended the memorial service when she died in 1935.

But what of the German yeoman families that the ill-fated Nietzsche-Förster couple had persuaded to come with them? The history books are blank. So late one afternoon, with the light disappearing fast, I found myself in the impoverished cemetery at Nueva Germania gazing at small iron crosses draped in lace, carrying the names of people born at the turn of the century: names like Werner Neumann and Carlos Fischer.

I ask a small boy on a bicycle where I might find the 'cura', the Catholic priest. There isn't one, he says, but there are some 'hermanas', sisters or nuns. He shows me the way to their house and I introduce myself to Hermana Gloria. She comes from Spain but has been in Paraguay for 19 years.

For a while we talk politics. All the people round here are Liberales, historically opposed to the Colorados of General Stroessner and his successor General Andres Rodriguez. That's probably why there isn't a decent road here, she says, ruefully, when I explain just how long it has taken me to get to this distant spot down a trail churned with mud. So it's not altogether true, I suggest, as some opinion polls maintain, that the rural areas are sewn up by General Rodriguez? Not at all, she replies. She'd gone to a political rally recently organized by the Liberales in the nearby town of San Pedro and been surprised by how many people had been there.

Quantities of peasants had arrived by the lorry load. But there is still much mistrust of the government's intentions. People say the elections may be *libre* (free) but will they be *limpio* (clean)?

Then I bring up the question of Nietzsche. Aha, she says, it's the Pastor you need to talk to. He knows all about the history of the place and only a couple of years ago was organizing centenary celebrations. So there is no Catholic *cura* here, only a Lutheran pastor. I say thank you and goodbye and she shows me how to reach his house.

By now the rain is settling down for a good soak, and walking down a back track I come across a flaxen-haired *fräulein* under the verandah of a single-storied house teaching a group of ten tiny blond children how to sing German nursery rhymes: *Ach du liebe Augustin, alles ist hin.*

I apologize for interrupting, but it's really incredibly wet and could I pop in for a moment and have a word with the Pastor? The *fräulein* smiles sweetly, the children stop singing and giggle, and I come in out of the tropical downpour. She finds an umbrella and takes me across a yard at the back of the house to where the Pastor is doing the accounts of the co-op.

He is a young German of about 30, very serious, and says he's really only a deacon, and a health assistant by training. But he's the first Lutheran pastor this community has ever had. He's a bit mistrustful of me at first, but then warms to his theme. He thinks that Elizabeth Nietzsche, fed up with impractical theorizing, goaded her husband into putting his utopian principles into practice. If Germany wasn't ready to establish a 'pure race' republic on socialist lines then perhaps they might have better luck in the virgin territories of South America. And so they ended up in this benighted and virtually inaccessible spot. They came with a few intellectuals and 14 families from Saxony recently thrown off their land and arrived in Berlin with nothing to do and nowhere to go.

'We have found the nearest thing to Paradise on earth,' Elizabeth Nietzsche wrote to her brother. And that's what we think sometimes, said the Pastor wistfully, listening to the rain on the roof. But looking around today, it is not difficult to see why the first colonists might have been angry with Förster. Even today, the area is poor and isolated, and it remains so because its products cannot reach the outside world except with immense difficulty and uncertainty.

The Pastor thinks that Förster has been somewhat

maligned, and that many things that occurred here 100 years ago were genuine misfortunes, like the size of the boats for example. Large boats had been built in Hamburg to come up the rivers on which the settlement is based, to carry away the produce of the colonists. But the rivers are only large enough for boats in the wet season. Most of the year they proved useless.

So what happened to the survivors? After Förster committed suicide and Elizabeth went back to Germany, others too returned. But some trickled down to Argentina, and some stayed.

Although most people today in Nueva Germania are Catholics, there are 50 families in the Lutheran congregation here. Between them they only have 11 family names, five of which go back to the names of the original settlers. At school, they are taught in Spanish. On the street, you see a lot of fair-haired children speaking Guarani. But at home they talk to each other in German, with a Saxon accent.

So the experiment, in a way, survives. Early the next morning, through the heavy mist, I watch while the children go off to school in their white shifts. They all look very serious and purposeful.

A few piglets rootle around, a rooster crosses the road, a large white bullock wanders aimlessly about. If it wasn't for the orchard of grapefruit trees, the stands of bananas and sugarcane, the plantations of yerba mate, it might be a farm in north Germany. But it isn't. For Förster, with all his nutty ideas about the superiority of the German race and his plans to spread his ideas all over South America, found himself faced with what is, perhaps, a genuinely superior race: the Guarani Indians, who have shown themselves through history to possess an unusual capacity to survive adversity. Nueva Germania, today, belongs to them.

Out of the ghetto . . .

MICHAEL BILLINGTON
29 April 1989

Joshua Sobol wryly admits in the National Theatre programme that the genocide of European Jews is a subject he
tried to resist. But he tackles it head on in *Ghetto*, written
in Hebrew and given in an English version by David Lan
at the Olivier; and not the least remarkable feature of this
astonishing play is that it debates moral issues in a form
that has the headlong exuberance one associates with
Yiddish theatre. But such paradoxes are partly what the
play is about.

On one level, the play concerns the tactics of survival.
The setting is the Vilna ghetto between January 1942 and
September 1943. Jacob Gens, the leading figure on the
Jewish Council, adopts a policy of pragmatic accommodation with the Germans and sanctions the formation of a
Vilna theatre troupe. Hermann Kruk, the ghetto librarian,
is a fierce proponent of underground resistance and produces a poster saying 'No theatre in a graveyard'. Meanwhile Kittel, a young, music-loving SS officer, rules over
the city with a saxophone in one hand and a gun in the
other.

Sobol is not the first dramatist to debate the ethics of
accommodation. Arthur Miller's moving TV film, *Playing
For Time*, dealt with the women's orchestra forced to play
in Auschwitz. Jim Allen's *Perdition* used a pseudo-forensic
approach to discuss the complicity of Hungarian Zionists
in extermination policies.

But Sobol's achievement is that (like Miller) he does not
use hindsight to adopt a comfortable moral stance but
recreates the dilemma faced by people like Gens at the
time. In one agonizing scene, Gens is ordered by Kittel (in

the midst of an orgiastic party) to murder half of the 4000 Jews in a neighbouring ghetto. Gens bargains with Kittel until he gets the number down to 410. Rather than judge Gens, Sobol empathizes with him and makes us comprehend his motives.

In the end, Sobol shows that, whether you negotiate with tyranny or adopt a policy of armed resistance, you cannot counter its arbitrary cruelty: for all Gens's accommodation, the Vilna ghetto was liquidated in 1943. But Sobol's real point is that there is a life of the spirit – here embodied by members of the Vilna Troupe – that is less easily crushed. Sobol has seized on and intelligently used the historical fact that the troupe put on plays and revues even as Jews were deported to the camp at Ponar five miles up the road.

Auden, pointing to the practical impotence of art, famously wrote that no line of poetry ever saved a Jew from the gas chamber. But Sobol's point is that art, and specifically theatre, can simultaneously provide spiritual comfort, symbolic defiance and communal solidarity. Theatre is the abiding metaphor of the play; and Sobol makes brilliant use of it, from a satirical sketch about a Nazi rally, to the inclusion of eight songs written by members of the ghetto and varying from plangent lyricism to a celebratory hymn to survival.

But Sobol's fascinating play also touches on something deeply mysterious: the relationship between oppressors and oppressed. As part of his damage-limitation exercise, Gens practises a Germanic efficiency. Conversely, Kittel is hypnotized not only by the troupe's lead singer but by the vivacity and energy of Jewish culture. It is as if he is seduced by what he is bound to destroy; and in one memorably queasy sequence initiates a lively group rendering of Gershwin's 'Swanee'.

Sobol has, in fact, found a fluid form, blending dialectic, drama, dance and cabaret, that precisely embodies what his play is about: the consolation and tenacity of art. And Nicholas Hytner has matched it with a richly expressive production that combines moral seriousness with theatrical exuberance. Bob Crowley's design, based on converging, multi-windowed ghetto walls, likewise has a pointed inventiveness: the librarian Kruk, for instance, is framed against a huge tower of books which says everything about the importance of written culture in the ghetto. And Jeremy Sams's arrangement of the ghetto music moves easily from lyrical fervour to Weill-like irony.

In a communal achievement, there are some strong individual performances. John Woodvine rightly plays Gens not as an obliging trimmer but as a man who brings an impassioned commitment to his belief that 'jobs mean lives'. Alex Jennings as Kittel also avoids all the usual war-movie clichés by playing the German officer as a smooth-faced figure who is parasitically dependent on the ghetto for spiritual sustenance. Maria Friedman as the ghetto's singer delivers her numbers with stunning directness and not a whisper of false pathos. And Paul Jesson makes the socialist librarian a figure of plausible rectitude.

Given the subject matter, you expect a punishing evening. The triumph of *Ghetto*, as both play and production, is that it takes an historical event and turns it into a testament to spiritual defiance, the durability of memory and the saving power of art.

Doonesbury

BY GARRY TRUDEAU

The death of a son

ED VULLIAMY
29 April 1989

Alberto Guarini had entrusted his 17-year-old sister, Paola, to make a video recording of the 1985 European Cup final for which he and his father, Bruno, had tickets; he would see the match live and the video would be his memento.

It was a particularly good time in Alberto's life: his 21st birthday was three weeks away, he and Paola had recently won the mixed doubles tennis trophy in their home town of Mesagne, and Alberto had just passed his second-year dentistry exams at the university in Bari – the trip to Brussels was a congratulatory gift from his father. Best of all, Juventus were in the European Cup final.

'He adored Juventus,' recalls Mr Guarini, 'Sport was his life and they were his idols. We're in the south, yes, but supporting Juventus in Italy is like being a fan of the Beatles. I've supported them since I was a boy, and Alberto after me. Juventus were his dreams.'

Paola had switched on the television and set the tape. 'They were saying that there was trouble, people hurt, problems,' said her mother, Lucia. 'I couldn't watch it. I hadn't wanted them to go, right up to the last moment I said "don't go" and Alberto was all "oh mamma, mamma". No, not because of the English, just because it was so far away and I was afraid. So I switched it off and we waited ... until Bruno's brother came and told us [Alberto was dead]. Then the house was full of people.'

Mesagne is a small agricultural town on a low plain of deep-red soil which stretches back inland from the port of Brindisi in the far south. Its factories package olives and artichokes, make wine, and process tomatoes into pasta sauces. As in most southern towns, there is a Juve Club

Sede Sociale – Juventus social centre – and a modest municipal sports complex where Alberto was known as a footballer, tennis champion and the proud owner of a small 'moto', a powered cycle. 'We gave it to him when he was eighteen,' said Mr Guarini. 'My wife and all his grand-parents were worried because it was dangerous.'

Mr Guarini is a pharmacist employed by a drug company based in Milan. When he bought tickets for Brussels through a tour agency in Brindisi, he asked for seats and was told only terrace tickets remained. Alberto phoned from Bari – 'Make sure we get tickets, ring again, make sure, he told me. It was like a festival, flags and singing in the aeroplane.'

It is hard to imagine Mr Guarini, who always leaves his house in a black tie and has a distant, deadened look in his eyes, singing on an aeroplane.

Bruno and Alberto reached the stadium early. 'The Eng-lish had their shirts off, we saw them lying on the grass with their beer, so we went straight inside. They did not search us, or tear our tickets. Alberto had his Juventus bag, to carry his binoculars and packed lunch. No one looked inside it.

'We saw the hooligans, they were at the other entrance, drinking and shouting, and I said to Alberto: "We'll go away from them – they might throw things at us." So we went towards the wall at the side. It was the worst thing I ever did, because those next to the English were the ones who escaped from them.

'When the English came running at us through the fence, which was ridiculous protection, Alberto was caught against a barrier. He shouted at me: "I don't know whether to go under or over". I shouted at him to go under it. His last words were: *Papa, mi stanno schiaccando* – Daddy, they're crushing me.

I remember it all, like a film, right up to the last moment when the film stops and you don't see it any more. At night, suddenly I am awake and I see it all again.'

Nothing has been moved in Alberto's bedroom since the

morning he left for Brussels. By his bed there is still a Juventus magazine, on top of the wardrobe are cups and trophies; inside it hang his clothes and the Juventus shoulder bag which came back with his body on the military plane. Paola has taken his Juventus hat. There are photographs of Alberto all over the house and in the hallway a candle burns beneath one of them.

The Guarinis are a religious family. Alberto used to serve at Mass in a little church across the street. Lucia Guarini goes every day to put fresh flowers on his tomb in the cemetery. 'But I only go on Saturday and Sunday,' says Mr Guarini. 'She did not see him die. She needs to believe it's true, to touch him. But I prefer to walk around the tennis courts, because there I can remember him alive.'

It is a soft evening at the tennis courts, the end of a day that began with a tempest and settled into a southern Italian late afternoon with its deep tangerine light on the whitewashed buildings. There is a bronze plaque on the fencing which reads 'Campo Alberto Guarini'. With money from the Agnelli Foundation (Mr Gianni Agnelli, head of Fiat, owns the club) and the local bishop and headmaster, there is now an Alberto Guarini scholarship at Bari University, a Guarini tennis cup and an Alberto Guarini soccer tournament in Mesagne.

'We did everything together – football, tennis. If I bought a car he always came. This was the education I gave him, where sport is clean and good for people. Of course he knew about Liverpool, a good team. We wanted them to be like us, just crazy about football and see who wins. I wanted my children to learn English. Alberto went twice to England; first Torquay then Bournemouth, to the language schools. Lucia was afraid because it was so far away, but I believed England was a civilized country – until that terrible night.

'If you had come here before, we would have been chatting about football and Alberto might have gone to London one day. That's what I call life. We live well in Italy, in the south. But I've lost mine now because I know how bad the world can be and I have to keep asking why? Why did he die?

'I think that for a father to have his son and then to watch him die and to have him no more is the greatest sorrow that exists. But to lose your son for this. Because he's killed by drunks and hooligans at a football match.' Mr Guarini presses his forefingers against his temples. 'This creates madness, like a rabies, it cannot be cured, it is beyond the maximum sorrow, you are dead in your heart.'

Unlike some of the families bereaved at Heysel, the Guarinis were not going to Brussels for the verdict. 'The trial? It doesn't interest me. Prison for the hooligans? The money? He was my richness, so now I am poor. Heysel, that word will make me mad.'

Save the Rose

LEADER
13 May 1989

The discovery of the remains of the 'Rose' theatre in Southwark – on which Shakespeare, Jonson and Marlowe trod the boards – is one of the most exciting archaeological finds of the century. It was the first of the four great Tudor/Jacobean playhouses on the South Bank and the only one whose remains have come to light. It stands yards from the site of the Globe theatre, on which excavations are due to start shortly, and next door to the site of the Bear Gardens where Mr Sam Wanamaker is constructing a replica of the Globe. It would be an act of cultural vandalism on a monstrous scale if the pile drivers were allowed in on Monday to turn it into the underground car park for London's latest office block.

Thus far the developers, Imry International, have acted impeccably in conjunction with the Museum of London and English Heritage to allow archaeologists time and money to uncover the treasures beneath. But what has been unearthed, though it only stands a few feet above the ground, is simply too important to be resolved in a few days by the collision of commercial pressures and political compromises. Yesterday Mrs Virginia Bottomley, junior minister at the Department of the Environment, announced that Imry had agreed a scheme under which the remains would be preserved so they could be viewed in future. Obviously better than bulldozing the site completely. But not enough. The site will be handed over at 6 a.m. on Monday to the contractors for 'preparatory' work to begin. Under any of the schemes on offer this will still involve eight piles being driven into the inner section of the theatre, including one through the stage. It is difficult to see how the developers can actually construct the building without causing profound damage to a unique national treasure. This is not only a living monument to the most influential Englishman who ever lived, but its conservation would pay for itself in extra tourist revenue before the new building has reached the end of its useful life. The last building on the site lasted all of 30 years. The arts, as an industry, earns £4 billion a year for the balance of payments (while the motor industry is negative).

There is every reason to sympathize with the property company, which should be compensated in some way; but it would be an unforgivable cultural tragedy if the site preparations involved anything which wrecked the Rose before a proper solution can be worked out. The Government has been taunting Mr Kinnock this week over whether he would press the nuclear button. A more immediate question is whether the Prime Minister will press the button which will send the first pile down the middle of Shakespeare's stage. The minutes are ticking away.

Holding on

JULIE FLINT
16 May 1989

One weekend early in 1942 – the exact month has long been forgotten – a group of young war veterans with terrible burns were dining at the Dorchester with a clutch of pretty girls. It was their first time back 'in society' and they were shy and embarrassed.

'Suddenly,' recounts their hostess, 'the head waiter came over and said: "I'm so sorry. We've had a complaint from one of our oldest customers that they can't continue their dinner with your boys here."'

The hostess – old now, but still slim, blonde and terribly feisty – approached the squeamish diners. 'I said, "You're English, aren't you?" They said, "Of course." I said, "You're sitting eating your dinner and these boys have been fighting to save your life. And because they have burned faces you can't enjoy your dinner? Too damned bad." And I picked up their drink and threw it in their faces. We never had any trouble after that . . .

'It was the beginning of the war and they'd never seen anyone like that. They looked terrible. It was the very early days of plastic surgery.'

The woman was Sunnie, now the wife of Capt Jackie Mann – the 74-year-old Battle of Britain pilot and holder of the Distinguished Flying Medal who was kidnapped in Syrian-controlled West Beirut on Friday. She had been driving ambulances during the blitz when a friend said, 'We're not doing enough.' And so they put their heads together and charmed a wealthy friend who owned 55 Park Lane into offering them a suite, and the Dorchester next door into offering them free meals, once a month, for burns patients from East Grinstead hospital.

In the third month of Dorchester weekends, one of the patients was a 27-year-old pilot whose career flying Spitfires had ended when he crash-landed in a Kentish field after being shot down for the sixth time.

'The plane blew up,' Mrs Mann recalls. 'But he got out – apparently feeling no pain. He even took a photograph of the plane before collapsing. We still have the photograph . . .'

After 43 years in Lebanon, the Manns remain a very British couple – the last British couple in West Beirut. He sports a Pickwickian moustache, speaks no Arabic, hates Lebanese food and insists on an English breakfast every day. She teaches riding, cares for stray dogs, wears a hairnet and drinks gin. The Beirut they knew in the Forties, even in the Seventies, was a Beirut of sand dunes and palm trees, swimming, skiing and fashion shows. But it was also a Beirut where people like Sunnie Mann raised funds, as the old newspaper cuttings say, 'for the people and children of south Lebanon who are without homes to live in and funds to live on because of the continuous harrassment of Israeli bombardments . . .'

'We both loved it here,' she says. 'You could have gone a million miles without finding such a lovely place to live. The people are wonderful.'

Jackie Mann continued to love it, content with his beer, his cigarettes and his much-reduced circle of friends. But Sunnie, after the Israeli invasion of 1982, was ready to go.

'We had more than forty horses at the stables. After the war we had two – thirty-eight were killed. The worst of it is that they weren't killed outright. They had broken legs and broken backs and half the stables down on top of them and there were no vets. I used to do the best I could for them – which wasn't a great deal – and come home crying.'

The Manns' small flat was hit and Sunnie Mann 'didn't really want to start again, buying again. But Jackie said: "We're not going to buy again. We'll live like this, with a few chairs . . ."'

There are still 'a few chairs': the Manns live on pensions

and the last instalment disappeared with Capt. Mann on Friday. The beer in the fridge has been hot since General Michel Aoun's 'war of liberation' against Syria led to a city-wide blackout. There is no water in the taps, no gas for cooking. A week ago, a shell destroyed Mrs Mann's little runabout.

'It went up in the air, turned over about four times like a leaf in the wind and came down burning. There were pieces of Renault all over the road.'

Two of her three strays were killed and the third, a hunter bitch called Stella, had shrapnel through her leg.

'I found her in a terrible state. I bandaged the leg up and gave her aspirin for the pain. She's just beginning to put the foot on the ground again and I'm so happy.'

Jackie Mann, his wife says, has not been awfully well lately. 'He has a certain amount of discomfort from his face and leg and the time we've had – carrying cans of water upstairs without electricity – hasn't helped.

'He didn't have his pills with him on Friday. I don't know how he's going to manage. I suppose he's just lying there, trying to pass the time. He doesn't do much. He likes to play cards . . . But who with?

'I don't know if he will be able to survive this.'

Kinnock doesn't need to press for action

DAVID FAIRHALL
16 May 1989

According to Mr Ken Livingstone, the sight of his party's leader being chased round the country by television reporters intent on knowing whether or not he would ever press The Button – the nuclear one that is, not the lift button over which he was hesitating in one sarcastic cartoon – is thoroughly humiliating. If so, the humiliation is largely self-inflicted.

After half a lifetime recording official pronouncements on nuclear deterrence, from heads of state down to the middle-ranking army officers who would operate Rhine Army's 'modernized' Lance missiles, I can assure him that they all contain contradictions and usually also a large measure of deliberate ambiguity. By comparison with the Israeli position on nuclear weapons, for instance, Mr Neil Kinnock's looks crudely categorical.

Israel has for many years sustained an effective policy of nuclear deterrence without even admitting that it possesses a nuclear bomb. The only answer any Israeli government official would give those television reporters if they put similar questions in Tel Aviv is the cryptic formulation: 'Israel will never be the first to introduce nuclear weapons into the Middle East'; to which the late General Moshe Dayan added the crucial phrase: 'And she will not be the third to introduce them either.'

The policy works because the Israelis' Arab neighbours know they have the technology to make and deliver a bomb, coupled with a national attitude which suggests that in desperation they might well use it. The Arabs also know that Israeli generals believe the best form of defence for a small country like theirs is often pre-emptive attack, a predilection which contradicts their retaliatory nuclear formula but nevertheless reinforces its message.

The fact remains that Tel Aviv's policy is deliberately clouded in uncertainty. Its effect depends on how others choose to interpret its ambiguity. Like a good actor, an Israeli Prime Minister leaves room for his audience's imagination to work. Mr Yitzak Shamir would never expect to be criticized, let alone humiliated, for failing to say whether or not he would ever use a weapon that does not officially exist.

It is true that the opposite approach may also inspire fear. I recall a spine-chilling conversation with a German general, who happened also to be a senior Nato official, who argued that the only way to be sure that nuclear weapons were never used was to be absolutely determined to use them. An American general was equally sure the Germans would, if necessary, 'die for freedom'.

But the Rhine Army's commanders, in my experience, make no such glib assumption. British defence officials were clearly embarrassed by this year's Wintex Nato war game, which ended with a tremendous nuclear firework display. They explained apologetically that the scenario was written several years ago when the Surpeme Commander was General Rogers – a soldier who believed politicians should face up to the implications of their policy directives.

None of this, however, need prevent a British government taking a characteristically understated line. Aldermaston clearly has the technology to make its own nuclear warheads, and it would still have that capability if Mr Kinnock became Prime Minister and successfully negotiated away Trident and the rest. Britain would continue to be regarded internationally as potentially a nuclear power even if he stayed in office as long as Mrs Thatcher, and followed through his policy by physically dismantling the Berkshire research establishment and dispersing its scientific staff.

While we still possessed the actual bombs, Soviet strategists would be bound to offer their leader a worst-case analysis in which they might be used, whatever views the British Prime Minister was believed to hold. Instead of taking refuge in explicit uncertainty, Mr Kinnock could have stated quite firmly that he personally had no intention of ever pressing the button, without removing that fear.

Labour's nuclear defence policy would then be symmetrical with Mrs Thatcher's. No rational Prime Minister of either party would order a nuclear attack on the Soviet Union because it would either invite annihilation or simply be a futile gesture after that event. With Mrs Thatcher, who says for deterrent effect that she might ready to commit national suicide, we have to hope she is lying. If Mr Kinnock were formally to renounce such suicidal tendencies, we would be left worrying he might change his mind in the heat of the moment.

The gold-diggers of '89

DEREK MALCOLM
18 May 1989

We're over the halfway mark at Cannes this year, and few of us have the remotest idea of what film is likely to win. Probably the jury, headed by Wim Wenders, is equally at a loss. It is one of those years. A rather good Cannes, as a matter of fact, with a better-than-average competition section. But nobody is very eager to bet on either the Palme D'Or or the wider financial fortunes of the hundreds of movies on display.

My three favourite films in the competition so far are Bertrand Blier's accomplished *Too Beautiful For You*, one of his very best films, young Steven Soderbergh's *Sex, Lies and Videotapes*, a highly promising serious comedy of sexual manners, and Jerry Schatzberg's moving *Reunion*, written by Harold Pinter.

We always knew Blier was a good film-maker, but those who actually like his work are opposed by some who simply don't get on with it. Sometimes I don't, but *Too Beautiful For You*, a sexual triangle between a man, his beautiful wife and dumpy mistress (the surprise twist in the plot), is so well made as to convince me at last that he really is one of France's very best film-makers. And this time there is heart as well as cleverness in the film too, since Blier takes the part not of Gerard Depardieu's unfaithful husband but of the 'ordinary' housewife he so amazingly falls for.

Love, even sex, he seems to be saying, are absolutely nothing to do with the outward appearances with which we are nowadays so transfixed. And the performance of Josiane Balasko as the surprising mistress amply justifies his theory. If Meryl Streep didn't have her number against the Best Actress award for *Cry In the Dark*, Balasko would certainly be a popular winner for most people, though Carole Bouquet as the beautiful wife who cannot understand the strange relationship is pretty good too.

The Soderbergh film, a stunningly proficient debut, also examines what makes us tick, through some splendid performances and in this case comes, via considerable irony and wit, to the conclusion that the people we generally treat most vilely are those who are nearest to us. To tell the truth to them, he suggests, might force us to be more accountable for our own lives – something we want to avoid at all costs.

This is the kind of debut which ought to be noted, but whether it is actually a major prize-winner at the premier festival in the world is another matter. We'll hear a lot more of Soderbergh, that's for sure.

Schatzberg's *Reunion* was another very pleasant surprise from this uneven but clearly talented director of *Panic In Needle Park* and *Scarecrow*. It is really his first European film and his sure hold on a very well written story provides a highly distinctive piece of cinema. In fact, if I had to bet on the Palme D'Or, my money would thus far be on this story of the friendship between an Aryan aristocrat and a bourgeois Jewish boy in the Germany of Hitler's pre-war bully boys.

The two young men are beautifully played by Christian Anholt and Samuel West – and Jason Robards plays the elderly man the Jewish boy becomes, having emigrated to America. He frames the story perfectly, and Pinter writes it with an intelligent economy that gets to the heart of this tale about friendship, class and antisemitism. Even so, I think it is Schatzberg's picture. Like Blier, he really knows what he is doing, and turns what might have been a quite ordinary piece of cinema into something that remains in the memory.

The one major disappointment in the competition, at least for me, is Jim Jarmusch's *Mystery Train*, which some thought might be the eventual prize-winner if the jury was going to settle for the new rather than the old cinema.

Jarmusch calls the film a temporal comedy and set its three stories in Memphis where, of course, the great Elvis remains a legend. In the first, a young Japanese couple wander the streets, in the second an Italian girl meets up with them and in the third Joe Strummer plays a British Elvis in serious trouble with his psyche.

Mystery Train is beautifully shot by Robby Muller and has a nice John Lurie score. But the screenplay sounds as if it has been written on the back of an envelope and the whole thing has an improvisatory air about it, as if it was intended as a home movie for Jarmusch's friends. That's precisely what some people here like about it, but I found the new film often self-indulgent and frequently rather carelessly made. It is certainly no advance at all on *Stranger Than Paradise* and *Down By Law*.

Outside the competition, there was an extraordinary Chinese film called, *Chine, Ma Douleur* about a young boy who is sent during the Cultural Revolution to a detention camp for 'enemies of the people'. He has been caught playing a record of forbidden capitalist music. The film is not so much angry as gently determined to tell a few home truths about those terrible years through its depiction of character and circumstance, and there are some wonderful moments when it sums itself up in this way. One of them has a group of the detained watching a travelling magic show put on by the party for the glorious peasantry. But they, of course, are the wrong audience and when it is discovered the show is instantly stopped amid great confusion.

The truly amazing thing about Dai Sijie's film, however, is that it was actually made with French help not in China but the Pyrenees. All I can say is that the art director deserves an Oscar, since you would absolutely never have guessed it.

Two more films from the so-called Third World have waved the flag with some success – Idrissa Ouedraogo's *Yaaba* from Burkina Faso, the second poorest country in the world but one of the most anxious to encourage African cinema, and Shaji's *Piravi* from South India.

The African film, again assisted with European money and some technical expertise, is a simple but by no means naïve story of village life and, in particular, the friendship between a young boy and an old woman who is an outcast from the community. It isn't a master work like *Yeelen*, but it reminded some critics of early Ray, and you couldn't get a much better compliment than that.

Shaji is the cameraman for Aravindan, one of the senior South Indian directors, and his first feature is suffused with the same beauty and charm of expression. Indeed, for anyone who knows Trivandrum and Kerala, this story about an old man who can't find his son, who has disappeared from university after a political demonstration, is clearly not to be missed.

At times the story-telling is magical, and the superb shooting makes the beautiful countryside almost the chief character in the story. But *Piravi* (*The Birth*) isn't just a nice, eloquent debut. Kerala is a Marxist state, and it is very critical of the government, who may not be too sure about Shaji in future. But I am. He is obviously a natural director, and the performance of the old man (Premji) is almost beyond praise.

Looking ahead, there is one film we all expect to figure in the jury's final deliberations – Shojei Immamura's *Black Rain*, which the Japanese say is his best film for years. I have the feeling that this film will be the key to the competition, but you never know.

Ashen-faced in seedy Soho

STEPHEN COOK
26 May 1989

'Make no mistake,' ashen-faced financial supremo Dave Cash told a crisis meeting at his seedy London headquarters yesterday. 'We are here to see if the magazine can continue – its future is by no means certain.'

That reads like a *Private Eye* satire on pop journalese, but comes near to describing what happened on the fourth floor of the magazine's cramped offices near Soho Square. The seriousness of Cash's statements about a jury's decision that the *Eye* must pay £600,000 in libel damages to Mrs Sonia Sutcliffe was temporarily undermined, however, by the arrival of Peter Cook, comedian and main shareholder.

Sporting a Torquay United rosette and blue-tinted sunglasses, he blamed his hangover on the shock of the court award in favour of the Yorkshire Ripper's wife, and kicked off with an in-depth discussion about his team's chances against Bolton Wanderers in the Sherpa Van trophy at Wembley on Sunday.

Fifteen minutes ticked away among the peeling posters and piles of back numbers. Eventually the nervous-looking Cash and the *Eye*'s editor, Ian Hislop, steered Cook to the matter in hand and the meeting got under way, with telephone advice from the *Eye*'s former editor and Hislop's mentor, Richard Ingrams.

Hislop emerged to tell representatives of the Street of Shame about the decision to launch legal and financial appeals. Cook was not far behind, cracking jokes about how the *Eye* would henceforward be running controversial stories about kind vicars spending nice days at the seaside, but wouldn't be naming the vicars or committing itself to the weather for fear of comebacks.

'I can't see the point of running a magazine like this if you're going to allow it to become bland,' he said, in a moment of what looked like seriousness.

Within minutes he had been propelled by Fleet Street's finest into the Nellie Dean for some large vodka and tonics and a little gentle pumping. As reporters edged him towards hard information about the *Eye*'s (and his own) cash reserves, Cook said he was 'a very vague proprietor' and just came in to help write the jokes.

In the end there was general agreement that libel damages were beyond a joke, that the *Eye*'s future was in the lap of the law, and that someone ought to make it clear whether the winning or losing players would be given a Sherpa Van each at the weekend.

No chance in the Maze

DAVID HEARST
30 May 1989

We walked up to the sign over the front door of HMP Maze and looked up to the watch-tower. We had already been photographed and the mugshots had become our passes. Even visitors leave their identity behind when they enter the Maze. Our escort reported our progress in feet and inches to an unseen control room. Several seconds later, a siren whined, a light flashed, and the first set of pneumatic steel doors opened with electronic reluctance. Our external passes had to be exchanged for internal ones.

A sign on the chipped wooden counter of the gate-house warned prison staff of the latest supermarket to be watched by the IRA. We were searched. Only then did the long grey march into the Maze begin. It was not so much the rattle of keys as the pauses at each gate which put distance between us and the outside world. Each pause was a new request, each request had to be considered, and your ident-ity reconfirmed. Permission came only with the click of the lock.

More steel doors led to a waiting blue minibus. A journey on foot between the administration block and some cells can take up to 25 minutes. The bus moved slowly down the long tarmac avenues. One senior member of the prison staff said: 'I often have to ask where I am.' The same grey vista of tarmac, concrete, and steel opened at each turn. After five minutes, we were completely disoriented.

The sign on the gate said H3. Another steel door edged open, and there, dwarfed by the walls, was a single-storey H Block. This is where ten men died on hunger strike in 1981, and from where 38 IRA men escaped in 1983. Inside, they still refer to that as 'the great escape'.

However, the situation may be changing. The Northern Ireland Prison Service is engaged on an ambitious pro-gramme of reviewing and releasing Special Category lifers and those held at the Secretary of State's pleasure. The change has been hailed by Dublin as the one unsung achievement of the Anglo-Irish Agreement.

A total of 132 lifers have been given release dates, 90 have been released and 55 cases are pending. The IRA claims that the purpose is to smash its support in the prisons, but it is co-operating with the review.

It had needed 18 gates and barriers to open before I – the first journalist to be allowed to interview such lifers – could walk down the narrow corridor of the Provisional IRA's segregated B wing, but when I did I was greeted with a smile, and ushered into the IRA's association room, an empty cell with a library of republican and socialist litera-ture.

Leo Green, the Provo officer commanding, and Mickey McMullan, his third in command, wanted to know why I had asked to see Tony Catney. All were lifers, how did I get his name? Was it my choice or that of the Northern Ireland Office? There is no such thing as chance in the

Maze, and it was difficult to persuade them that I had been given a free hand in choosing whom to interview.

They thought for a while, and Tony Catney deferred to Mickey McMullan who had served longer – 16 years for killing a British soldier – and as yet had no date for his release. The topic of conversation was the Life Sentence Review Board. Apart from another 'great escape', this is the only way to get out. When a man gets an indeterminate life sentence for murder, he can expect to serve ten to twenty years. Annual internal reviews are conducted both by the governor of his block and of the prison, and external reviews are conducted every three, six and ten years.

The first major review comes at ten years. This is conducted by the board, an anonymous body chaired by Sir John Blelloc, Permanent Under-Secretary at the Northern Ireland Office. Members include senior officials of the prison service, social and probation officers, and a psychiatrist. Apart from the chairman, membership is a closely guarded secret.

The only information a lifer gets after the hearing is a three-line letter, stating either that his case has been referred to the judiciary – which means the board has recommended his release, subject to approval of his trial judge and the Secretary of State – or that his case will be reviewed again in up to five years' time. The latter is known as a 'knock-back'.

The system has been criticized as arbitrary. Tony Catney's co-accused – who pulled the trigger in the shooting – has been released, whereas Catney, convicted for having a 'common purpose', is still inside. Private Ian Thain, the only British soldier to be convicted of murder during the 20 years of the present violence – for the shooting of Thomas Reilly, road manager of the Bananarama pop group – served 26 months. One lifer held at the Secretary of State's Pleasure, because he was under 18 at the time of his conviction, is now in his 17th year of detention.

Senior members of the Northern Ireland Prison Service have spoken for the first time about the review process.

There are two criteria for release. The first is that of retribution, and whether the punishment has fitted the crime. They consider how young the offender was, his part in the crime, and his psychological state at the time.

The second, more difficult, criterion is to assess the risk of reinvolvement. This entails analysing the lifer's behaviour in prison. Does he organize threats against prison staff? Is he a 'dedicated terrorist'? That phrase leads the prison service into the biggest minefield of all. Over 90 per cent of the lifers, particularly on the republican wing, have no criminal background at all. Their families can be middle-class professionals, whose only link with the republican movement is the imprisonment of their son. Father Dennis Faul, a Dungannon priest, has been campaigning for release of the majority of lifers on the grounds that it would end the IRA almost at a stroke. The IRA now refuses to see Father Faul during his weekly visits to take mass.

The review board sees a Royal Ulster Constabulary intelligence assessment of the family and home area. One senior member of the prison service said: 'We are not convicting a man because of his politics. Some families have been republican for generations. On the other hand, are we going to send someone back when we know his brother is active?'

Back in the cell, Mickey McMullan, aged 37, said: 'I was reviewed at the end of the last year. I received a two-year knock-back. I will have done seventeen and a half years by the time my next review comes. I know absolutely nothing about why I was knocked back. At the end of the day, there is a hidden agenda, which nobody can see or do anything about.'

McMullan was convicted of killing a soldier, but is reluctant to talk about it and even more so to consider the question of remorse for what he regards as a political act. 'They keep asking me the same questions, and I keep on giving them the same answers. It won't change what I did. I have not changed my beliefs.'

Leo Green comes in: 'Nobody who has done thirteen or

fourteen years is going to get reinvolved. They knock you back because they want their pound of flesh, and they want to break our families.'

But why then are the IRA prisoners co-operating with a review system they once refused to recognize, and why did a prison campaign which they tried to mount last year over the review process collapse? Green said: 'It didn't. We identified areas which represent a meaningful improvement in the prison regime and we are still involved in talks with the governor.'

The atmosphere between prison officers and the IRA is relaxed down this wing. But the war continues on the psychological front. For prisoners, the smallest change of regime is a gain that must be followed by other demands. The Northern Ireland Office denies that its object is to break the paramilitary hold of loyalists and republicans in the Maze.

'Our aim is not to smash the IRA in the Maze. If we can unglue a foot soldier from the ranks, so much the better. Our aim is to give everyone a choice,' a senior member of the prison staff said. However, 100 republican lifers have opted to transfer from the segregated paramilitary wings of the H Blocks into the new integrated prison of Maghaberry. In doing so, some are turning their backs on the movement; others are saying that they have done their bit.

The battle in the Maze is a battle for control. No one wants to say the IRA is losing; least of all is the Northern Ireland Office claiming victory. But everyone knows the consequences of what is going on in the Maze affects life on both sides of the wire. One prison governor said: 'My ambition is to persuade my seniors that you can run a normal prison in Northern Ireland.' But nobody is giving him any odds.

In place of revolutionary romance

MARTIN KETTLE
25 May 1989

If you read just one book this year to mark the two hundredth anniversary of the French Revolution, then the one you are going to have to get is by a 44-year-old, London-born descendent of a Jewish spice merchant from Izmir who now teaches at Harvard and who doesn't intend to visit France this summer for fear of being labelled a revolutionary party-pooper.

Simon Schama's *Citizens: a Chronicle of the French Revolution* (Viking), published this week, is by far the most important English language book of the 1789 bicentenary. It is important because it offers a complete and unashamed reinterpretation of events which for so long have been the subject of Left v Right political trench warfare on a historic scale.

Other writers have challenged these orthodoxies before – notably Alfred Cobban in this country and François Furet in France itself – but, unlike them, Schama has done it in a brilliantly readable narrative history style. This popular accessibility means that the revisionist interpretation of the French Revolution is now poised to reach a much wider public than it has ever done before.

The revisionists' targets are the twin pillars of the traditional Marxist interpretation of the convulsive events of 1789–94 which held almost absolute sway among French academics – and among the Left worldwide – from the late nineteenth century until around 1968. The first held that a revolution in France was historically *necessary* in order to catapult France from a feudal into a bourgeois society, and that there was a definable French bourgeoisie which was, in Schama's phrase, 'the carrier of that historical necessity'.

At the heart of Schama's version of the Revolution is the argument that this was simply untrue. In late ancien régime France, he argues, the bourgeoisie were not only not denied the status they sought, it was also easier for them than ever before to rise in society. Pre-revolutionary France was a society alive with ideas, science, initiative, new business and mobility. It was an era of a 'bourgeoisified' aristocracy, says Schama. Whatever did happen in 1789, it was not the rising of a socially and economically frustrated middle-class.

'I'm not arguing that 1789 was a non-event,' Schama said in London this week. 'It was the collapse of a state. It happened as a result of the belief that only representative institutions would make France solvent again. It was a total non sequitur, actually. It produced overwhelming and profound effects. Even I, a strong revisionist, am not saying that there were no differences afterwards. But 1789 was an event in political culture, and the changes it created were changes in political culture.'

The second pillar of the Marxist interpretation is that the violence of the revolutionary years was justifiable on grounds of political necessity. For Schama, this is simply an unacceptable proposition for a liberal historian to endorse. The violence of the revolutionary years went well beyond sufficiency to the circumstances. It was altogether more vengeful and punitive, and the great deception was the belief of the political elite that it could be controlled. Schama calls that 'a sacrament of blood'.

These are familiar charges against the Terror of 1793–4. They are less commonly aplied to the so-called liberal period of the Revolution. But, in Schama's hands, 1789 is the ancestor of the Terror. 'How do you explain the Governor of the Bastille's head being sawn through with a pen-knife and stuck on a pike? Violence sufficient to the cause? No. It was punitive display. It didn't change things. It was just somehow necessary to assuage the popular instinct for punishment and anger.

'I am very bleak about 1789,' he continues. 'As I encountered 1789 and 1790 I got more alarmed. For example, no sooner was the ink dry on the Declaration of the Rights of Man [in 1789] than the National Assembly – not the revolutionary Convention, remember – set up committees to report on potential counter-revolutionary plots and to open mail, stop people without warrant, detain people without due process and prevent freedom of movement. In the so-called golden age of 1791 there's already an incredibly sweeping definition of a political crime.'

Something along these lines has, of course, been the stock-in-trade of conservative critiques of the French Revolution since the time of Burke. But Schama is clear that he himself is not a conservative. He angrily rejects the charge. A root-and-branch revisionist, yes; a right-winger, absolutely not. 'A concern about the conflict between freedom and violence is central to liberal self-understanding,' he says.

The bicentenary of the French Revolution poses difficult problems for a traditional left-wing audience. Schama thinks they must simply face the facts about events like the September Massacres of 1792. 'Historians at this point tend to avert their eyes,' he writes, or, even worse, to contort themselves into apologetics which amount to 'the scholarly normalisation of evil'. This is one of the reasons why he has used the narrative technique. 'If you feel indignant at certain points – say so,' he argues. 'You don't have to say that this renders nothing legitimate except conservatism. That absolutely is not the message of the book and it's not my own politics.'

By extension, Schama argued this week, his approach has a lesson for the European Left today. 'It's a liberating thing. You are so much more empowered to attack Mrs Thatcher or to say "Of course there's an alternative to the Right" if you are honest with your own history.' Schama's message is that historical honesty and revolutionary romance don't mix. 'It's an historical hallucination,' he says.

Judging judges

HUGO YOUNG
25 May 1989

Judges, unlike lawyers, occupy an extraordinarily high place in public esteem. They have a special brand of influence. Although they have all been barristers, the moment they arrive on the High Court bench they are transformed. People whom the public tend typically to see as money-grubbing, self-interested exponents of myriad restrictive practices become the faceless repositories of almost super-human, and certainly non-political, wisdom.

This clout is now being mobilized against the Lord Chancellor's radical plans to change the way in which law is practised. It is a riveting spectacle. The issue is great, the contest unique. It is against the very nature of judges – an affront, one might say, exactly to the independence on which each separate judge so prides himself – to sign collective manifestos. For them not only to violate precedent, but to do so with the concentrated object of opposing the head of their own profession, suggests a crisis of unsettling proportion.

In this novel role, however, the judges have shown certain limitations. It is a political situation, and these paragons of the non-political turn out to be not very good at politics. They have, in part, an excellent case, which deserves to attract the support of anyone who cares about the quality of justice. But they run the serious risk of losing it because of their blind misunderstanding, which presumably derives from the magisterial detachment in which they are accustomed to living.

They seem to imagine that, merely by assembling their collective clout, they can stop change occurring. Their response reveals as much. It is relentlessly negative. A grain of political sense would have told them to play it differently: acknowledge that the Government was serious, identify the issues which didn't matter much, and produce constructive drafts on the big issues, so that a debate could ensue between people who knew there had to be a compromise.

Permitting solicitors to argue in the higher courts would have been the perfect concession: maximum advantage at minimum cost. Exclusive advocacy is the Bar's single most visible restrictive practice. Surrendering it would be a grand gesture – and a wise one, since it's certain to be lost anyway. Comparatively few solicitors will in fact want to become advocates, for reasons well-rehearsed. By welcoming them, the judges would be better placed to fend off the more insidious and irrelevant piece of free-market cant: the plan inspired by the Department of Trade to permit any untutored jackanapes from any profession to hang out his shingle as a legal advocate.

Instead, the judges are about as grudging as they could be, venturing only that they be 'receptive' to a limited extension of solicitors' rights. Similarly, on the proposed ombudsman to hear public complaints against lawyers, the judges' *hauteur* gets the better of such common sense as they might be expected to possess. At times, their grand remonstrance may remind the Lord Chancellor of the antediluvian mind-set he was facing yesterday from his church elders.

It seems to be the judges' hope that this unique intervention will have a unique effect: causing the Thatcher government, at the instance of a producers' pressure-group, entirely to abandon a plan to which its leaders are starkly committed. They may not hold out much hope of the Commons, where the anti-lawyer prejudice of the Labour Party meets the free-market philistinism of the Tories. But they are expecting much of the House of Lords, where the judicial interest is heavily represented. Yet here too, I would place no faith in the reluctance of whipped Tories to defeat the special pleaders. If Lord Mackay wants his Bill, he will probably get it over dead bodies (Hailsham, Lane, Donaldson and the rest) that now constitute not an obstacle but a provocation.

If that happens, civic life will be the worse. For the Bar, and the judiciary who grow out of it, will in an important sense have ceased to be self-regulating and therefore truly independent. Instead of the law being responsible for the quality of advocacy it offers the litigant, the Mackay plan will hand this task to the State. A supervisory committee, not even to be dominated by lawyers (let alone judge/barristers), will lay down who may practise in the courts. To the already multiple conflicts of interest a Lord Chancellor experiences, another will be added, through the patronage he enjoys as the invigilator of this committee.

On this central point, Mackay's critics, including the judges, are almost too kind to him. Nothing wrong with *his* regime, they say; but imagine such a power in the hands of a more unscrupulous successor. Given the propensity of every minister in the Thatcher government to pack even the smallest quangoid sub-committee with its reliable placemen, I wouldn't be so charitable. One does not need to think forward to some unexperienced nightmare in order to see plainly what is prone to happen when a new power passes into the hands of politicians.

It is said that, since the Lord Chancellor already appoints the judges, this extension of his power should cause no offence. But the analogue is false. Indeed, it works in the opposite way. All higher judicial appointments, although the Lord Chancellor's responsibility, are made only after a lot of informal consultation. The judges are, in an important sense, self-regulators, vouching for the quality of their successors; a system which may have its weaknesses but has produced few duds and no felons, and makes no case for political control over who may practise at the Bar.

The judges understand all this, and make a cogent case against it. Reminding us of the vast expansion of judicial review, and therefore of legal issues which range the judiciary against government, they underline the particular point where their independence must be seen to be unimpeachable – and also where this Government will take pleasure in cutting them down. Equally, they are right to fear for the quality of legal services likely to result from a trend towards ever more massive, one-stop, all-purpose law firms, which will imperil the independent Bar and the dependent client alike.

In the real world of legal service, this entire argument sometimes seems like a side-show. If the judges, on the one hand, and Lord Mackay, on the other, are serious about the need for a better system, more readily available, more redolent of choice, how can any of their utterances compare with the most under-publicized large fact of the Thatcher decade: the removal, as Cyril Glasser has demonstrated, of between ten and thirteen *million* people from the scope of legal aid? So much for the availability of justice.

All the same, the independence of the Bar is worth fighting for. The judges have imperilled it themselves, during many years of restricting access to their trade and defending practices which were against the public interest. Now, for want of modest political competence, a hundred stiff-necked judges are threatening it again. I thought it was only the Prime Minister who did not hold with negotiation.

80 in the pink

FRANK KEATING
26 May 1989

Sir Matt Busby celebrates his 80th birthday in Manchester today with a warm, intimate family lunch. No interruptions, by request.

Not that world football's grandest old man is too tottery to take the public plaudits in person any more, far from it. The founding father of the dashing Red Devils is very much in the pink – and intends to remain so at least till the next week is over.

For, do not forget, on Monday he also celebrates the 21st anniversary of that golden Wembley night when Manchester United won the European Cup, and next Friday at Old Trafford his Association of Old Boys throws a banquet in his honour. From all points of the globe, Sir Matt's alumni will fly in to toast The Boss.

Eighty years ago today a miner's wife gave birth to a son in their two-roomed cottage at Orbiston near Motherwell. The boy was five when dad and three uncles left the village at the behest of king and country for the trenches of northern France. He never saw any of them again. 64 years ago today, on his 16th birthday, the boy went down the mine to become the family breadwinner while mother, at her wits' end, tried to get emigration papers for the United States, where her sister had settled in Pittsburgh. While they were waiting, a Mr Hodge, a talent scout from Manchester City, saw the kid playing amateur football for the Denny Hibernians.

Mother did not want him to go. Pittsburgh seemed to offer more prospects than Manchester. The young man had no father or uncle to turn to. He took the desperate decision himself; Manchester it was.

Fatherless at five, OK – but there was to be an even more stunning and grievous family trauma many years later. He was 48 when he lost 'all my lovely boys' as a BEA Elizabethan chartered aircraft skidded on a slushy runway in West Germany.

He was not even allowed to bury his 'Busby Babes', for he was desperately injured himself, the wall of his chest having caved in on his lungs. His Catholic faith fortified the convalescence, especially the Dominican acceptance: 'We seem to give them back to Thee, O God, who gavest them to us; yet as Thou didst not lose them in giving, so do we not lose them by return . . . for life is eternal and love is immortal.'

But even that wavered on his first, ghost-faced, hobbling,

solitary return to Old Trafford. 'I just looked at the empty field and in all my life I have never felt such a terrible vacuum,' he said. 'And so I cried, and afterwards I felt better for the tears and because I had forced myself to go back there. It was something I had done, something I had conquered.'

In less than a dozen years he strove to put together another team in his own image and likeness – a different team, harder and more brittle perhaps, but one that did what had to be done with astonishing panache at Wembley on the night of 29 May 1968. And then, to all intents, he stepped aside – to be successively general manager, caretaker-manager and now president of the club. For almost a quarter of a century, since Busby returned from the war to the bomb site at Trafford Park that was meant to be a football ground, he was Manchester United – and United was Matt Busby.

In fact, it all started long before 1945. Sixty years ago this summer, the Orbiston boy had arrived in the city to play at Maine Road for £5 a week through the season. In 1934 the *Manchester Guardian* football correspondent wrote on these pages the first fulsome profile – as far as I can dip into the files, anyway – of City's young wing-half: 'It is his bewildering footcraft which most delights the crowds. His crouching style may not be pretty but the control is perfect, the effect akin to conjuring. His dribble is a thing of swerves, feints and deceptions. Few opponents are not hoodwinked by his phantom pass . . . while Busby is not so sound in defence, who would have him different?

'He laughs equally at his blunders and his triumphs, which of course is the privilege as well as the proof of a great player. He is a certain choice for that Select XI of Footballers Who Obviously Love Football – and that is the highest praise of all.'

Eleven years later, on February 16, 1945, newsprint rationing kept the report of the United board meeting to a one-paragraph minimum: 'The United chairman, Mr James Gibson, has offered the post of team manager to Mr Matt

Busby, and although he has also received offers of a number of similar appointments elsewhere, he prefers the Manchester area for family reasons. Mr Gibson said he was impressed by Mr Busby's ideas and honesty of purpose.'

With such matter-of-fact prefaces are legends born.

The team, of course, still played at Maine Road. Old Trafford was rebuilt by 1949. A year later Busby's first – and, many a greybeard still says, grandest – team won the FA Cup in resplendent manner. Old men still recite in pubs those rhythmic semi-colons: Crompton; Carey, Aston; Anderson, Chilton, Cockburn; Delaney, Morris, Rowley, Pearson, Mitten.

The vision, however, remained in his breast. Give or take a player or two, that 1948 team won United the League Championship in 1952. But just as vital as knowing how to build a team is the knack of knowing when to dismantle it. Six months after winning the League title with those bold men who had aged together, Busby gave simultaneous debuts in a crucial match against Huddersfield to an un-known home-grown sextet of teenagers – Colman, Edwards, Whitefoot, Blanchflower, McGuinness and Pegg. The Babes were born. They were, as a confraternity, to have less than five years of life.

And then he built another team – to play for the ones that had gone, 'for life is eternal and love is immortal'. And they did it for him, 21 years ago this Monday. And though they were not all, by any means, the cottage-crafted, be-spoke young Babes who had been moulded so closely to his own character and personality, their dazzle at least helped Busby, and all of us, just a little to forget.

Sir Matt still watches United. You still see the rheumy, soft-boiled eyes full-beam a brighter blue when the Red Devils emerge from the tunnel of the stadium he first rebuilt, then made a stage for all the world.

Sir Matt's contemporary, confidant, and chronicler all down the purple pageant, the incomparable Geoffrey Green of *The Times* – himself, in his turn, the modern founding father of our trade – once asked Busby how he went about building a football team. Busby smiled that soft Scottish smile of his, and replied: 'A sculptor was once asked how he managed to turn a square slab of stone into, say, an elephant. He said "Easy. I just knock off the bits that don't look like an elephant".'

China versus China

JASPER BECKER
5 June 1989

It was only by the time we arrived at Fuxingmen Bridge, the last bridge in the west before the city centre, and heard the steady crackle-crackle of small arms fire and the intermittent thud-thud of heavy machine guns that the enormity of what was happening dawned on us. It was 1 a.m. and in the warm June night air the usual crowd in vests and summer skirts were waiting on the flyover crossing the second ring road.

Before we took the scene in, a plump middle-aged woman was carried through the crowd. She was shaking with shock, with a large gash across her forearm, and was bundled into a taxi. As the gunfire approached, the crowd behind became frantic and started ramming six articulated buses across the road into the hedgerows on either side.

Until then a tour of the suburbs had revealed the by now usual and farcical attempt by the army to enter. Out in the east towards the airport a few platoons of troops in battledress were shepherded by an excited crowd into barracks.

Swinging west along the third ring road, we found more convoys but now also signs of violence or force. The mood was sombre and edgier than it had been a fortnight ago when the soldiers had first come.

But even on Saturday afternoon there were ominous signs of the terror to come. Tiananmen Square was the usual spectacle of red flags blowing gaily, but behind the Great Hall of the People 1000 troops were surrounded by a jeering crowd and the mood was ugly. Occasionally a student emerged holding aloft a captured helmet or showing off a bloody wound.

Littering the street towards Fuxingmen were half a dozen smashed-up army trucks or buses. Troops were trapped in one. Another was crammed full of gear and an AK-47 machine gun had been erected on top as an exhibition. The stream of cyclists drifting up and down were in high spirits, but there was an air of hysteria. At around 2 p.m. police loudspeakers had warned the crowd it was illegal to steal equipment from the People's Liberation Army, amid announcements that the troops would not use force but were there to protect the people.

The 800 riot police stormed out of Zhongnanhai, the leadership's compound, firing tear gas and laying about them with clubs. The mêlée lasted half an hour and the police left. Later, by the square, more troops were hemmed in a crowd by the Revolutionary History museum. Students with 'V' for victory T-shirts led the troops and onlookers in singing the 'Internationale'.

Then at 7 p.m. troops began pouring in. Forty trucks pulled into the eastern approach to the square just by the main diplomatic compounds and were stopped again. The soldiers clutched their guns and twisted nooses in their hands as they were loudly berated by angry grandmothers. Leading them were trucks of toughs in plain clothes with yellow hardhats, wooden clubs and iron bars. They were surrounded by a crowd of 500 and several were almost beaten to death as they tried to escape. Unaware of this, diplomats brought their families out to watch the troops.

All of this had failed to give us an intimation of what was in store. As the gunfire at Fuxingmen came closer, we began to run back in fear as the crowd began to set fire to the buses. A tyre on our jeep had been slashed, but we rumbled down the street dodging in and out of the road barriers until we arrived at the Minzu Hotel, where an angry band of youths stormed our jeep, hurling stones and rocking us until we established our identity.

We dashed across to the hotel entrance, where a crowd was savagely beating a soldier. Another had found safety in the hotel and the crowd was trying to smash the doors. A police car was burning near by.

The road was littered with broken glass and bricks. Just before, a detachment of riot police had been attacked, and the air was thick with tear gas and smoke. The sound of gunfire and explosions grew closer and we tried to get into the hotel, finally finding a back entrance. First, a tank came past, then a dozen armoured personnel carriers, followed by hundreds of trucks from which troops fired constantly.

The crowd melted away, but there were constant tracers and sparks as bullets ricocheted across the road. Some of the bullets were just 'firecrackers', but others left holes in the lobby or dining-hall windows. Lines of soldiers with clubs followed the trucks and buses. On the truck stood a soldier cradling a machine gun. Some trucks were adorned with red banners saying, 'the army loves the people'.

From a window we could see shadowy figures, flitting through the dark, hurling stones, and after an hour the last trucks moved down. One man siphoned off petrol from our jeep and hurled a Molotov cocktail, setting himself on fire. Others smashed open the cars, including ours, trying to find transport to carry the wounded away. Later we found blood drying on the pavement, smeared across the car doors and drawn into circles under the hotel's revolving doors.

When the last truck had vanished towards the square, the crowd emerged clutching stones and sticks and moved off in pursuit. Gradually the chants of 'Tu Fei, Tu Fei' – the old nationalist cry of 'Communist bandit' – grew louder and louder. Then they stopped and men in tears began singing the 'Internationale'. People tore down the red pro-government banners draped down the sides of the hotel and burned them.

More and more wounded were being taken to hospital near by. We went to the small People's Hospital and it looked like an abattoir. There were bodies on benches and beds or on blood-soaked mattresses on the floor. Many had gaping bullet wounds on the chest, legs, or head. A doctor, voice hoarse with emotion, told us that 300 wounded had come in. 'Most were so bad we sent them on elsewhere. There were thirty-five seriously wounded and seventy others. Four have died, including a nine-year-old girl shot through the throat,' he said.

Students had rescued badly beaten soldiers and we saw one covered in blood who was clearly not going to live. It was the same story at the nearby post office hospital. I began to feel sick. Another doctor said 12 people had died under his hands; out of 300 injured, 30 had died. There was not enough blood, and many bled to death as the exhausted staff could only operate three times in an hour. He thought 50 had died in every one of the 20 major hospitals in the capital.

The horror only worsened as we stood outside the hotel and people told us more and more stories. At the central post office, a journalist from the state news agency had been beaten to death; a family had been killed in their home by stray gunfire, another man in his bathroom, a girl by a tear gas shell as she looked out of her window; four police had been dragged out of their car and beaten to death.

Students had been bayoneted to death, others had set fire to two armoured personnel carriers and trucks, tanks had crushed to death 11 students who had left the square and were lagging behind the others, more students had been crushed to death in their tents. People showed us huge shells, six inches long and half an inch in diameter, as well as .303 bullets.

'How could the Communist Party do this? How could they shoot children?' asked a worker in blue overalls. Others pleaded with us to tell the world what happened. The West must stop all investments, they said, and condemn their government. No one, not even the Japanese or the Kuomintang or the warlords, had ever done this and this was their own government. But many were mute with horror. Nobody could find the words.

'All we wanted was some democracy,' said a student who had been whipped across the face, his shoulders trembling with anger.

They must not get away with it

LEADER
5 June 1989

It is, for all who watch and wonder about the Communist world, the ultimate obscenity. Worse even than Hungary or Czechoslovakia or Afghanistan; for there the tanks and troops were alien invaders, rolling across borders in the fashion through time immemorial of big powers knocking little powers into line. But in China it is the People's Army turned against the people: shooting them indiscriminately in Tiananmen Square, on the streets, on their doorsteps; crushing them beneath the tracks of the tanks; sweeping them from sight in a sea of bloodshed. A bankrupt, desperate, geriatric government; an edifice of ideology and aspiration flaking and toppling before our eyes.

At such a moment the normal calculations of political analysis – can Li last? is Deng peripheralized? – fall from the board. We have been confronted, this week-end, by one of the great punctuation marks of twentieth century history. No one in the largest nation in the world will ever forget the first week of June in Beijing; and the whole world is enmeshed in these events. In Chinese terms, a surge of desire for greater freedoms – not democracy as we know it, but an opening of society, a spirit of glasnost – has posed ultimate questions to a group of old men; and, ultimately, at whatever cost, they have moved to stamp it out. There was a chance, only a handful of days ago, that a more liberal strain of thinking within the Chinese Communist Party could, by its success in the backroom struggle for power, have harnessed the yearning for glasnost. But the old men won.

It matters hugely what happens next. If the politicians who ordered a manifestly stricken army into action survive, if they can still the cities and choke information to the distant countryside, *if they can get away with it*, then a second set of great questions will dominate debate. Are the manifest death throes of the Communist monoliths manageable? Can they be predicted and relied on? Could Tiananmen Square come to Red Square and savagely end a period of burgeoning hope?

The point is a starkly simple one. We, sitting comfortably in the West, assume that a spark in the individual human condition – a spark called freedom – must, in the end, make a bonfire of the system that seeks to snuff it out. We assumed, from the peripatetic Nixon on, that China – by its own, complex lights – would gradually evolve into a nation which had made its peace with liberty; that the business culture, the Americans with cheque books, would inevitably bring some form of democracy in their wake. How else could the British sign away Hong Kong and millions of its citizens to the old enemy to the north? Beijing, surely, needed and would nurture Hong Kong's wealth.

Tell that, this bloody, awful morning, to the marines. The human beings who walk the streets of Hong Kong can no longer be thought of as pawns, signed away and forgotten. And meanwhile, patrolling the Berlin wall, looking East, we must suck our thumbs. Gorbachev has put glasnost ahead of perestroika. His people have increasing freedom to demand a better life but not yet the system to provide it; the reverse of Deng's approach in China. How frail is the Soviet spark?

There is comfort in dwelling on the different roads towards capitalism. The Soviet people – because glasnost came first – may have acquired a patina of sophistication that the students of Beijing, seeking to destroy a regime by peaceful but utterly confrontational protest, lack. The

Soviet Union, driven on from the top, is seeking to devolve power, to provoke argument, to manage change. The pensioners of the Chinese establishment had, long since, run out of ideas. You have a different generation and a different impetus. But still: there is the conundrum of desperation, of men backed to the wall by a tide of events.

As the rest of the world, therefore, moves today beyond statements of shock and horror, there is a common interest never hitherto perceived. *They must not get away with it*; in the eyes of the West, because of the spark. And in the eyes of those who watch from Moscow, too, because the nightmare of Deng is theirs as well. We all, at root, know that the Chinese march towards liberty must be resumed. We must see the old men, constitutionally and not in further chaos, defeated and removed. We have a duty, to the Chinese people, to make a thunderous voice of revulsion insistently heard.

Defiance in a burning city

JASPER BECKER
6 June 1989

All night the tanks and armoured vehicles rumbled past my bedroom window. In the silence in between, I could hear people outside talking and reassembling pitiful barriers. About 40 men from the housing blocks opposite had tipped steel tables and sundry metal junk in a line across the broad avenue. They stood there hammering the tables, but when the tanks came they withdrew to the hedgerows, peering out and lobbing stones and occasionally a petrol bomb.

The tanks drove across, oblivious, and the men reassembled to discuss new tactics. They were not wild youths but middle-aged workers in vests and summer shorts.

The point, they explained to me, was not to stop the tanks

– they knew that was futile – but to show they were unwelcome and to express their anger. At lunchtime next day they were still there. I cycled out towards the Jianguomenwai flyover where three trucks were still burning.

An army convoy had stopped below and troops were lying on the grass, washing themselves in basins. Others stood guard with sub-machine guns at the ready. Behind one of the burning trucks, half covered in canvas, was a dead demonstrator, his head smashed to a bloody pulp. A diplomat who lived opposite said that in the early morning the authorities had turned off the street lights to collect more bodies. This demonstrator must have died later.

I cycled past the near-deserted railway station to the south of the square where people stood watching rows of police armed with wooden clubs. At the north-west corner of the square, by the huge Beijing Hotel, another crowd stood warily, some 300 yards from the troops. We could see the tanks in the distance and the helicopters landing. There was sporadic gunfire and everyone would scatter in panic, and then return laughing in a nervous, frightened way. A student had been shot dead half an hour earlier and, while I was there, another schoolchild was beaten and dragged away. He or she had run too slowly.

'Animals, animals,' screamed the crowd.

On the other side of the square, people were wreaking a terrible vengeance among the burning vehicles and rubble. An army officer had been burned and hanged. His naked corpse dangled in a charred bus. No one felt any pity. 'He deserved it. He murdered the people of Beijing,' a middle-aged worker said. 'Blood for blood,' said posters pasted up near by.

Heading back west, I saw 20 tanks and armoured personnel carriers burst out of Tiananmen Square towards Jianguomenwai. They were safeguarding the only route in or out of the city. In the late afternoon, we drove along the deserted streets, passing convoys of troops, burning vehicles, army and citizens' road-blocks, to the university quarter in the north-west.

Inside the university all was calm. Students were playing badminton and relaxing. There were plenty of posters and banners but no signs of panic. No troops had tried to enter, but many students wore black armbands and white flowers in mourning. 'There are constant rumours about the troops. We are all very frightened,' one student said.

Another from the press office told us seven students were dead, 140 missing, uncounted wounded. In Qinghua University four were dead and 60 missing. In the west of the city where the troops had smashed their way through early on Sunday morning, we understood why no tanks were coming in from the west any more – they did not dare to try.

It looked like a war zone. Along two miles of road we counted at least 100 burnt-out army vehicles, including 50 armoured personnel carriers destroyed on Sunday night after the first onslaught. Many had clearly smashed into each other. Others had crashed into trees. People were still systematically wrecking the smouldering hulks.

How unarmed civilians had managed to destroy a convoy of this size defied the imagination. At around 10.30 last night normal television programmes were interrupted to transmit pictures of the rioting, taken by the traffic monitors. They showed hundreds of citizens attacking and defeating heavily armed riot police and dragging and punching troops.

Then the screen suddenly went blank and all transmissions stopped.

Valedictory for Khomeini

DAVID ROSE
6 June 1989

Dressed in a white shroud, his Imam's turban placed neatly on his stomach, Ayatollah Khomeini lay in state yesterday before a million of his people. High above the surging, ragged tides of grief, the superstructure of his penultimate place of repose glinted in the sun: the outer layer, an air-conditioned crystal cuboid, and within, prosaically, closely covering the Imam's body, a chilled glass fridge, of the kind used in supermarkets for displaying fresh food. The whole rested on a black dais, decked in giant, elliptical wreaths, built in turn on a high wooden stage, a hundred yards square, guarded by soldiers.

At the opposite end of the platform, Mullahs took turns to sing dirge-like, solemn verses from the Koran, broadcast over a public address system to the multitude below and, simultaneously, live across the country on radio and TV. Eight of the mourners gathered around Khomeini's body died yesterday, crushed to death or overcome with exhaustion in the sweltering frenzy of their grief. Hundreds more were treated in the waiting fleets of ambulances, carried prostrate over the heads of the crowd, some still chanting as they collapsed.

By dawn, the vast new prayer field of Mossallah, an arid plateau of stones and dust above Tehran's northern suburbs, was packed with hundred of thousands of mourners. As the day wore on, mothers and children slipped away to be replaced by thousands more who had travelled from outlying cities. Revolutionary Guards marched in ordered phalanxes to take their positions, singing battle songs from the Iran–Iraq war. But there was no hostility, this time, to the Western reporters and TV crews who mingled freely with the crowd.

As the mourners reached each new crescendo of expression, dancing furiously in time to their chants, beating their breasts and faces, firemen sprayed them from the tops of tenders with power hoses in an attempt to limit the numbers falling prey to the heat. The women were less violent, standing solemnly with pictures of the Ayatollah. But sometimes, a group of them would suddenly change from silent contemplation to passionate fury in a moment, clasping each other, wailing and weeping, taking up the self-flagellation of the men. 'Khomeini, Khomeini, who is like the Prophet, we are still living, we are still living,' one chant ran. 'Goodbye Imam, goodbye.'

Another invoked the name of God, beseeching him to take the Imam's body upward to heaven. The Revolutionary Guards, who gathered briefly around a group of war veterans in wheelchairs, sang: 'We are orphans, the Revolutionary Guard our orphans, we have lost our father.'

Hassa Shiri, aged nineteen, who spent fourteen months at the front against Iraq, said: 'Like the great men of history, like Shakespeare, he will not die. In the war, the Iraqis had only machine guns, but we had another kind of machine gun, the weapon of Islamic ideology.' Yar Mohameddi, who lost fingers and part of an arm in the war, said: 'We are sad that we have lost our leader. But all human beings will come to see that he taught us the best way of behaving that is possible for humanity.'

Few among yesterday's crowd were willing to speculate on Iran's political future. 'Our new leader can never be as great as Khomeini,' one young man said, 'but he is from the same line. That gives us strength.'

As dusk fell, businesses remained closed, while the population prepared itself for today's funeral, in which the Ayatollah's cortège will travel the 15 miles to the Cemetery of the Martyrs. On street corners, shrines of flowers, coloured lights and photographs of Khomeini were beginning to spring up, built as places of contemplation for the remaining 39 days of mourning.

Pay now, die later

NANCY BANKS-SMITH
7 June 1989

The young man dancing, denying a line of 20 tanks in Tiananmen Square, had an imaginative power which imprints him on the retina. You close your eyes and see them still. The leading tank seemed to try to limit his movements, clumsily lumbering to left and right. He skipped to face it as a dancer faces his partner. We will know his name one day but now he has the elasticity of astronauts on the moon, who bounce from the joy of sudden new power. Look at me. Look at what I can do. Look what I have done.

What a jolly enterprising idea. Choose your own funeral. In *Enterprise Culture* (BBC2) Howard Hodgson marketed the idea as 'Dignity in Destiny'. This means nothing at all but it has a good hollow ring, like a kicked oil drum. Mr Hodgson is an undertaker or, as he prefers to think of it, a businessman. 'It is quite interesting how businessmen have replaced footballers as the bed-fellows of rock stars and film stars. As important people.' Mr Hodgson is the sort of man who thinks the bed-fellow of a rock star is an important person.

What Dignity in Destiny boils down to is 'You pay now and die later'. This takes the burden of sorrow from your loved ones. It also prevents them settling for veneered pine when you fancied the solid oak with the Jacobean handles.

Few of us get the send-off we expect. Look at the poor old Ayatollah. Shaw, a vegetarian, wanted his cortège to be followed by all the animals he hadn't eaten, wearing white scarves. Chesterton amiably offered to stand in for the elephant. W. C. Fields, an atheist, stipulated he should have no funeral. His wife and mistress between them had three: non-conformist, Catholic and spiritualist.

My great-grandfather had what sounds a lively affair after having had, in life, several lively affairs. His cortège was followed by a carriage of fallen women. 'And no man raised his hat as they passed,' my grandmother used to say weightily, being somewhat miffed as the fallen women had got the money. Dignity in Destiny hardly seems to describe any of these. You go to Mr Hodgson and he will fix you up with the full hygienic treatment and a Volvo. What? Oh, embalming, but, as he says, everyone is terribly sensitive now about the word.

The trouble with burying people is that we are not in an

on-going organic growth situation here. They have to be dead first. It is difficult to treble your turnover, if they won't lie down. Hence Dignity in Destiny. As a sadly unserious reporter put it to Mr Hodgson: 'You could say you're the only undertaker who makes a killing even if people don't die.' I fear the frivolity of the media must have been a disappointment to Mr Hodgson, who came down from Birmingham 'to take the media head-on and totally transform the whole profession'. Out goes 'the little old man with the ulcerated alcoholic nose' and in comes the dashing young man with the long hair and a large cigar. Out goes the family firm and in 'the solid, secure corporate image like banks or insurance companies or building societies. The public warm to that.'

Not if they're dead they don't.

TYBURN: even after 200 years there is a shudder along the blood at the name of the great London gallows near Marble Arch. There is a Benedictine Convent there now which, day and night, sends up a silent disinfection of prayer. In the crypt is a replica of the gallows and relics of Catholic martyrs. Part of a finger of John Roberts, a Benedictine. A finger nail of Thomas Holland, a Jesuit. Phials of blood and a shirt, the blood stain faded to a mud splash.

Sister Mary Martin described all these to callers with the utmost matter-of-factness. She was shortly to take her first vows. Her family came down from Bootle all dressed up for her spiritual marriage. 'She was coming in after twelve o'clock. To me it was too late,' said her father. 'I was a bit frightened. Now I know she's quite safe. I sleep easy now.' She was 35 when she entered the convent.

The traffic draws across the throat of the place like a knife. They are a silent order. They do not watch television or listen to the radio. They still whip themselves on Friday night. The novice mistress chooses their books. For recreation they skip, play scrabble and – of all things – snooker. They seem to take the *Guardian Weekly*. They all have the definitive nun's smile: wide, washed and guileless.

Sister Martin's Profession (First Tuesday, Yorkshire) was as peaceful as sleep and as mysterious. It told you little, nothing really, about the secret at the heart of the silence. It is, in any case, not unheard of for a few women to stand underneath the gallows.

Telling it like it was?

JOHN GITTINGS
12 June 1989

Foreign correspondents in Beijing, urged to tell the world about what they have seen, have so far been able to answer with complete sincerity that they will do so. But three weeks after martial law was declared, it is swiftly becoming very difficult. In a disconcerting but logical progresssion, as the danger of being shot by a stray army bullet has receded, the threat of a severe beating and perhaps of a deliberately aimed revolver has risen as the authorities reassert their control.

The foreign correspondents, radio reporters, and film and camera personnel ignored with virtual impunity the martial-law regulations for the first fortnight. They were very vaguely worded: they stipulated that journalists were 'strictly forbidden to utilize press coverage to make instigating and inciting propaganda'. Interviews in schools, workplaces, et cetera were forbidden, but not those out in the open.

A later clarification tightened the grip, specifying that the government's interpretation was final. But the text of this clarification was never delivered to foreign correspondents, and the Chinese foreign ministry seemed careful to avoid getting involved. Indeed, officials of the information department were greeting amiably foreign journalists whom they must have known were breaking the regulations. But the press corps did not rely on the legal ambiguities when it ignored the regulations. The chief view would be that the restrictions were designed to conceal the evidence of a fundamentally immoral attempt to cow the students and citizens of Beijing by military means. It is much the same principle on which those students and citizens relied in holding at bay that force for a fortnight. Based on an order signed only by Mr Deng Xiaoping, martial law was seen to be 'against what is right'.

The foreign press has also been sustained by an amazing wave of popular approval. 'We felt that if there was any difficulty with the authorities,' one of the BBC's team recalls, 'the people would certainly defend us.' Even after the military takeover a week ago, the people wherever possible continued to encourage us. When a camera team was detained by armed police on Friday, a crowd materialized within a few minutes and the team was allowed to depart to the cheers of the spectators.

If they had been soldiers with Chinese AK47s, it would have been very different. The equation had been fatally tipped against free reporting by the sheer firepower of the army and the orders it had evidently received to shoot to deter. The print journalist is still able to rely on a pair of eyes from the seat of a bicycle. But after a series of ugly incidents towards the end of last week, some television men were concluding it was too dangerous to shoot anything at all.

The stake-out positions were also getting more hazardous: the Beijing Hotel, nearest to the square, has top-security guards armed with cattle prods and a strict pass system. And the foreigners' flats in the diplomatic quarter were hit with dum-dum bullets when they army alleged they were concealing a sniper.

How to find out what is happening has long been more difficult than how to get the news out. With historical hindsight the foreign press will be found to have gone over the hill in pursuit of some very wispy stories. The circular process that elevates a rumour into alleged fact extends from Beijing to Hong Kong and back again. For a fortnight, as stories from the Hong Kong newspapers were faxed in through sympathizers at local hotels, and retailed by the masses, they were too often quoted back as from Chinese sources by the networks and the Voice of America.

Until the power struggle was resolved, the supporters of Zhao Ziyang sometimes tried to boost the reformist case by leaking his version of the argument in the party's politburo. The stories of fierce antagonism between different armies – particularly the famous 'conflict' between the 27th and 38th – had some basis other than wishful thinking. Armed squadrons of tanks do not rush to and fro for no reason. But Chinese history is too full of tales of armies that manoeuvre without ever joining arms to influence the intrigues of the emperor's ministers in the capital.

We shall also have to revise downwards some of the statistics of deaths in the square, though that should not weaken our judgment on the army's use of killing force. Those hospital counts that are known point to hundreds rather than thousands, although there is uncertainty about the large number of wounded.

The regime that ordered the troops in has news-media problems of its own. Strange goings-on at Central Television seem to indicate passive resistance by the staff: programmes have gone off the air, film has been shot out of focus, wavering from side to side, and a week ago the news readers wore black; their news bulletins were read flatly; there are still awkward breaks and signs of passages being dubbed.

Sometimes the picture seems to contradict the commentary. Last week a film showing how the army was cleaning up Tiananmen Square lingered silently on a bullet hole in a wall of the Martyrs Memorial. It also traversed a pile of rubbish with evident patches of blood. It is only a few days since hundreds of Chinese journalists demonstrated for the right of a free press. 'Don't force us to tell lies,' was their most popular slogan. The newspapers that are reappearing print little else but martial-law communiqués.

The struggle has taken a long step backwards. The

government is showing some concern now for public opinion. Long films on television of public confrontations with the army are designed to show that everything could be blamed on the 'counterrevolutionary hooligans'.

But the martial tone of their announcements, the readiness to show tanks moving through the streets, and the energetic denunciation of evil elements, all suggest a readiness to remould truth as required. 'Somehow we wounded, by mistake, a number of people,' one smiling lieutenant said. He expressed his sorrow and regret. He then went on to explain that the army's guns were not intended for use against the public and the students. That evening the army moved into Beijing University.

Index